A Handbook *for an* INDIAN PHILOSOPHY

Dr. Ch. Venkata Sivasai

PRASHANT PUBLISHING HOUSE
DELHI-110094

Published by :
Prashant Publishing House
C-34, 28 Foota Road, Gali-3,
West Karwal Nagar, Delhi-110094
Phone : 011-22963970, Mob. : 9810396373
e-mail.: prashantpublishinghouse@gmail.com

A Handbook for an Indian Philosophy
Reserved
First Published 2015

ISBN 978-93-80565-61-3

PRINTED IN INDIA
Published by Mr. R.K. Jha M/s Prashant Publishing House and Published at H.S. Offset House Press, Delhi.

Preface

The philosophy is concerned with the understanding of the life and the universe. It is aimed at comprehending the nature of existence. Philosophy is a human endeavor that leads to the Ultimate Truth. The English word 'philosophy' has its root in the Greek term – 'philo–sophia'. The term 'philo' refers to 'love' and 'sophia' refers to human reason.. In Sanskrit, the philosophy is referred to as ' darshana'. The Sanskrit word 'darshana' has its root in the word 'drs' that means 'to see', 'to look' or 'to view'. "Seeing" or "viewing" the reality and the facts of experience forms the basis of philosophy. According to Indian view, the word 'philosophy' is concerned with 'the revelation of the nature of reality' or 'the vision of Ultimate Truth and Reality'.

Indian Philosophy: The Indian philosophy has its roots in the Vedic period. The great Rishis, settled in the peaceful, invigorating environment of the forests, meditated over the fundamental questions of existence: What is the world? If it's a creation, what are its constituents? Who is the creator? What is life? What is 'truth'? What is 'the nature of reality'? What was revealed to them was expressed in hymns. With the passage of time, the systematized collection of these hymns constituted the Vedas and the Upanishads.

The Systems of Indian Philosophy: The Vedas are the oldest scriptures in the world. The Indian philosophical systems are classified according as they accept the authority of the Vedas or not. The systems of Indian philosophy are classified into two groups:

(1) The Orthodox Systems

(2) The Heterodox Systems (Unorthodox)

The orthodox systems are: Nyaya, Vaisheshika, Samkhya, Yoga, Purva-Mimamsa, and Uttar-Mimamsa.

The Heterodox (unorthodox) systems are: Charvakism, Jainism and Buddhism.

Very often, Purva-Mimamsa is referred to as "Mimamsa" only and Uttar-Mimamsa as "Vedanta". The orthodox systems uphold the supremacy of the Vedas. The unorthodox systems reject the authority of the Vedas. Truly speaking Vaisheshika, Nyaya, Samkhya and Yoga are neither orthodox nor unorthodox. These four systems, while originating, neither accepted nor rejected the Vedas. This book discuss about these systems in brief manner.

I think this book help to everybody, both scholars and the layman, students who are interested to know about Indian Philosophy and its systems.

— *Dr. Ch. Venkata Sivasai*

Contents

Introduction

The philosophy is concerned with the understanding of the life and the universe. It is aimed at comprehending the nature of existence. Philosophy is a human endeavour that leads to the Ultimate Truth. The English word 'philosophy' has its root in the Greek term – 'philo–sophia'.

The term 'philo' refers to 'love' and 'sophia' refers to human reason. The Greek terms can be literally translated in English as "love of reason" or "love of human judgment and discrimination."

From the Indian viewpoint, the word 'philosophy' suggests "observing and surveying" the existence.

In Sanskrit, the philosophy is referred to as 'darshana'. The Sanskrit word 'darshana' has its root in the word 'drs' that means 'to see', 'to look' or 'to view'. "Seeing" or "viewing" the reality and the facts of experience forms the basis of philosophy. Senses, mind and even consciousness are involved in this 'seeing'. "Seeing" also encompasses "contemplation". Seeing is not simply a sensory activity. 'Seeing' may primarily be a perceptual observation. But it may also concern the conceptual knowledge or an intuitional flash. Thus 'darshana' suggests vision. In other words, 'darshana' is a whole view revealed to the inner self, what we term as the soul or the spirit or the inner being. Philosophy or 'darshana' is concerned with the vision of 'truth and reality'.

In Sanskrit, the 'philosophy' is also referred to as 'tatva'. The Sanskrit word 'tatva' is concerned with 'the nature of reality.'

In India, the philosophy is not restricted to the intellectual pursuit. According to Indian view, the word 'philosophy' is concerned with 'the revelation of the nature of reality' or 'the vision of Ultimate Truth and Reality'.

Indian Philosophy: The Indian philosophy has its roots in the Vedic period.

The great Rishis, settled in the peaceful, invigorating environment of the forests, meditated over the fundamental questions of existence: What is the world? If it's a creation, what are its constituents? Who is the creator? What is life? What is 'truth'? What is 'the nature of reality'?

What was revealed to them was expressed in hymns. With the passage of time, the systematized collection of these hymns constituted the Vedas and the Upanishads.

Indian philosophy distinctly exhibits a spiritual bent. The essence of religion is not dogmatic in India. Here, religion develops as philosophy progressively scales higher planes.

Some of the fundamentals expressed in the Indian philosophy and the Western philosophy may be similar. However, Indian philosophy differs from the Western philosophy on several counts. While the Western philosophy deals with metaphysics, epistemology, psychology, ethics etc. separately, Indian philosophy takes a comprehensive view of all these topics.

For an Indian philosopher, philosophy is something beyond an intellectual pursuit. The Indian philosopher exemplifies philosophy in his life. His intelligence, knowledge and wisdom are reflected in his life. This is why his life positively influences the life of masses.

The Indian philosophy uniquely describes four *purusharthas* of life.

Purusharthas:

The four basic ends (*purusharthas*) of human life, as recognized by the Indian tradition, are as follows:

artha, kama, dharma and *moksha.*

(1) *Artha*: The Sanskrit word *artha* means 'that which one seeks.' Whatever activity and physical material a man needs to support life can be considered as *artha. Artha,* in a broad sense, covers man's professional activities, job, business, wealth, property and all such earthly material helpful in maintaining his life.

(2) *Kama*: Man seeks pleasure in various activities and material objects. Pursuit of happiness and pleasure is a basic, natural

instinct in man. Man derives pleasures from relationships and material objects like food, drink etc. This is *kama*. Man largely accumulates *artha* for *kama*. But *artha* and *kama* should be closely linked with the *dharma*. They should be directed towards *dharma*.

(3) *Dharma*: 'That which sustains' is *dharma*. The word *dharma* stems from the Sanskrit root '*dhr*' meaning 'to sustain' or 'to support'. *Dharma* sustains or maintains life. *Dharma* supports the society. Man lives in the society with fellow-men and various life forms. *Dharma* lays down duties and obligations expected of man. An individual and the society, for their conduct and actions, get guidance from *dharma*. Man has obligation to his own self, to the fellow-men and to the society, in fact, to the whole environment of the world. All the mutual obligations of these inter-relationships are spelt out by *dharma*.

(4) *Moksha*: *Moksha* means liberation or total freedom. The Sanskrit word *moksha* is derived from the root '*muk*'. This root means 'to emancipate' or 'to release' or 'to free'. Indian tradition considers *moksha* as the ultimate goal of life. The sufferings of man are due to *avidya*, his original ignorance about self. He has been oblivious of his true identity. He attaches himself to worldly objects. Tempted and pressed by everlasting lust and insurmountable desires, he remains bonded to the mundane objects. When knowledge (*vidya*) dawns on him, he overcomes the dualities of the world and identifies himself as the infinite, eternal Being. Having been completely free from all attachments, expectations and desires, the liberated soul attains *moksha*.

THE SYSTEMS OF INDIAN PHILOSOPHY

The Vedas are the oldest scriptures in the world. The Indian philosophical systems are classified according as they accept the authority of the Vedas or not. The systems of Indian philosophy are classified into two groups:

(1) The Orthodox Systems

(2) The Hetrodox Systems (Unorthodox)

The orthodox systems are: Nyaya, Vaisheshika, Samkhya, Yoga, Purva-Mimamsa, and Uttar-Mimamsa.

The Hetrodox (unorthodox) systems are: Charvakism, Jainism and Buddhism.

Very often, Purva-Mimamsa is referred to as "Mimamsa" only and Uttar-Mimamsa as "Vedanta".

The orthodox systems uphold the supremacy of the Vedas. The unorthodox systems reject the authority of the Vedas. Truly speaking Vaisheshika, Nyaya, Samkhya and Yoga are neither orthodox nor unorthodox. These four systems, while originating, neither accepted nor rejected the Vedas.

The orthodox systems form pairs as follows:

Nyaya-Vaisheshika, Yoga-Samkhya, Mimamsa-Vedanta. In each of the pairs, the first system is concerned with the practice and the second system focuses on the theoretical aspects.

It becomes difficult, sometimes, to name a single founder or a promoter of a system. However, the following are widely acknowledged as proponents of the above systems: Gautama for Nyaya, Kanada for Vaisheshika, Patanjali for Yoga, Kapila for Samkhya, Jaimini for Purva-Mimamsa and Shamkara for Uttar-Mimamsa.

Charvakism is believed to have been promoted by Charvaka. Vardhamana Mahavira is acknowledged as the founder of Jainism and Gautama Buddha as the founder of Buddhism.

The Common Characteristics in Indian Philosophies

The systems of Indian philosophies, with a singular exception of Charvakism, have certain common characteristics. Charvakism remarkably differs from other systems as it promotes materialism.

The following characteristics are common to all other systems:

(1) All the schools emphasize that the philosophy must have a positive impact on life of man. The schools have a general agreement on the importance of the *Purushartha*. All the schools agree that the philosophy should help man in realizing the main ends of human life: the*purusharthas*, i.e. *artha, kama, dharma* and *moksha*.

(2) All the systems reflect that the philosophy should lead a man from darkness and ignorance to light and knowledge.

(3) There is a general agreement among the systems that the truth and reality should be verifiable. They should be substantiated with reasoning and experience. An experience may be sensory, conceptual or intuitional.

(4) It is accepted by all the schools that man's suffering results from his ignorance. Man can conquer ignorance and attain total freedom (*moksha*) in this bodily existence.

(5) There is a general agreement on man's essential spirituality.

The History of Indian Philosophy: The historians go on debating about the origin of the Aryans and the time-period when the Vedic civilization developed in India.

It is believed by the Western scholars that the Aryans descended from the regions of the North-Central Asia sometime around 1500 B.C., though this has been challenged by some other learned scholars. Some of the eminent Indian scholars also differ from their Western counterparts, saying that the Aryans were natives of India for long and that the Vedic civilization developed about 4000 to 8000 years ago. The renowned Indian scholar Lokamanya Tilak contends that the first Vedic hymns could have been composed nearly 6000 years ago and the later works like the Upanishads themselves could be nearly 3000 years old.

The philosophies develop over long spells of time. It is difficult for the historians to ascertain the period for the development of a particular philosophy.

However, we can safely outline the history of Indian philosophies, as per Dr. Radhakrishnan, as follows:

(1) The Vedic period (1500 B.C. to 600 B.C.)

(2) The Epic period (600 B.C. to 200 A.D.)

(3) The *Sutra* period (200 A.D. to 1700 A.D.)

(4) The Scholastic period (From Sutra Period to 17th century)

Let us get an idea of these periods:

(1) The Vedic Period: This period can be regarded as the dawn of civilization in the world. It witnessed the real transformation of man from a *prakrit* man to a *Sanskrit*

man. The Vedic period covers the rise and the development of the Aryan culture and civilization. The literature of the Vedic period is considered to be the most ancient in the world. It consists of the four Vedas, namely, Rig Veda, Yajur Veda, Sama Veda and Atharva Veda. Each of the Vedas is divided into four parts: The *Samhitas* (the *Mantras*) , the *Brahmanas*, the *Aranyakas* and the *Upanishads*.

(2) The Epic Period: It is the period of the development of the early Upanishads and the *darshanas* and is concerned with the enriching of intellect of man. The *darshanas* paved the way for the growth of the systems of philosophies in India. The invaluable *dharma -shastras*, the great treatises on ethical and social philosophy, are the gifts of this period. Apart from the extra-ordinary philosophical doctrines, the "non-systemic and the non-technical" literature appeared in this age. The great epics Ramayana and Mahabharata are the gifts of this period. The period is very significant because it witnessed the rise and early development of *Shaivism* and *Vaishnavism* as well as that of *Jainism* and *Buddhism*. The *Jainism* and the *Buddhism* are considered as heterodox religious philosophies as they do not endorse the authority of the Vedas.

(3) The *Sutra* Period: Over a period of time, the Vedic literature and the subsequent works grew to a massive scale. The great scholars made efforts to safeguard the rich heritage. That is how the illustrious *Sutras* were written. The *Sutras* are, mostly, epigrammatic sentences in the verse-form. They helped to preserve and transmit the treasure of philosophies expressed in the voluminous ancient works. Badarayana (*Veda Vyasa*), one of the greatest scholars, wrote Brahma-Sutra, also known as Vedanta-Sutra. The *Sutras* laid the foundation of the different systems of philosophies in India. The six orthodox systems based on the Sutras are Vaisheshika, Nyaya, Samkhya, Yoga, Purva-Mimamsa and Uttar-Mimamsa.

(4) The Scholastic Period: This period coinciding with the Sutra period, witnessed the distinguished scholars like

Shamkaracharya, Kumarila, Madhavacharya, Ramanujacharya, Sridhara and others. With the passage of time, the ancient literature became nearly incomprehensible. The Vedas, expressed in the *Chhandas*, the old form of Sanskrit, became difficult to follow. Even the interpretation of the *Sutras* posed challenges to the learned scholars. Hence the scholars wrote commentaries on the ancient literature in general and on the *Sutras*in particular. Then a number of commentaries were written. Very often a commentary was written on the original commentary or on an earlier one. Various scholars wrote commentaries on Brahma-Sutra according to their own interpretation. Chief among them were Shamkaracharya, Ramanujacharya and Madhavacharya. Incidentally, three schools of Vedanta were developed: Shamkaracharya's *Advaita Vedanta*, Ramanujacharya's Vishishtadvaita *Vedanta* and Madhavacharya's *Dvaita Vedanta*.

1

History of an Indian Philosophy

INTRODUCTION

"Hinduism" is a term used to designate a body of religious and philosophical beliefs indigenous to the Indian subcontinent. Hinduism is one of the world's oldest religious traditions, and it is founded upon what is often regarded as the oldest surviving text of humanity: the Vedas. It is a religion practiced the world over. Countries with Hindu majorities include Bali, India, Mauritius and Nepal, though countries in Asia, Africa, Europe and the Americas have sizable minorities of practicing Hindus.

For historical and doctrinal reasons, some modern Indologists have adopted the convention of distinguishing between traditional Hinduism and "Neo-Hinduism" (cf. Hacker; Halbfass, *India and Europe*). Against this distinction, "Hinduism" is often reserved for some traditional philosophical and religious beliefs indigenous to the Indian subcontinent, and "Neo-Hinduism" is reserved for a modern set of religious and philosophical beliefs articulated by Indians who defined their religious views in contrast to a perceived Western preoccupation with scientism and sectarianism. For many Western educated individuals in the world today (particularly those who count themselves as "Hindus"), the philosophy captured under the term "Neo-Hinduism" designates their religious and philosophical belief set. While Neo-Hinduism is no doubt a part of the Hindu philosophical tradition, it constitutes a distinct development within the tradition. Here the terms "Neo-Hindu" and "Neo-Hinduism" will be used to single out this recent development of Hindu thought. "Hindu" and "Hinduism" will be used to designate any portion of the tradition. The label "Hindu philosophy" will be reserved for the philosophical elements of Hinduism.

The history of Hindu philosophy can be divided roughly into three, largely overlapping stages:

1. Non-Systematic Hindu Philosophy, Found in the Vedas and Secondary religious Texts(beginning in 2nd Millennia B.C.E)
2. Systematic Hindu Philosophy (begining in the 1st millennia B.C.E)
3. Neo-Hindu Philosophy (beginning in the 19th Century C.E.

Hindu philosophy is difficult to narrow down to a definite doctrine because Hinduism itself, as a religion, resists identification with any well worked out doctrine. This may not be so surprising when we consider that the term "Hinduism" itself is not in traditional, pre-colonial Hindu literature. Prior to the modern period of history, authors that we think of as Hindus did not identify themselves by that title. The term itself is not rooted in any Indian language, but likely derives from the Persian term "*sindhu,*" cognate with the Latin "*Indus,*" used to refer to inhabitants of the Indian subcontinent (cf. Monier-Williams p.1298). Its historical usage is thus an umbrella term that identifies many related religious and philosophical traditions that are not clearly part of another Indian tradition, such as Buddhism and Jainism.

Owing to the geographical proximity of the views grouped under the term "Hinduism" we might expect that such views have some comprehensive doctrinal similarities. However, many of the ideas and practices commonly associated with Hinduism can be found in adjacent Indian religio-philosophical traditions, such as Buddhism and Jainism. Moreover, some of them are not common to all Hindu thinkers. The rich diversity of views within the Hindu tradition that overlap with non-Hindu views makes identifying "Hinduism" on the basis of a shared, comprehensive doctrine difficult if not impossible.

a. Defining Hinduism: Salient Features and False Starts

i. Karma

A common thesis associated with Hinduism is the view that events in a person's life are determined by karma. The term literally means "action," but in this context it denotes the moral, psychological spiritual and physical causal consequences of morally significant past choices. If it were the case that a belief in karma is common to all Hindu philosophies, and only Hindu philosophies, then we would have a clear doctrinal criterion for identifying Hinduism. This approach is unsuccessful because a belief in karma is common to many of India's religious traditions—including Buddhism and Jainism. Moreover, it is not evident that it is embraced by all sources that we consider Hindu. For instance, the doctrine of karma seems to be absent from much of the Vedas. Karma is not a sufficient criterion of Hinduism, and it likely is not a necessary condition either.

ii. Polytheism

Polytheism, or the worship of many deities, is often identified as a distinctive feature of Hinduism. However, it is not true that all Hindus are polytheists. Indeed, many Hindus belong to sectarian traditions (such as Vaisnavism, or Saivism) that specify that only one deity (Visnu, in the first case, or Siva, in the second), or a very small set of deities, are genuine Gods, and subordinate the rest of the pantheon associated with Hinduism to the status of exalted beings. We could identify Hinduism as the set of religious views that recognize the divinity or exalted status of a core set of Indic deities, but this too would not provide a way to separate Hinduism from Buddhism and Jainism.

Many "Hindu" deities, such as Brahmâ (the Creator God), are recognized and treated as exalted beings and deities in the Buddhist Pâli Canon (cf. *Majjhima Nikâya* II.130; *Samyutta Nikâya* I.421-23). Likewise, the popular Hindu deity Krsna is treated in the early Jain tradition as a Jain Ford Maker, and a tradition of worshiping the Goddess Laksmî (a goddess revered by Hindus as the consort of Visnu) continues amongst Jains today (see Dundas pp. 98, 183).

Belief in certain deities might constitute a necessary condition of Hinduism, but it is not a sufficient criterion.

iii. Purusârthas : dharma, artha, kâma and moksa

Hinduism might be identified with a core set of values, commonly known in Hindu literature as the Purusârthas , or ends of persons. The *Purusârthas* are a set of four values: dharma, *artha, kâma* and *moksa*. "Dharma" in the *Purusârtha* scheme and throughout much of Hindu literature stands for the ethical or moral (in action, or in character, hence it is often translated as "duty"), "*artha*" for economic wealth, "*kâma*" for pleasure, and "*moksa*" for soteriological liberation from rebirth and imperfection. Hinduism, one might argue, is any religious view from the Indian subcontinent that recognizes that human beings ought to maximize the *Purusârthas* at the appropriate time and in the appropriate ways. This approach will not do, for not all views that we consider Hindu recognize the validity of all of these values. While many of the systematic Hindu philosophical schools seem to be critical of *kâma,* understood as sensual pleasure, the early stage of one Hindu philosophical school—Pûrvamîmâmsâ—does not recognize the idea that there is anything like liberation as a possible end for individuals.

The *Purusârthas* are important for any study of Indian thought, however, for they constitute the value-theoretic backdrop against which Indian thinkers articulated their views: typically, most all Indian philosophers recognized the validity of all four values, though some, like the Materialists (Cârvâka) are on record as holding that *kâma* or sensual pleasure is the only dharma or morality (*Gunaratna* p.276), and that there is no such thing as liberation. Others such as the early Pûrvamîmâmsâ ignore the idea of personal liberation but emphasizes the importance of dharma. As all Hindu philosophical schools appear to recognize something that might count as "dharma" or morality, we might attempt to understand Hinduism in terms of its allegiance to a particular moral theory. This attempt to define Hinduism in terms of a simple doctrine fails, for some of what passes for dharma (ethics, morality or duty) in the context of particular schools of Hindu philosophical thought share much with non-Hindu, but Indian schools of thought. This is particularly apparent in the case of the Hindu philosophical school of Yoga, whose moral theory shares much with Jainism, and with Buddhist Mahâyâna thought. Also, there is sufficient variation amongst the schools of Hindu philosophy on moral matters that makes defining Hindu philosophy *solely*on the basis of a shared moral doctrine impossible. If there is a core moral theory common to all Hindu schools, it is likely to be so thin that it will also be found as a component of other Indian religions. Thus, an ethical theory might be a necessary criterion of Hinduism, but it is insufficient.

iv. Varna (Caste)

Finally, one might attempt to identify Hinduism with the institution of a caste system that carves society into a specified set of classes whose natures dispose them and obligate them to certain occupations in life. More specifically, one might argue that Hinduism is any belief system wedded to the idea that any well ordered society is composed of four castes: Brahmins (priestly or scholarly caste), *Ksatriya* (marshal or royal caste), *Vaisyas* (merchant caste) and *Sûdras* (labor caste).

This approach to defining Hinduism is essentially a rehabilitation of the idea that some core moral doctrine cements Hinduism together. There are two problems with this approach that renders it unhelpful to identifying Hinduism. First, anyone familiar with Indian society will know that caste (*"varna,"* or more commonly *"jâti"*) is an Indian phenomenon that is not restricted to Hindu sections of society. One might argue that the approving use of the term *"Brahmin"* in Buddhist and Jain texts shows that even these socially critical movements were comfortable with a caste structured society provided that obligations and privileges accorded to the various castes were justly distributed (cf. *Dhammapada* ch. XXVI; cf. Sûtrakrtânga I.xii.11-21). Secondly, and more importantly, it is not clear that caste is philosophically important to many schools that are conventionally understood under the heading of "Hindu philosophy." Some schools, such as Yoga, appear to be implicitly critical of life in conventional society guided by the values of social and ecological domination, while some schools, such as Advaita Vedânta, are openly critical of the idea that caste morality has any relevance to a spiritually *serious* aspirant.

b. A Textual Definition of Hinduism and Hindu Philosophy

Because the term "Hinduism" has no roots in the self-conceptualization of people that we in retrospect label as "Hindus," we are unlikely to find anything very significant in the way of philosophical doctrine that is essential to Hinduism. Yet, the term continues to be useful because it centers on a stance that separates Hindu thinkers from Buddhist, Jain, or Sikh thinkers. The stance in question is openness to the provisional validity of a core set of Hindu texts. At the center of the canon of Hindu texts is the Vedas, followed by a large body of literature of secondary religious importance, which largely derive their legitimacy from Vedic thought. Non-systematic Hindu philosophy is comprised of the philosophical elements of the primary and secondary bodies of canonical Hindu texts, while the systematic Hindu philosophies, which also adopt the congenial disposition towards the Vedas, find their definitive expressions in formal philosophical texts authored by professional philosophers. Finally, Neo-Hindu philosophy of late likewise adopts a positive disposition to the Vedas, and hence constitutes the latest offering in the history of Hindu philosophy.

2. STAGE ONE: NON-SYSTEMATIC HINDU PHILOSOPHY: THE RELIGIOUS TEXTS

a. The Four Vedas

The Vedas are a large corpus, originally committed to memory and transmitted orally from teacher to student. The term *"veda"* means "knowledge" or "wisdom" and embodies what was likely regarded by its original attendants as the sum-total of the knowledge of their people. On the basis of linguistic variations in the corpus, contemporary scholars are of the opinion that the Vedas were composed at various points during approximately a 900 year span that can be no later than 1500 B.C.E. to 600 B.C.E.. The Vedas are composed in an Indo-European language that is loosely referred to as Sanskrit, but much of it is in an ancient precursor to Sanskrit, more properly called Vedic.

The Vedic corpus is comprised of four works each called "Vedas." The four Vedas are *Zg Veda, Sâma Veda, Yajur Veda* and *Atharva Veda,* respectively. Each of the four Vedas is edited into four distinct sections: *Mantras, Brâhmanas, Âranyakas,* and *Upanisads.*

i. Karma Khanda or Action Section of the Vedas

The main portion of the Veda (which the term "Veda" most properly refers to) consists of *mantras,* or sacred chants and incantations. A section called the *Brâhmanas,* which contains ritual instruction, and speculative discussions on the meaning of Vedic rituals, follows this. These first two portions comprise what is often called the *karma Khanda* or "action portion" of the Vedas, or alternatively, the Pûrvamîmâmsâ ("former inquiry"). (The philosophical school of Pûrvamîmâmsâ takes its name from its focus on the early part of the Vedas.)

Many of the hymns of the *karma Khanda* ask for special favors from deities, and emphasize the worldly rewards of *artha* (economic prosperity) and *kâma* (sensual pleasure) that come from propitiating gods through prescribed sacrifices. However, the earlier portion of the Vedas is not entirely devoid of lofty or philosophical significance. Many of the mantras resurface in the latter portion of the Vedas as dense expressions of metaphysical theses. Moreover, many portions of the *karma Khanda* elaborate the significance of the various Vedic deities, which surpass the role that could be attributed to them in a polytheistic context. Instead, what one finds frequently is the elevation of a single deity to the level of the cosmic soul (for example, see the *Srî Rudra*).

A recurrent cosmological and ethical vision appears to emerge in the *karma Khanda.* This is the idea that the universe is a closed ethical system, supported by a system of reciprocal sacrifice and obligation. In this context, the *karma Khanda* promotes the practice of animal sacrifices to the gods, to ensure that conditions on earth are livable and fruitful for all of its inhabitants. A related doctrine that begins to emerge in portions of the *karma Khanda* is the four-fold caste system that sets out strict obligations for all to fulfill, along with the idea that the caste-social order is divinely ordained. This is most clearly related in the *Purusa Sûkta*, a section of mantras from the *Zg Veda*. According to the *Purusa Sûkta*, the universe, as we know it, is a result of the self-sacrifice of a Cosmic Person (an ultimate God, later identified with Visnu or Siva, depending upon sectarian contexts). Upon being bound and sacrificed by the gods, the various portions of the Cosmic Person become the various castes: the head becomes the Brahmins, the arms become the *Ksatriya* caste, the thighs become the *Vaisya* caste, and the feet become the *Sûdra* caste. While the caste system may be a pervasively Indian phenomenon, the idea that the caste system is divinely ordained appears to be found in Hindu philosophies in proportion to the weight they give to the authority of the *karma khanda*.

ii. Jñana Khanda or Knowledge Section of the Vedas

The *karma khanda* is followed by the *Âranyakas*, or forest books, which for the most part eschew rituals, and are far more speculative. After the *Âranyakas* come the section of the Vedas known as the "*Upanisads*," which consist of a dialogue between a teacher and student on metaphysical, axiological and cosmological issues. Whereas the goal of the early portion of the Vedas is action, the goal of the latter portion of the Vedas is *jñâna* (knowledge) of *Brahman* (a neuter term for the Ultimate, depicted in the Upanisads as the ultimate God). Further, the *Upanisads* identify *Brahman* with *Âtma* (Self) and suggest that knowing this entity will save one from all sorrow (cf. *Mundaka Upanisad* 7) and result in liberation. *Brahman* or *Âtma* is additionally presented as the omniscient, omnipotent and omnipresent entity hidden from plain view, but known through philosophical speculation that is driven by dissatisfaction with earthly rewards. This latter part of the Vedas is often referred to as the *uttara mîmâmsâ* ("higher inquiry"), or the *vedânta*, which means "end of the Vedas." Alternatively, it is known as the *jñâna khanda*, or "knowledge portion" of the Vedas. (The Hindu schools known as Vedânta take their name from their focus on this portion of the Vedas). The sustained theme of the *uttara mîmâmsâ* is that the cosmos as we know it is the result of the causal efficacy of *Brahman*, or *Âtma*, that the results of works are ephemeral, and that knowledge of reality brings everlasting reward. The *uttara mîmâmsâ* is characterized by a pervasive dissatisfaction with ritual (cf. *Mundaka Upanisad* I.ii.10).

The specific relationship between the individual and *Brahman*, or *Âtma*, is a matter of controversy amongst commentators on the latter portions of the Vedas. Four major commentarial schools evolved to interpret the import of the later portions of the Vedas. This confirms the suspicion that the actual position of the *Upanisads* is less than clear, or at least debatable.

b. Secondary Texts: *Smrti* Literature

On many traditional Hindu accounts (specifically the account found in the Pûrvamîmâmsâ and Vedânta schools), the Vedas are regarded as "*sruti*", "heard" or revealed texts, and are contrasted with *smrti* or remembered texts. The *smrti* texts are far more numerous, but purport to be based upon the learning of the Vedas. Unlike the Vedas, the *smrtis* were traditionally regarded as appropriate for general consumption, while the Vedas were regarded as the sole preserve of the high castes. The *smrti* literature, as a rule, was originally authored in Sanskrit. Over time, however, translations into vernacular languages became popular, and additional texts were authored in vernaculars.

The tradition of *smrti* literature stretches back to the end of the Vedic period, and in some ways is still very much alive today. The *smrti* texts can all be read as attempting to unify the seemingly divergent goals of the action section of the Vedas (being morality, or dharma) and the knowledge section of the Vedas (being liberation or *moksa*). The overall strategy offered in the various *smrti* texts is to affirm a moral scheme known traditionally as *varna âsrama dharma*, or the morality of caste (*varna*) and station in life (*âsrama*). This scheme reconciles the demands of dharma and *moksa*, as well as *artha* and *kâma*, by apportioning different stages of life to the pursuit of different ends. At the end of childhood, and before the beginning of adolescence, an individual is typically expected to be a celibate student (*brahmacarya*), and learn one caste's ways. Then at an appropriate age they are to marry and become a householder (*grhastha*). During this stage an individual is permitted and expected to pursue the ends of *kâma* or sensual pleasure through married life and *artha* or economic prosperity through caste occupations. After raising a family, a couple is to retire to the forest and become forest dwellers (*vânaprastha*), to facilitate their transition from a life focused on *kâma* and *artha* to a life geared towards liberation. Finally, individuals give up all possessions, renounce society and become a ascetic (*sannyâsa*) at which point they are to focus solely on *moksa* or spiritual liberation.

There are three prominent varieties of *smrti* literature that are important to the study of Hindu philosophy. Though they for the most part express and extol the doctrine of *varna âsrama dharma*, they are composed in different styles, and with different audiences in mind.

i. Itihâsas

The best known of the *smrti* literature are the great Hindu epics, such as the *Mahâbhârata* and *Râmâyana*. The focal plot of the *Mahâbhârata* is a fratricidal war between the children of two princes. The deity Krsna figures prominently in this epic, as a mutual cousin of both warring factions, though he is not the protagonist. The *Râmâyana* is an account of the life story of the crown prince Râma up until he vanquishes the tyrant King Râvana and successfully rescues his wife and the crown princess Sîtâ from Râvana's grips. Both Krsna and Râma are traditionally regarded as human incarnations of Visnu. Both the *Mahâbhârata* and *Râmâyana* are grouped under the heading of *itihâsa* ('thus spoken') literature. The focal events of the two epics likely occurred between 1000 B.C.E. and 700 A.D. (Thapar p. 31) though the epics themselves appear to have gone through a long process of revision and evolution before their final Sanskrit versions appear on the scene in the first two centuries of the common era.

Itihâsas, though recorded in the form of a narrative, are littered with philosophical discussions on cosmology, and ethics. The most philosophically famous portion of the *itihâsa* literature is the *Bhagavad Gîtâ*. The *Bhagavad Gîtâ* forms a portion of the *Mahâbhârata*, but owing to its importance in the tradition it is often regarded as a stand-alone text.

ii. Bhagavad Gîtâ

The *Bhagavad Gîtâ* consists of a discourse given by Krsna on the eve of the battle of the fratricidal war of the *Mahâbhârata* to his cousin Arjuna, who becomes despondent at the thought of engaging in a war whose main aim is resting control over the throne, at the expense of the destruction of his family. Krsna exhorts Arjuna to do his duty as a *Ksatriya* and fight the war that he has been charged with (*Bhagavad Gîtâ* 2:31). For "[b]etter is one's own duty, though ill done, than the duty of another well done...." (*Bhagavad Gîtâ* 18:47; cf. Manu X. 97). In keeping with the general theme of the *smrti* literature, Krsna focuses on reconciling the goal of *moksa* with that of dharma. Krsna's first solution to the problem of the conflict of dharma and *moksa* involves doing one's duty with a strong deontological consciousness, which attends to duty for duty's sake, and not for its rewards. This deontological attitude not only perfects moral action, on Krsna's account, but it also constitutes true renunciation, which is a prerequisite to *moksa*. Krsna calls the deontological renunciation of rewards of dutiful action *karma yoga,* or the discipline (yoga) of action (karma) (*Bhagavad Gîtâ* ch.3). This is not the only type of yoga that Krsna prescribes. He also propounds what he identifies as distinct yogas (*Bhagavad Gîtâ* chs. 4-11) that might be grouped under the heading of *jñâna yoga,* or the discipline (yoga) of knowledge (*jñâna*), whereby one develops a detached attitude towards the fruits of works through knowledge of the excellences and unchanging nature of the transcendent (sometimes spoken of as "*Brahman*" in this text), and the ephemeral and temporary nature of worldly accomplishments. To this end, Krsna calls upon the philosophy of Sânkhya and Yoga, as well as the philosophical concepts of the *Upanisads* to explicate the nature of the changing and the transcendent. Finally, Krsna also prescribes what he calls *bhakti yoga* or the "discipline (yoga) of devotion (*bhakti*)" (*Bhagavad Gîtâ* chs. 12-18). Whereas in karma yoga, one merely gives up fruits of actions, in *bhakti yoga* one offers the fruits of one's actions to God. Whereas in *jñâna yoga* one pursues knowledge for its own sake, in *bhakti yoga* one pursues knowledge for the sake of a loving relationship with the Ultimate. Krsna appears to hold that any of the ways that he prescribes will result in liberation for all three varieties of yogas will ensure that the obstacle to liberation—attachment to fruits of actions—is over come.

iii. Purânas

"Purâna" means *history* and is the term applied to a group of texts that share a few features: (a) they typically provide a detailed history of the origin of the various gods and the Universe, and (b) they are written in praise of the exploits of a particular deity. Unlike the *itihâsas,* the *Purânas* are not restricted to incarnations of deities, but describe the activities of the deities, including their incarnations. The *Purâna* literature comes down to us from a time that post dates the composition of the Vedas, though their precise dates of composition are not known (cf. Thapar p.29). There are many *Purânas,* though the most famous is likely the *Bhâgavata Purâna.*

The *Bhâgavata Purâna* is distinguished amongst *Purânas* for being regarded by Gaudiya Vaisnavism, founded by the medieval Bengali saint Caitanya, as the ultimate revelation on all doctrinal matters. This tradition has come into prominence in recent times in the form of the International Society for Krsna Consciousness, commonly known as the Hare Krsna movement. According to the *Bhâgavata Purâna,* the Ultimate (*Brahman*) is both identical with and distinct from creation: on this account, *Brahman* converts itself into the universe but maintains a distinct identity all the same. The *Bhâgavata Purâna* also identifies Visnu with *Brahman,* and holds that *bhakti* (devotion) is the chief means of attaining liberation, which consists in the personal absorption of the individual (*jîva*) in *Brahman.* The *Bhâgavata Purâna* thus presents one of the famous and enduring theistic expressions of the Bhedâbheda philosophy. In the way of ethics, the *Bhâgavata Purâna* strays little from the *Varna âsrama dharma* found in most *smrti* literature (*Bhâgavata Purâna* I.ii.9-12), though it advocates what it calls *"bhâgavata dharma"* (*bhâgavata* ethic) which is a combination of the *karma yoga* and *bhakti yoga* of the *Gîtâ* supplemented with an emphasis on living the life characteristic of a devotee of Krsna as described in the *Bhâgavata Purâna* (XI.iii.23-31).

iv. Dharmasâstra

The term *"Dharmasâstra"* literally means treaties or science (*sâstra*) of dharma. The term refers to a corpus of literature clearly authored by Brahmins with the aim of reinforcing a particular conception of *Varna âsrama dharma*: a moral theory that critics will note ensures that Brahmins are allotted a privileged or crowning position in the caste scheme. The *Dharmasâstras* contain many features of other *smrti* literature that make them philosophically interesting.

Like the *Purâna* literature, many of the *Dharmasâstras* provide accounts of the origins of the universe, and sometimes they delve into the question of the means to liberation. Their dominant concern however is to prescribe the specific duties and privileges of each caste. After attending to the political question of the proper ordering of society, the *Dharmasâstras* typically focus on the matter of *prayascitta,* or ritual expiation (see Kane vol.4 ch.1 pp. 1-40).

The idea of ritual expiation can be understood as a procedure concerned with alleviating ritual impurity. However, it also has clear moral implications: *prayascittas* are prescribed for every manner of offence, and if an agent undertakes the appropriate *prayascitta,* they can atone for their moral transgressions. Aprayascitta can take the form of a ritual, an act of charity, or corporal punishment. The idea that one can ritually atone for moral transgressions is unique to the *Dharmasâstras,* and related texts in the history of Hindu philosophy.

3. STAGE TWO: SYSTEMATIC HINDU PHILOSOPHY: THE DARSANAS

Core Hindu canonical texts—the Vedas—form the textual backdrop against which many of the systematic Hindu philosophies are articulated. However, they do not exhaust the import of Hindu philosophy for two main reasons. First, the Vedas are not composed with the intention of being systematic treaties on philosophical issues. They leave many issues of philosophy relatively untouched. Secondly, the core Hindu canonical texts are not canonical in the same way for all Hindus. By and large, those we tend to regard as Hindu accord some type of provisional authority to both the Vedas, and the secondary Vedic literature. However, the authority accorded is something that Hindu thinkers have disagreed upon. Some of the foundational works in systematic Hindu philosophy do not explicitly mention the Vedas (for example, the Sânkhya Kârikâ), leaving the impression that these schools were tolerant of the authority of the Vedas, but not philosophically wedded to it in any deep sense.

The term "*darsana*" in Sanskrit translates as "vision" and is conventionally regarded as designating what we are inclined to look upon as systematic philosophical views. The history of Indian philosophy is replete with *Darsanas*. The number of *Darsanas* to be found in the history of Indian philosophy depends largely on the organizational question of how one is to enumerate *Darsanas*: how much difference between expressions of philosophical views can be tolerated before we are inclined to count texts as expressing distinct *Darsanas*? The question seems particularly pertinent in cases like Buddhist and Jain philosophy, which have all had rich philosophical histories. The issue is relatively easier to settle in the context of Hindu philosophy, for a convention has developed over the centuries to count systematic Hindu philosophy as being comprised of *six* (*âstika*, or Veda recognizing) *Darsanas*. The six *Darsanas* are: Nyâya, Vaisesika, Sânkhya, Yoga, Pûrvamîmâmsâ, and Vedânta.

As a rule, systematic Indian philosophy (Hinduism, Jainism and Buddhism) was recorded in Sanskrit, the pan-Indian language of scholarship, after the end of the Vedic period. While scholars are confident about the approximate dates that the texts of systematic Indian philosophy handed down to us were written (cf. Potter, *"Bibliography," Encyclopaedia of Indian Philosophies,* vol.1) scholars are not in many cases as confident about the age of the schools themselves. Moreover, most of the schools of Hindu philosophy have existed side by side. Thus, the order of explication of the systematic schools of Hindu philosophy follows the conventional order of explication and not any particular historical order.

a. Nyâya

The term "*nyâya*" traditionally had the meaning "formal reasoning," though in later times it also came to be used for reasoning in general, and by extension, the legal reasoning of traditional Indian law courts. Opponents of the Nyâya school of philosophy frequently reduce it to the status of an arm of Hindu philosophy devoted to questions of logic and rhetoric. While reasoning is very important to Nyâya, this school also had important things to say on the topic of epistemology, theology and metaphysics, rendering it a comprehensive and autonomous school of Indian philosophy.

The Nyâya school of Hindu philosophy has had a long and illustrious history. The founder of this school is the sage Gautama (2nd cent. C.E.)—not to be confused with the Buddha, who on many accounts had the name "Gautama" as well. Nyâya went through at least two stages in the history of Indian philosophy. At an earlier, purer stage, proponents of Nyâya sought to elaborate a philosophy that was distinct from contrary *Darsanas*. At a later stage, some Nyâya and Vaisesika authors (such as Sankara-Misra, 15th cent. C.E.) became increasingly syncretistic and viewed their two schools as sister *darsanas*. As well, at the latter stages of the Nyâya tradition, the philosopher Gangesa (14th cent. C.E.) narrowed the focus to the epistemological issues discussed by the earlier authors, while leaving off metaphysical matters and so initiated a new school, which came to be known as Navya Nyâya, or "New" Nyâya. Our focus will be mainly on classical, non-syncretic, Nyâya.

According to the first verse of the *Nyâya-Sûtra*, the Nyâya school is concerned with shedding light on sixteen topics: *pramâna* (epistemology), *prameya* (ontology), *saCœaya* (doubt), *prayojana* (axiology, or "purpose"), *drstânta* (paradigm cases that establish a rule), *Siddhânta* (established doctrine), *avayava* (premise of a syllogism), *tarka* (*reductio ad absurdum*), *nirnaya* (certain beliefs gained through epistemically respectable means), *vâda* (appropriately conducted discussion), *jalpa* (sophistic debates aimed at beating the opponent, and not at establishing the truth), *vitanda* (a debate characterized by one party's disinterest in establishing a positive view, and solely with refutation of the opponent's view), *hetvâbhâsa* (persuasive but fallacious arguments), chala (unfair attempt to contradict a statement byequivocating its meaning), jâti (an unfair reply to an argument based on a false analogy), andnigrahasthâna (ground for defeat in a debate) (Nyâya-Sûtra and Vâtsyâyana's Bhâsya I.1.1-20).

With respect to the question of epistemology, the *Nyâya-Sûtra* recognizes four avenues of knowledge: these are perception, inference, analogy, and verbal testimony of reliable persons. Perception arises when the senses make contact with the object of perception. Inference comes in three varieties: pûrvavat (a priori), sesavat (a posteriori) and sâmanyatodrsta (common sense) (*Nyâya-Sûtra* I.1.3–7).

The Nyâya's acceptance of both arguments from analogy and testimony as means of knowledge, allows it to accomplish two theological goals. First, it allows Nyâya to claim that the Veda's are valid owing to the reliability of their transmitters (*Nyâya-Sûtra* II.1.68). Secondly, the acceptance of arguments from analogy allows the Nyâya philosophers to forward a natural theology based on analogical reasoning. Specifically, the Nyâya tradition is famous for the argument that God's existence can be known for (a) all created things resemble artifacts, and (b) just as every artifact has a creator, so too must all of creation have a creator (Udayanâcârya and Haridâsa Nyâyâlamkâra I.3-4).

The metaphysics that pervades the Nyâya texts is both realistic and pluralistic. On the Nyâya view the plurality of reasonably believed things exist and have an identity independently of their contingent relationship with other objects. This applies as much to mundane objects, as it does to the self, and God. The ontological model that appears to pervade Nyâya metaphysical thinking is that of atomism, the view that reality is composed of indecomposable simples (cf. *Nyâya-Sûtra* IV.2.4.16).

Nyâya's treatment of logical and rhetorical issues, particularly in the *Nyâya Sûtra,* consists in an extended inventory acceptable and unacceptable argumentation. Nyâya is often depicted as primarily concerned with logic, but it is more accurately thought of as being concerned with argumentation.

b. Vaisesika

The Vaisesika system was founded by the ascetic, Kanada (1st cent. C.E.). His name translates literally as "atom-eater." On some accounts Kanada gained this name because of the pronounced ontological atomism of his philosophy (*Vaisesika Sûtra* VII.1.8), or because he restricted his diet to grains picked from the field. If the Nyâya system can be characterized as being predominantly concerned with matters of argumentation, the Vaisesika system can be characterized as overwhelmingly concerned with metaphysical questions. Like Nyâya, Vaisesika in its later stages turned into a syncretic movement, wedded to the Nyâya system. Here the focus will be primarily on the early Vaisesika system, with the help of some latter day commentaries.

Kanada's *Vaisesika Sûtra*'s opening verses are both dense and very revealing about the scope of the system. The opening verse states that the topic of the text is the elaboration of dharma (ethics or morality). According to the second verse, dharma is that which results not only in *abhyudaya* but also the Supreme Good (*nihreyasa*), commonly known as *moksa* (liberation) in Indian philosophy (*Vaisesika Sûtra* I.1.1-2). The term "*abhyudaya*" designates the values extolled in the early, action portion of the Vedas, such as *artha* (economic prosperity) and *kâma* (sensual pleasure). From the second verse it thus appears that the Vaisesika system regards morality as providing the way for the remaining *Purusârthas* . A reading of the obscure third verse provided by the latter day philosopher Sankara-Misra (15th cent. C.E.) states that the validity of the Vedas rests on the fact that it is an explication of dharma. (Misra's alternative explanation is that the phrase can be read as asserting that the validity of the Vedas derives from the authority of its author, God—this is a syncretistic reading of the *Vaisesika Sûtra*, influenced by Nyâya philosophy.) (Sankara-Misra's *Vaisesika Sûtra Bhâsya* I.1.2, p.7).

From the densely worded fourth verse, it appears that the Vaisesika system regards itself as an explication of dharma. The Vaisesika system holds that the elaboration or knowledge of the particular expression of dharma (which is the Vaisesika system) consists of knowledge of six categories: substance (*dravya*), attribute (*guna*), action (karma), genus (*sâmânya*), particularity (*visesa*), and the relationship of inherence between attributes and their substances (*samavâya*) (*Vaisesika Sûtra* I.1.4).

The dense fourth verse of the *Vaisesika Sûtra* gives expression to a thorough going metaphysical realism. On the Vaisesika account, universals (*sâmânya*) as well as particularity (*visesa*) are realities, and these have a distinct reality from substances, attributes, actions, and the relation of inherence, which all have their own irreducible reality.

The metaphysical import of the fourth verse potentially obscures the fact that the Vaisesika system sets itself the task of elaborating dharma. Given the weight that the *Vaisesika Sûtra* gives to ontological matters, it is inviting to treat its insistence that it seeks to elaborate dharma as quite irrelevant to its overall concern. However, subsequent authors in the Vaisesika tradition have drawn attention to the significance of dharma to the overall system.

Sankara-Misra suggests that dharma understood in its particular presentation in the Vaisesika system is a kind of sagely forbearance or withdrawal from the world (Sankara-Misra's *Vaisesika Sûtra Bhâsya* I.1.4. p.12). In a similar vein, another commentator, Chandrakânta (19th cent. C.E.), states:

> Dharma presents two aspects, that is under the characteristic of *Pravntti* or worldly activity, and the characteristic of *Nivntti* or withdrawal from worldly activity. Of these, Dharma characterized by *Nivntti*, brings forth *tattva–jñana* or knowledge of truths, by means of removal of sins and other blemishes. (Chandrakânta p.15.)

Thus the view of the commentators appears to be that the Vaisesika system, which yields "knowledge of truths," "knowledge of the categories," or "knowledge of the essences" (cf. Sankara-Misra, p.5) is a moral virtue of the person who is initiated into the system—that is, a "particular dharma" of that person. Hence, in elaborating the nature of reality, the Vaisesika system seeks to extinguish the ignorance that obstructs the effects of dharma, and it thus also constitutes a moral virtue of the proponent of the Vaisesika system. This virtue will not only yield the fruits of works, such as *kâma* and *artha* (which the Vaisesika sage will know to appreciate at a distance) but it will also yield the highest good: *moksa*.

c. Sânkhya

The term "Sânkhya" means 'enumeration' and it suggests a methodology of philosophical analysis. On many accounts, Sânkhya is the oldest of the systematic schools of Indian philosophy. It is attributed to the legendary sage Kapila of antiquity, though we have no extant work left to us by him. His views are recounted in many *smrti* texts, such as the *Bhâgavata Purâna* and the *Bhagavad Gîtâ,* but the Sânkhya system appears to stretch back to the end of the Vedic period itself. Key concepts of the Sânkhya system appear in the *Upanisads* (*Katha Upanisad* I.3.10–11), suggesting that it is an indigenous Indian philosophical school that developed congenially in parallel with the Vedic tradition. Its relative antiquity appears to be confirmed by the references to the school in classical Jain writings (for instance, *Sûtrakrtânga* I.i.1.13), which are known for their antiquity. Unlike many of the other systematic schools of Hindu philosophy, the Sânkhya system does not explicitly attempt to align itself with the authority of the Vedas (cf. *Sânkhya Kârikâ* 2).

The oldest systematic writing on Sânkhya that we have is Îsvarakrsna's *Sânkhya Kârikâ* (4th cent. C.E.). In it we have the classic Sânkhya ontology and metaphysic set out, along with its theory of agency.

According to the Sânkhya system, the cosmos is the result of the mutual contact of two distinct metaphysical categories: *Prakrti* (Nature), and *Purusa* (person). *Prakrti,* or Nature, is the material principle of the cosmos and is comprised of three *gunas,* or "qualities." These are *sattva, rajas,* and *tamas*. *Sattva* is illuminating, buoyant and a source of pleasure; *rajas* is actuating, propelling and a source of pain; *tamas* is still, enveloping and a source of indifference (*Sânkhya Kârikâ* 12-13).

Purusa, in contrast, has the quality of consciousness. It is the entity that the personal pronoun "I" actually refers to. It is eternally distinct from Nature, but it enters into complex configurations of Nature (biological bodies) in order to experience and to have knowledge. According to the Sânkhya tradition, mind, mentality, intellect or *Mahat* (the Great one) is not a part of the *Purusa,* but the result of the complex organization of matter, or the *gunas*. Mentality is the closest thing in Nature to *Purusa,* but it is still a natural entity, rooted in materiality. *Purusa,* in contrast, is a pure witness. It lacks the ability to be an agent. Thus, on the Sânkhya account, when it seems as though we as persons are making decisions, we are mistaken: it is actually our natural constitution comprised by the *gunas* that make the decision. The *Purusa* does nothing but lend consciousness to the situation (*Sânkhya Kârikâ* 12-13, 19, 21).

The contact of *Prakrti* and *Purusa*, on the Sânkhya account, is not a chance occurrence. Rather, the two principles make contact so that *Purusa* can come to have knowledge of its own nature. A *Purusa* comes to have such knowledge when *sattva*, the illuminating *guna*, assumes a governing position in a bodily constitution. The moment that this knowledge comes about, a *Purusa* becomes liberated. The *Purusa* is no longer bound by the actions and choices of its body's constitution. However, liberation consists in the end of karma tying the *Purusa* to *Prakrti*: it does not coincide with the complete annihilation of past karma, which would consist in the disentangling of a *Purusa* from *Prakrti*. Hence, the *Sânkhya Kârikâ* likens the self-realization of the *Purusa* to a potter's wheel, which continues to spin down, after the potter has ceased putting energy to keep the wheel in motion (*Sânkhya Kârikâ* 67).

Students of ancient Western philosophy are apt to note that the Sânkhya *gunas*, and the dualistic theory of personhood, appear to have echos in Plato (4th cent. B.C.E.). Plato held that the body is the casing of the soul (though Plato, at *Phaedo* 81 and *Phaedrus* 250c suggests it is a prison, which the Sânkhya system does not), and that the embodied soul is composed of three characteristics: an earthy quality geared toward menial tasks that is appetitive (corresponding to bronze), a high-spirited quality geared towards accomplishment and competition (silver), and a reflective or rational portion that is in a position to put in order the constitution of the soul (gold) (*Republic* 3.415, 4.435–42). *Prima facie*, the bronze quality appears to correspond to *tamas*, silver to *rajas*, and *sattva* to gold. Owing to the antiquity of the Sânkhya system, it is historically implausible that it was influenced by Platonistic thought. This of course invites the contrary proposal, that Plato was influenced by the Sânkhya system. While Indian philosophers had an important impact on the course of ancient Greek philosophy (through Pyrrho of Elis, who travelled to India in the 3rd cent. B.C.E. and was impressed by a type of dialectic nihilism characteristic of some Buddhist philosophies, promoted by gymnosophists—naked wise people—who resemble Jain monks) (see Flintoff), there is no historical evidence to suggest that Sânkhya thought made its way to ancient Greece. This suggests that both Plato (4th cent. B.C.E.), and the Sânkhya system (dating back to the 6th cent. B.C.E. in the Vedas) articulate an ancient Indo-European philosophical perspective that predates both Plato and the Sânkhya system, *if* the similarities between the two are not purely coincidental.

d. Yoga

The Yoga tradition shares much with the Sânkhya *darsana.* Like the Sânkhya philosophy, traces of the Yoga tradition can be found in the *Upanisads*. While the systematic expression of the Yoga philosophy comes to us from Patañjali's *Yoga Sûtra,* it comes relatively late in the history of philosophy (at the end of the epic period, roughly 3rd century C.E.), the Yoga philosophy is also expressed in the Bhagavad Gîtâ.

The Yoga philosophy shares with Sânkhya its dualistic cosmology. Like Sânkhya, the Yoga philosophy does not attempt to explicitly derive its authority from the Vedas. However, Yoga departs from Sânkhya on an important metaphysical and moral point—the nature of agency—and from Sânkhya in its emphasis on practical means to achieve liberation.

Like the Sânkhya tradition, the Yoga *darsana* holds that the cosmos is the result of the interaction of two categories: *Prakrti* (Nature) and *Purusa* (Person). Like the Sânkhya tradition, the Yoga tradition is of the opinion that *Prakrti,* or Nature, is comprised of three *gunas,* or qualities. These are the same three qualities extolled in the Sânkhya system—*tamas, rajas,* and *sattva*—though the *Yoga Sûtra* refers to many of these by different terms (cf. *Yoga Sûtra* II.18). As with the Sânkhya system, liberation in the Yoga system is facilitated by the ascendance of *sattva* in a person's mind, which permits enlightenment on the nature of the self.

A relatively important point of cosmological difference is that the Yoga system does not consider the Mind or the Intellect (*Mahat*) to be the greatest creation of Nature. A major difference between the two schools concerns Yoga's picture of how liberation is achieved. On the Sânkhya account, liberation comes about by Nature enlightening the *Purusa,* for *Purusas* are mere spectators (cf. *Sânkhya Kârikâ* 62). In the contexts of the Yoga *darsana,* the *Purusa* is not a mere spectator, but an agent: *Purusa* is regarded as the "lord of the mind" (*Yoga Sûtra* IV.18): for Yoga it is the effort of the *Purusa* that brings about liberation. The empowered account of *Purusa* in the Yoga system is supplemented by a detail account of the practical means by which *Purusa* can bring about its own liberation.

The *Yoga Sûtra* tells us that the point of yoga is to still perturbations of the mind—the main obstacle to liberation (*Yoga Sûtra* I.2). The practice of the Yoga philosophy comes to those with energy (*Yoga Sûtra* I.21). In order to facilitate the calming of the mind, the Yoga system prescribes several moral and practical means. The core of the practical import of the Yoga philosophy is what it calls the *Astânga yoga* (not to be confused with a tradition of physical yoga also called *Astânga Yoga,* popular in many yoga centers in recent times). The *Astânga yoga* sets out the eight (*asta*) limbs (*anga*) of the practice of yoga (*Yoga Sûtra* II.29). The eight limbs include:

- *yama* – abstention from evil-doing, which specifically consists of abstention from harming others (*Ahimsâ*), abstention from telling falsehoods (*asatya*), abstention from acquisitiveness (*asteya*), abstention from greed/envy (*aparigraha*); and sexual restraint (*brahmacarya*)
- *niyamas* – various observances, which include the cultivation of purity (*sauca*), contentment (*santos*)) and austerities (*tapas*)
- *âsana* – posture
- *prânâyâma* – control of breath
- *pratyâhâra* – withdrawal of the mind from sense objects
- *dhâranâ*– concentration
- *dhyâna* – meditation
- *samâdhi* – absorption [in the self] (*Yoga Sûtra* II.29-32)

According to the *Yoga Sûtra,* the *yama* rules "are basic rules.... They must be practiced without any reservations as to time, place, purpose, or caste rules" (*Yoga Sûtra* II.31). The failure to live a morally pure life constitutes a major obstacle to the practice of Yoga (*Yoga Sûtra* II.34). On the plus side, by living the morally pure life, all of one's needs and desires are fulfilled:

When [one] becomes steadfast in... abstention from harming others, then all living creatures will cease to feel enmity in [one's] presence. When [one] becomes steadfast in... abstention from falsehood, [one] gets the power of obtaining for [oneself] and others the fruits of good deeds, without [others] having to perform the deeds themselves. When [one] becomes steadfast in... abstention from theft, all wealth comes.... Moreover, one achieves purification of the heart, cheerfulness of mind, the power of concentration, control of the passions and fitness for vision of the *Âtma* [self, or *Purusa*]. "(*Yoga Sûtra*II.35–41)

The steadfast practice of the *Astânga yoga* results in counteracting past karmas. This culminates in a milestone-liberating event: *dharmameghasamâdhi* (or the absorption in the cloud of virtue). In this penultimate state, the aspirant has all their past sins washed away by a cloud of dharma (virtue, or morality). This leads to the ultimate state of liberation for the yogi, *kaivalya* (*Yoga Sûtra* IV.33). "*Kaivalya*" translates as "aloneness."

Critics of the Yoga system charge that it cannot be accepted on moral grounds for it has as its ultimate goal a state of isolation. On this view, *kaivalya* is understood literally as a state of social isolation (see Bharadwaja). The defender of the *Yoga Sûtra* can point out that this reading of "*kaivalya*" takes the final event of liberation in the Yoga system out of context. The penultimate event that paves way for the state of *kaivalya* is a wholly moral event (*dharmameghasamâdhi*) and the path that leads to this morally perfecting event is itself an intrinsically moral endeavor (*Astânga yoga*, and particularly the *yamas*). If the concept of '*kaivalya*' is to be understood in the context of the Yoga system's preoccupation with morality, it seems that it must be understood as a function of moral perfection. Given the uncommon journey that the yogi takes, it is also natural to conclude that the state of *kaivalya* is the state characterized by having no peers, owing to the radical shift in perspective that the yogi attains through yoga. The yogi, at the point of *kaivalya*, no longer sees things from the perspective of individuals in society, but from the perspective of the *Purusa*. This arguably is the yogi's loneliness.

e. Pûrvamîmâmsâ

The Pûrvamîmâmsâ school of Hindu philosophy gains its name from the portion of the Vedas that it is primarily concerned with: the earlier (*pûrva*) inquiry (*Mîmâmsâ*), or the *karma Khanda*. In the context of Hinduism, the Pûrvamîmâmsâ school is one of the most orthodox of the Hindu philosophical schools because of its concern to elaborate and defend the contents of the early, ritually oriented part of the Vedas. Like many other schools of Indian philosophy, Pûrvamîmâmsâ takes dharma ("duty" or "ethics") as its primary focus (*Mîmâmsâ Sûtra* I.i.1). Unlike all other schools of Hindu philosophy, Pûrvamîmâmsâ did not take *moksa*, or liberation, as something to extol or elaborate upon. The very topic of liberation is nowhere discussed in the foundational text of this tradition, and is recognized for the first time by the medieval Pûrvamîmâmsâ author Kumârila (7th cent. C.E.) as a real objective worth pursuing in conjunction with dharma (Kumârila V.xvi.108–110).

The school of philosophy known as Pûrvamîmâmsâ has its roots in the *Mîmâmsâ Sûtra*, written by Jaimini (1st cent. C.E.). The *Mîmâmsâ Sûtra*, like the *Vaisesika Sûtra*, begins with the assertion that its main concern is the elaboration of dharma. The second verse tells us that dharma (or the ethical) is an injunction (*codana*) that has the distinction (*laksana*) of bringing about welfare (*artha*) (*Mîmâmsâ Sûtra* I.i.1-2).

The Pûrvamîmâmsâ system is distinguished from other Hindu philosophical schools—but for the Vedânta systems—in its view that the Vedas are epistemically foundational. Foundationalism is the view that certain knowledge claims are independently valid (which means that no further justificatory reasons are either possible or necessary to justify these claims), and moreover, that these independently valid knowledge claims are able to serve as justifications for beliefs that are based upon them. Such independently valid knowledge claims are thought to be justificatory foundations of a system of beliefs. While all Hindu philosophical schools recognize the validity of the Vedas, only the

Pûrvamîmâmsâ and Vedânta systems explicitly regard the Vedas as foundational, and being in no need of further justification: "... instruction [in the Vedas] is the means of knowing it (dharma)—infallible regarding all that is imperceptible; it is a valid means of knowledge, as it is independent..." (*Mîmâmsâ Sûtra* I.i.5). The justificatory capacity of the Vedas serves to ground the *smrti* literature, for it is the sacred tradition based on the Vedas (*Mîmâmsâ Sûtra* I.iii.2). If a *smrti* text conflicts with the Vedas, the Vedas are to be preferred. When there is no conflict, we are entitled to presume that the Vedas stand as support for the *smrti* text (*Mîmâmsâ Sûtra* I.iii.3).

Pûrvamîmâmsâ perhaps more than any other school of Indian philosophy made a sizable contribution to Indian debates on the philosophy of language. Some of Pûrvamîmâmsâ's distinctive linguistic theses impact on theological matters. One distinctive thesis of the Pûrvamîmâmsâ tradition is that the relationship between a word and its referent is "inborn" and not mediated by authorial intention (*Mîmâmsâ Sûtra* I.i.5). The second view is that words, or verbal units (*sabda*), are eternal existents. This view contrasts sharply with the view taken by the Nyâya philosophers, that words have a temporary existence, and are brought in and out of existence by utterance (*Nyâya Sûtra* II.ii.13, cf. *Mîmâmsâ Sûtra* I.i.6-11). The commentator Sabara (5th cent. C.E.) explains the Pûrvamîmâmsâ view thus:

...the word is manifested (not produced) by human effort; that is to say, if, before being pronounced, the word was not manifest, it becomes manifested by the effort (or pronouncing). Thus it is found that the fact of words being "seen after effort" is equally compatible with both views.... The Word must be eternal;—why?—because its utterance is for the purpose of another.... If the word ceased to exist as soon as uttered then no one could speak of any thing to others.... Whenever the word "*go*" (cow) is uttered, there is a notion of all cows simultaneously. From this it follows that the word denotes the Class. And it is not possible to create the relation of the Word to a Class; because in creating the relation, the creator would have to lay down the relation by pointing to the Class; and without actually using the word "*go*" (which he could not use before he has laid down its relation to its denotation) in what manner could he point to the distinct class denoted by the word "go".... (*Sabara Bhâsya* on *Mîmâmsâ Sûtra* I.i.12-19, pp. 33–38)

Hence, the only solution to the problem of how words have their meaning, on the Pûrvamîmâmsâ account, is that they have them eternally. If they do not have their meaning eternally and independent of subjective associations between referents and words, communication would be impossible. These strikingly Platonistic positions on the nature of meaning allows the Pûrvamîmâmsâ tradition to argue that the Vedas are an eternally existing, unauthored corpus, and that it's validity is beyond reproach: "... if the Veda be eternal its denotation cannot but be eternal; and if it be non-eternal (caused), then it can have no validity..." (Kumârila XXVII–XXXII, cf. V.xi.1).

Views in the history of Hindu philosophy that contrast with the Pûrvamîmâmsâ view, on the question of the source and nature of the Vedas, is the view implicit in the *Nyâya Sûtra*, and stated more clearly by the later syncretic Vaisesika (and Nyâya) author Sankara-Misra (*Vaisesika Sûtra Bhâsya*, p.7): the Vedas is the testimony of a particular person (namely God). This is a view that also appears to be echoed in the theistic schools of Vedânta, such as Visistâdvaita, where God is alluded to as the author of the Vedas (cf. Râmânuja's *Bhagavad Gîtâ Bhâsya* 18:58).

f. Vedânta

Like the Pûrvamîmâmsâ tradition, the Vedânta school is concerned with explicating the contents of a particular portion of the Vedas. While the Pûrvamîmâmsâ concerns itself with the former portion of the Vedas, the Vedânta school concerns the end (*anta*) of the Vedas. Whereas the principal concern of the earlier portion of the Vedas is action and dharma, the principal concern of the latter portion of the Vedas is knowledge and *moksa*.

Philosophies that count technically as expressions of the Vedânta philosophy find their classical expression in a commentary on a synopsis of the *Upanisads*. The synopsis of the contents of the *Upanisads* is called the *Vedânta Sûtras*, or the *Brahma Sûtras*, and its author is Bâdarâyana (1st cent. C.E.). The latter portion of the Vedas is a vast corpus that does not elaborate a single doctrine in the manner of a monograph. Rather, it is a collection of speculative texts of the Vedas with overlapping themes and images. A common thread that runs through most of the *Upanisads* is a concern to elaborate the nature of the Ultimate, or *Brahman, Âtma* or the Self (often equated in these texts with *Brahman*) and what in the subsequent tradition is known as the *jîva,* or the individual psychological unity. The *Upanisads* are relatively clear that *Brahman* stands to creation as its source and support, but its unsystematic nature leaves much to be specified in the way of doctrine. While Bâdarâyana's *Brahma Sûtra* is the systematization of the teachings of the *Upanisads,* many of the verses of the *Brahma Sûtra* are obscure and unintelligible without a commentary.

Owing to the cryptic nature of the *Brahma Sûtra* itself, many commentarial subtraditions have evolved in Vedânta. As a result, it is possible to misleadingly use the term "Vedânta" as though it stood for one comprehensive doctrine. Rather, the term "Vedânta" is best understood as a term embracing within it divergent philosophical views that have a common textual connection: their classical expression as a commentary on Bâdarâyana's text.

There are three famous commentaries (*Bhâsyas*) on the *Brahma Sûtra* that shine in the history of Hindu philosophy. These are the 8th century C.E. commentary of Sankara (Advaita) the 12th century C.E. commentary of Râmânuja (Visistâdvaita) and the 13th century C.E. commentary by Madhva (Dvaita). These three are not the only commentaries. There appears to have been no less than twenty-one commentators on the *Brahma Sûtra* prior to Madhva (Sharma, vol.1 p.15), and Madhva is by no means the last commentator on the *Brahma Sûtra* either. Important names in the history of Indian theology are amongst the latter day commentators: Nimbârka (13th cent. C.E.), Srkantha (15th cent. C.E.), Vallabha (16th cent. C.E.), and Baladeva (18th cent. C.E.). However, the majority of the commentaries prior to Sankara have been lost to history. The philosophical positions expressed in the various commentaries fall into four major camps of Vedânta: Bhedâbheda, Advaita, Visistâdvaita and Dvaita. They principally differ on the metaphysics of individual selves and *Brahman,* though there are also some striking ethical differences between these schools as well.

i. Bhedâbheda

According to the Bhedâbheda view, *Brahman* converts itself into the created, but yet maintains a distinct identity. Thus, the school holds that *Brahman* is both different (*bheda*) and not different (*abheda*) from creation and the individual *jîva*.

The philosophical persuasion that has produced the most commentaries on the *Brahma Sûtra* is the Bhedâbheda philosophy. Textual evidence suggests that all of the commentaries authored prior to Sankara's famous Advaita commentary on the *Brahma Sûtra* subscribed to a form of Bhedâbheda, which one historian calls "Pantheistic Realism" (Sharma, pp. 15-7). And on natural readings, it appears that most of the remaining commentators (but for the three famous commentators) also promulgate an interpretation of the *Brahma Sûtra* that falls within the Bhedâbheda camp.

ii. Commonalities of the Three Famous Commentaries

While the three major commentators on the *Brahma Sûtra*'s differ on important metaphysical questions like the nature and relationship of *Brahman* to creation and *jîvas,* or the important moral questions on the priority of Vedic morality, there are some common views that they all share.

All of the three major schools of Vedânta hold that the Vedas are the ultimate source of knowledge of *Brahman,* and that the Vedas have an independent validity, not reducible or contingent upon the validity of any other means of knowledge (Sankara's, Râmânuja's and Madhva's *Brahma Sûtra Bhâsyas,* I.i.1-3). This interpretation of the *Brahma Sûtra* pits the Vedânta tradition against the Nyâya optimism aboutnatural theology. For the major schools of Vedânta, natural reason cannot, on its own, arrive at knowledge of the existence of God (*Brahman*). (For a detailed criticism of the Nyâya natural theology, see Râmânuja's *Brahma Sûtra Bhâsya* pp. 162-74.)

Râmânuja and Sankara both regard the individual *jîva* as being uncreated; and having no beginning (Sankara's *Brahma Sûtra Bhâsya*

II.iii.16; Râmânuja's *Brahma Sûtra Bhâsya* II.iii.18). Madhva concurs that individual souls are eternal, but yet insists that it is correct to regard *Brahman* as the source of individual souls (Madhva's *Brahma Sûtra Bhâsya* II.iii.19).

The three major commentators on the *Brahma Sûtra* see eye to eye on the nature of the individual *as*agent. According to Sankara, Râmânuja and Madhva, the individual, or *jîva,* is an agent, with desires and goals. However, in and of itself, it has no power to make its will manifest. *Brahman,* on all three accounts, steps in and grants the fruits of the desires of an individual. Thus while on this account individuals are agents, they are really also quite impotent. (Sankara's and Râmânuja's *Brahma SûtraBhâsyas* I.iii.41; Madhva's *Brahma Sûtra Bhâsya* II.iii.42). All three authors are sensitive to the fact that *Brahman*'s help in bringing about the fruits of desires of individuals implicates *Brahman* in the evils of the world, and hence opens up the problem of evil. The theodicy of all three relies upon the doctrine of the eternality of the individual *jîva.* Since there is always some prior choice and action on the part of the individual according to which *Brahman* has to dispense consequences, at no point can *Brahman* be accused of partiality, cruelty, or making persons choose the things that they do (Sankara's and Râmânuja's *Brahma Sûtra Bhâsyas* II.i.34; *Madhva Bhâsya* II.i.35, iii.42).

Finally, Râmânuja and Sankara both appear to take a position on the propriety of animal sacrifices as prescribed in the Vedas that is reminiscent of the Pûrvamîmâmsâ deferral to the Vedas on all matters of morality. According to both Sankara and Râmânuja, animal sacrifices cannot be regarded as evils for they are enjoined in the Vedas, and the Vedas is the ultimate authority on such matters (Sankara's and Râmânuja's *Brahma Sûtra Bhâsya* III.i.25). Madhva in contrast is reputed to have been a staunch opponent of animal sacrifices, who held that such rituals are a result of a corruption of the Vedic tradition. He interprets the *Brahma Sûtra* in such a way that the question of animal sacrifices does not arise.

iii. Advaita

Combining the negative particle "*a*" with the term "*dvaita*" creates the term "*advaita*". The term "*dvaita*" is often translated as "dualism" as the term "*advaita*" is often translated as "non-dualism." In the case of Dvaita Vedânta, this convention of translation is misleading, for Dvaita Vedânta does not, like the Sânkhya system, propound a metaphysical dualism. Indeed, Dvaita Vedânta holds an explicitly pluralistic metaphysics. Rather, "*dvaita*" in the context of Vedânta nomenclature is an ordinal, meaning "secondness." Dvaita Vedânta, thus, holds that there is such a thing as secondness—something extra, that comes after the first: *Brahman*. Advaita Vedânta, in contrast, holds that *Brahman* is one without a second. "Advaita" can thus be translated as "monism," "non-duality" or most perspicuously as "non-secondness" (Hacker p.131n21).

The principal author in the Advaita tradition is Sankara. In addition to writing several philosophical works, Sankara the commentator on the *Brahma Sûtra,* set up four monasteries in the four corners of India. Successive heads of the monasteries, according to tradition, take Sankara's name. This has contributed to great confusion about the views that Sankara, the commentator on the *Brahma Sûtras* held, for many of his successors also authored philosophical works with the same name. On the basis of comparing writing style, vocabulary, and the colophons of the various works attributed to "Sankara," the German philologist and scholar of Indian philosophy, Paul Hacker, has concluded that only a portion of the works attributed to Sankara are by the author of the commentary on the *Brahma Sûtras* (Hacker pp. 41-56). These genuine works include commentaries on the *Upanisads*, and a commentary on the *Bhagavad Gîtâ*. The following explication will be restricted to such works.

It is commonly held that Sankara argued that the common sense, empirical world as we know it is an illusion, or *mâyâ*. The term "*mâyâ*" does not figure prominently in the genuine writings of Sankara. However, it is an accurate assessment that Sankara holds that the majority of our beliefs about the reality of a plurality of objects and persons are ultimately false.

Sankara's philosophy and criticism of common sense rests on an argument unique to him in the history of Indian philosophy—an argument that Sankara sets at the outset of his commentary on the *Brahma Sûtra*. From this argument from superimposition, the ordinary human psyche (which self identifies with a body, a unique personal history, and distinguishes itself from a plurality of other persons and objects) comes about by an erroneous superimposition of the characteristics of subjectivity (consciousness, or the sense of being a witness), with the category of objects (which includes the characteristics of having a body, existing at a certain time and place and being numerically distinct from other objects). According to Sankara, these categories are opposed to each other as night and day. And hence, the conflation of the two categories is fallacious. However, it is also a creative mistake. As a result of this superimposition, the *jîva* (individual person) is constructed complete with psychological integrity, and a natural relationship with a body (*Sankara Brahma Sûtra Bhâsya*, Preamble to I.i.1). All of this is brought about by beginningless nescience (*avidyâ*)—a creative factor at play in the creation of the cosmos.

In reality, all there really is on Sankara's account is *Brahman*: objects of its awareness, such as the entire universe, exist within the realm of its consciousness. The liberation of the individual *jîva* occurs when it undoes the error of superimposition, and no longer identifies itself with a body, or a particular person with a natural history, but with *Brahman*.

It is worth stressing that Sankara's view is not a form of subjective idealism, or solipsism in any ordinary sense. For those sympathetic to Sankara's account, superimposition is an objective occurrence that happens most anywhere there is an ordinary organism with a living body. However, Sankara's system is properly characterized as a form of Absolute Idealism, for on its account only the undifferentiated Absolute is ultimately real, while affairs of the world are its thoughts.

Sankara's Advaita tradition is known for giving a nuanced, and two-part account of the 'self' and '*Brahman*.' On Sankara's account, there is a lower and higher self. The lower self is the *jîva*, while the higher self (the real referent of the personal pronoun "I," used by anyone) is the one real Self: *Âtma*, which on Sankara's account is *Brahman*. Likewise, on Sankara's account, there is a lower and a higher *Brahman* (Sankara *Brahma Sûtra Bhâsya* IV.3.16.

pp. 403-4). The lower *Brahman* is the personal God that pious devotees pray to and meditate on, while the Higher *Brahman* is devoid of most all such qualities, is impersonal, and is characterized as being essentially bliss (*ânanda*) (Sankara *Brahma SûtraBhâsya* III.3.14) truth (*satyam*) knowledge (*jñânam*) and infinite (*anantam*) (cf. Sankara, *Taittitrîya Upanisad Bhâsya* II.i.1.).

The lower *Brahman*, or the personal God that people pray to, can be afforded the title of "*Brahman*" owing to its proximity to the Highest *Brahman*: in the world of plurality, it is the closest thing to the Ultimate (Sankara *Brahma Sûtra Bhâsya* IV.3.9). However, it too, like the concept of the individual person, is a result of the error of superimposing the qualities of objectivity and subjectivity on each other (Sankara, *Brahma Sûtra Bhâsya* IV.3.10). In the Advaita tradition, the lower *Brahman* is known as the *saguna Brahman* (or *Brahman* with qualities) while the highest *Brahman* is known as the *nirguna Brahman* (or *Brahman* without qualities) (Sankara *Brahma Sûtra Bhâsya* III.2.21).

Sankara takes a skeptical attitude towards the importance of dharma, or morality. On Sankara's account, so long as one exists as a construction of necessience, operating under the erroneous assumption that one is a distinct object from *Brahman* and other objects, then one ought to follow the Vedas and its injunctions regarding dharma for it will help form tendencies to look within (Sankara, *Bhagavad GîtâBhâsya* on 18:66). However, for the serious aspirant, Sankara regards dharma as an impediment to liberation—it too must be abandoned, lest an individual reinforce their self-identification with a body in contradistinction to other bodies and persons (Sankara, *Bhagavad Gîtâ Bhâsya* on 4:21). Those sympathetic to Sankara's philosophy often regard Sankara's skepticism about dharma as a liberal and progressive aspect to his philosophy, for it devalues the importance of Vedic dharma, which contains within it caste morality. Critics of Sankara are likely to regard Sankara's skepticism about the importance of dharma as troubling, not because it implies that we should forsake Vedic dharma, but because it suggests that we ought to give up moral concerns, altogether, for the sake of spiritual pursuits (lest we fall back into the fallacy of superimposition).

iv. Visistâdvaita

The term "Visistâdvaita" is often translated as "Qualified Non-Dualism." An alternative, and more informative, translation is "Non-duality of the qualified whole," or perhaps 'Non-duality with qualifications." The principal exponent of this school of Vedânta is Râmânuja, who attempted to eschew the illusionist implications of Advaita Vedânta, and the perceived logical problems of the Bhedâbheda view while attempting to reconcile the portions of the *Upanisads* that affirmed a substantial monism and those that affirmed substantial pluralism. Râmânuja's solution to his problematic is to argue for a theistic and organismic conception of *Brahman*.

The theism of Râmânuja's Visistâdvaita shows up in his insistence that *Brahman* is a specific deity (Visnu, also known as "Nârâyana") who is an abode of an infinite number of auspicious qualities. The organismic aspect of Râmânuja's model consists in his view that all things that we normally consider as distinct from *Brahman* (such as individual persons or *jîvas*, mundane objects, and other unexalted qualities) constitute the Body of *Brahman*, while the *Âtman* spoken of in the *Upanisads* is the non-body, or mental component of *Brahman*. The result is a metaphysic that regards *Brahman* as the only substance, but yet affirms the existence of a plurality of abstract and concrete objects as the qualities of *Brahman*'s Body and Soul (*Vedârthasangraha* §2).

Râmânuja holds that in the absence of stains of passed karma the *jîva* (individual person) resembles *Brahman* in being of the nature of consciousness and knowledge (Râmânuja, *Brahma Sûtra Bhâsya*, I.i.1. "*Great Siddhânta*" pp. 99-102). Past actions cloud our true nature and force us to act out their consequences. On Râmânuja's account, the prime way of extricating ourselves from the beginningless effects of karma involves *bhakti*, or devotion to God. But *bhakti* on its own is not sufficient, or at least, *bhakti* if it is to bring about liberation must either be combined with the *karma yoga* mentioned in the *Bhagavad Gîtâ*, or it must turn into *bhakti yoga*. For attending to one's dharma (duty) is the chief means by which one can propitiate God, on Râmânuja's account (Râmânuja, *Gîtâ Bhâsya*, XVIII.47 p.583). Moreover, in attending to one's dharma in the deontological spirit characteristic of *karma yoga* and consonant with *bhakti yoga* one prevents the development of new karmic dispositions, and can allow the past stores of karma to be naturally extinguished. This will have the effect of unclouding the individual *jîva*'s omniscience, and bringing the *jîva* closer to a vision of God, which alone is an unending source of joy (*Vedârthasangraha* §241). Unlike Sankara, Râmânuja insists that dharma is never to be abandoned (Râmânuja, *Bhagavad Gîtâ Bhâsya* XVIII.66, p.599).

v. Dvaita

Madhva is one of the principal theistic exponents of Vedânta. On his account, *Brahman* is a personal God, and specifically He is the Hindu deity Visnu.

According to Madhva, reality is characterized by a five fold difference: (i) *jîvas* (individual persons) are different from God; (ii) *jîvas* are also different from each other; (iii) inanimate objects are different from God; (iv) inanimate objects are different from other inanimate objects; (v) inanimate objects are different from *jîvas* (*Mahâbhâratatâtparnirnayah,* I. 70-71). The number of types of entities on Madhva's account appears thus to be three: God, *jîvas*, and inanimate objects. However, the actual number of objects on Madhva's account appears to be very high. This substantial pluralism sets Madhva apart from the other principle exponents of Vedânta.

A distinctive doctrine of Madhva's Vedânta is his view that *jîvas* fall into a hierarchy, with the most exalted *jîvas* occupying a place below Visnu (such as Visnu's companions in his eternal abode) to the lowest *jîvas*, who occupy dark hell regions. Moreover, on Madhva's account, the ranking of *jîvas* is eternal, and hence those who occupy the lowest hells are eternally damned. Amongst the middle level *jîvas*, the Gods and the most virtuous of humans are eligible for liberation. The average amongst the middle rung *jîvas* transmigrate forever, while the lowest amongst the middle level *jîvas* find themselves in the upper hells (*Mahâbhâratatâtparnirnayah* I.85-88).

Madhva holds that liberation comes to those who appreciate the five fold differences and the hierarchy of the *jîvas*

(*Mahâbhâratatâtparnirnayah,* 81-2). However, ultimately, whether one is liberated or not is completely at the discretion of *Brahman,* and *Brahman* is pleased by nothing more than *bhakti,* or devotion (*Mahâbhâratatâtparnirnayah* I.117).

g. Classical Hindu Philosophy in the Context of Indian Philosophy

Hindu philosophy did not develop in a vacuum. Rather, it is an inextricable part of the history of Indian philosophy. Hence, other Indian philosophical movements did not only influence Hindu philosophy, but it also arguably had an influence on their development as well.

The most salient manner in which Hindu philosophy was influenced by other Indian philosophical developments is in the realm of ethics. In its infancy, Hindu philosophy as set out in the action portion of the Vedas was wedded to the practice of animal sacrifices (see *Aitareya Brâhmana,* book II.1-2). Buddhism and Jainism were both critical of the practice. Buddhism as a philosophy devoted to the alleviation of suffering is disposed to see animal sacrifices as involving unnecessary suffering. Jainism, in contrast, had made *Ahimsâ,* or non-harmfulness, its chief moral virtue. Jainism might very well have been the first religio-philosophical movement in India staunchly wedded to vegetarianism. And while vegetarianism was alien to early Hindu practice, it has become an integral part of Hindu orthodoxy in many parts of India. Now, for many Hindus, the very idea of eating meat is the very archetype of immoral and irreligious behaviour. This attitude can be found amongst the most orthodox followers of both Sankara and Râmânuja, who, as noted, defended the propriety of animal sacrifices. The shift in the general attitude of many Hindus arguably goes to the credit of Jainism, a once prevalent religion in India, which has been a source of tireless criticism of violence.

A case might also be made for the influence of Jainism on the Yoga *darsana.* Specifically, the *yama* rules found in the Yoga *darsana,* which include *Ahimsâ,* are identical to the five Great vows of Jainism (*Âcâranga Sûtra* II.15.i.1–v.1). While it is possible that these precepts have a third common source, or that they are indigenous to the Yoga tradition, it is also highly probable that they were incorporated, early on, into the Yoga tradition by way of influence of Jain thought. The Yoga tradition also shows the mark of being influenced by Mahâyâna Buddhism in its account of *"dharmameghasamâdhi"*—a term that shows up in many latter day Buddhist texts (see Klostermaier).

In the realm of metaphysics, a controversial argument can be made that Hindu philosophy, as found in the *Upanisads,* has exercised a profound effect on the development of latter day Indian Buddhist thought. Increasingly, in the context of latter Indian Buddhism, there is a movement away from a seeming agnosticism to an affirmation of the Ultimate in terms of a master concept, which designates both the grounding and the source of all. For Buddhist Idealism (Yogâcâra, or Vijñânavâda) the master concept is that of Consciousness-Only, and in the context of Mâdhyamika Buddhism of Nâgârjuna (2nd cent. C.E.) the master concept is that of Emptiness, or Sûnyatâ. Such a move towards a master concept resembles the Upanisad's employment of the concept *"Brahman"* and is arguably an adaptation of some elements of the metaphysical picture of the Upanisads into Buddhist philosophy.

Similarly, a case might also be made that the notion of "Two-Truths" (the doctrine that there is a distinction to be drawn between conventional truth that operates in ordinary, domestic discourse that recognizes diversity, and Truth from the perspective of the Ultimate which rejects diversity) operative in latter Buddhist thought is also a doctrine that can be found in the *Upanisads* (cf. *Mundaka Upanisad,* I.i. 5-6). While this doctrine gets its clearest explication in the context of latter day Buddhist thought in India, it seems that it has its precursor in Vedic speculation.

4. STAGE THREE: NEO-HINDUISM

The term "Neo-Hinduism" refers to a conception of the Hindu religion formed by recent authors who were learned in traditional Indian philosophy, and English. Famous Neo-Hindus include Swami Vivekânanda (1863-1902) the famous disciple of the traditional Hindu saint Râma-Krsna, and India's first president, Sarvepalli Radhakrishnan (1888-1975) a professional philosopher who held academic posts at various universities in India and Oxford, in the UK.

A famous formulation of the doctrine of Neo-Hinduism is the simile that likens religions to rivers, and the oceans to God: as all rivers lead to the ocean so do all religions lead to God. Similarly, Swami Nirvenananda in his book *Hinduism at a Glance* writes:

All true religions of the world lead us alike to the same goal, namely, to perfection if, of course, they are followed faithfully. Each of them is a correct path to Divinity. The Hindus have been taught to regard religion in this light. (Nivernananda, p.20.)

Frequently, Neo-Hindu authors identify Hinduism with Vedânta in their elaboration of Neo-Hindu doctrine, and in this formulation we find another tenet of Neo-Hinduism: Hinduism is not simply another religion, but a meta-religion, or the philosophy of religion. Hence, we find Vivekânanda writes:

Ours is the universal religion. It is inclusive enough, it is broad enough to include all the ideals. All the ideals of religion that already exist in the world can be immediately included, and we can patiently wait for all the ideals that are to come in the future to be taken in the same fashion, embraced in the infinite arms of the religion of Vedânta. (Vivekânanda, vol. III p.251-2.)

Similarly, Radhakrishnan holds "[t]he Vedânta is not a religion, but religion itself in its most universal and deepest significance" (Radhakrishnan, 35).

The view identified as Neo-Hinduism here might be understood as a form of Universalism or liberal theology that attempts to ground religion itself in Hindu philosophy. Neo-Hinduism must be distinguished from another theological view that has a long history in India, which we might call Inclusivist Theology. According to Inclusivist Theology, there are elements in any number of religious practices that are consonant with the one true religion, and if a practitioner of a contrary religion holds fast to those elements in their religion that are correct, they will eventually attain the Ultimate. Often, this view finds expression in the widespread Hindu view that all the various deities are really lower manifestations of one true deity (for example, a Vaisnava who held an Inclusivist theology might interpret all deities, in so far as they are consonant with the qualities attributed to Visnu, to be lower manifestations of Visnu, and thus good first steps to conceptualizing the Ultimate). Neo-Hinduism, in contrast, makes no distinction between deities, religions, or elements within religions, for all religions operate at the level of the practical, while the Ultimate, *ex hypothesi*, is transcendent. There is no religion, or no portion of any religion, which is incorrect, on this view, for all are equally human efforts to strive for the Divine. Neo-Hindus do not typically regard themselves as forming a new philosophy or religion, though the doctrine expressed by Neo-Hinduism is characterized by theses and concerns not clearly expressed in classical Hindu philosophy. As a rule, Neo-Hinduism is a reformulation of Advaita Vedânta, which emphasizes the implicit liberal theological tendencies that follow from the two-fold account of *Brahman*.

Recall that on Sankara's account a distinction is to be drawn between a lower and higher *Brahman*. Higher *Brahman* (*nirguna Brahman*) is impersonal and lacks much of what is normally attributed to God. In contrast, lower *Brahman* (*saguna Brahman*) has personal characteristics attributed to deities. While the higher *Brahman* is the eternally existing reality, lower *Brahman* is a result of the same creative error that results in the construction of normal integrated egos in bodies: superimposition. Neo-Hinduism takes note of the fact that this account of lower *Brahman*'s nature implies that the deities normally worshipped in a religious context are really natural artefacts, or projections of aesthetic concerns on the Ultimate: they are images of the Ultimate formulated for the sake of religious progress. Neo-Hinduism thus reasons that no one's personal God is any more the real God than another religion's personal God: rather, all are equally approximations of the one real, impersonal *Brahman* that transcends the domestic qualities attributed to it. While personal deities are considerably devalued on this account, the result is a liberal theology that is closed to no religious tradition, in principle, for any religion that personalizes God will be approaching the highest *Brahman* through the lens of superimposed characteristics of object-qualities on *Brahman*.

Critics of Neo-Hinduism have noted that while Neo-Hinduism aspires to shun the sectarianism that characterises the history of religion in the West through a spirit of Universalism, Neo-Hinduism itself engages in a sectarianism, in so far as it identifies Hinduism with the true perspective that understands the quality-less nature of the Ultimate (cf. Halbfass, *Tradition and Reflection* pp. 51-86).

In defence of Neo-Hinduism, it could be argued that it is a genuine, modern attempt to re-understand the philosophical implications of earlier Hindu thought, and not an attempt to reconcile the various religions of the world.

Critics might also argue that Neo-Hinduism is bad history: many philosophers that we today regard as Hindu (such as Râmânuja or Madhva) would not accept the idea that all deities are equal, and that God is ultimately an impersonal entity. Moreover, Sankara, the commentator on the *Brahma Sûtras* did not argue for the type of Universalism characteristic of Neo-Hinduism, which regards all religious observance as equally valid (though this arguably is an implication of his philosophy). Neo-Hinduism, the critic might argue, is historical revisionism. In response, Neo-Hinduism might defend itself by insisting that it is not in the business of providing an account of the history of all of Hindu philosophy, but only a certain strand that it regards as the most important.

5. CONCLUSION: THE STATUS OF HINDU PHILOSOPHY

Hindu philosophers have taken varied views on many important issues in philosophy. Hindu philosophers, for instance, are not in agreement as to whether God is a person. They have not all agreed upon the nature and scope of the epistemic validity of the Vedas, nor have they all agreed on basic questions of axiology, such as the content of morality. Some affirm the importance of Vedicly prescribed acts, such as animal sacrifices, while others, such as the Yoga philosopher Patañjali, appear to suggest that violence is always to be avoided. Likewise, some Hindu philosophers hold that the content of the Vedas as always binding, such as Râmânuja. Others, such as Sankara, regard it as constituting provisional obligations, subject to a person not being serious about liberation. All Hindu philosophers are not in agreement on whether there is anything like liberation. Most recognize the existence of liberation, while the early Pûrvamîmâmsâ does not. While all Hindu philosophers hold that there is something like an individual self, they differ radically in their account of the reality and nature of this individual. This difference in ontology reflects the rich metaphysical diversity amongst Hindu philosophers: some affirm the existence of a plurality of objects; qualities and relations (such as the Vaisesika, Dvaita Vedânta) while others do not (Advaita Vedânta). Such differences have made Hindu philosophy into a sub-tradition of philosophy within Indian philosophy, and not simply one comprehensive philosophical view amongst many. Hindu philosophy is not a static doctrine, but a growing tradition rich in diverse philosophical perspectives. Contrary to some popular accounts, what is presented as Hindu philosophy in recent times is not simply an elaboration of ancient tradition, but a re-evaluation and dialectical evolution of Hindu philosophical thought. Far from detracting from the authority or authenticity of recent Hindu speculation, what this shows is that Hindu philosophy is a living and vibrant tradition that shows no sign of being fossilized into a curiosity from the past, any time soon.

REFERENCES:

a. Primary Sources

1. *Âcâranga Sûtra*. Trans. Harmann Georg Jacobi. Jaina Sûtras. Ed. Harmann Georg Jacobi. Vol. 1. 2 vols. Delhi: AVF Books, 1987.

2. *Aiterya Brâhmana. Aiterya Brâhmana of the Zg Veda*. Trans. Martin Haug. Sacred Books of the Hindus. Ed. B.D. Basu. Allahabad: Sudhindra Nath Vasu, 1922.

3. *Bhâgavata Purâna. Srîmad Bhâgavatam*. Trans. Tapasyânanda. Madras: Sri Ramakrishna Math, 1981.

4. Chandrakânta. *Vaisesika Sûtra (Gloss)*. Trans. Nandal Sinha. Allahabad: Sudhindra Nath Basu, 1923.

5. *Dhammapada. A Source Book in Indian Philosophy*. Eds. S. Radhakrishnan and Charles Alexander Moore. Princeton, N.J.: Princeton University Press, 1967. 292-325.

6. Gautama. *Nyâya Sûtra.* Trans. Satisa Chandra Viyabhusana. Sacred Books of the Hindus. Ed. Nandalal Sinha. 2nd rev. and enl. ed. Vol. 8. Allahabad: Panini Office, 1930.

7. Gautama, Vâtsyâyana, and *Uddyotakara. The Nyâya-Sûtras of Gautama: with the Bhâsya of Vâtsyâyana and the Vârtika of Uddyotakara.* Trans. Ganganatha Jha. Delhi: Motilal Banarsidass, 1984.

8. *Gîtâ. Srîmad Bhagavad Gîtâ; the Scripture of Mankind.* Trans. and Ed. Swâmi Tapasyânanda. Madras: Srî Ramakrishna Math, 1986.

9. Gunaratna. *Tarkarahasyadîpika.* Cârvâka/Lokâyata: an Anthology of Source Materials and Some Recent Studies. Ed. Debiprasad Chattopadhyaya. New Delhi: Indian Council of Philosophical Research in association with Rddhi-India Calcutta, 1990.

10. Îsvarakrsna. *Sânkhya Kârikâ.* Trans. S.S. Suryanârâyana-Sastri. Madras University Philosophical Series. no. 3. Ed. S.S. Suryanârâyana-Sastri. 2nd rev. ed. Madras: University of Madras, 1948.

11. Jaimini. *Mîmâmsâ Sûtra.* Trans. and Ed. Mohan Lal Sandal. Sacred Books of the Hindus. Vol. 27. Allahabad: Sudhindre Nath Basu, 1923.

12. Khanda. *Vaisesika Sûtra.* Trans. and Ed. Nandalal Sinha. Sacred Books of the Hindus. Ed. Nandal Sinha. 2nd rev. and enl. ed. Vol. 6. Allahabad: Sudhindra Nath Basu, Panini Office, 1923.

13. *Katha Upanisad.* Trans. and Ed. Swami Gambirananda. *Eight Upanisads, With the Commentary of Sankarâcârya.* Ed. Swami Gambirananda. Vol. 2: Advaita Ashrama, 1977. 91-220.

14. Kumârila. *Slokavârtika.* 1909 Bibliotheca Indica. Calcutta: Asiatic Society. Trans. Ganganatha Jha. Srî Garib Das Oriental Series. Vol. 8. Delhi: Srî Satguru, 1983.

15. Madhva. *Mahâbhâratâtparyanirnayah.* Trans. and Ed. K.T. Pandurang. Vol. 1. Chirtanur: Sriman Madhva Siddhantonnanhini Sabha, 1993. Madhva. *Vedânta Sûtras with the commentary of Srî Madhwacharya (Madva Brahma Sûtra Bhâsya).* Trans. S. Subba Rau. Madras: Thompson and Co., 1904.

16. *Majjhima Nikâya. The Collection of the Middle Length Sayings.* Trans. I. B. Horner. Pali Text Society Translation Series. Vol. 29–31. 3 vols. London: Published for the Pali Text Society by Luzac, 1957.

17. Manu. *The Laws of Manu (ManavaDharmasâstra).* Trans. G.Buhler. Sacred

Books of the East. Ed. Max Müller. Vol. xxv. Oxford: Oxford University Press, 1886.

18. *Mundaka Upanisad*. Trans. and Ed. Swami Gambirananda. *Eight Upanisads, With the Commentary of Sankarâcârya*. Vol. 2: Advaita Ashrama, 1977. 77-172.

19. Patañjali. *Yoga Sûtra*. Trans. and Ed. Swâmi Prabhavananda. Madras: Ramakrishna Math., 1953.

20. Plato. *Phaedo*. Trans. Hugh Tredennick. The Collected Dialogues of Plato, Including the Letters. Bollingen Series 71. Eds. Edith Hamilton and Huntington Cairns. New York: Pantheon Books, 1966. 40-99.

21. Plato. *Phaedrus*. Trans. R. Hackforth. The Collected Dialogues of Plato, Including the Letters. Bollingen Series 71. Eds. Edith Hamilton and Huntington Cairns. New York: Pantheon Books, 1966. 475-525.

22. Plato. *Republic*. Trans. Paul Shorey. The Collected Dialogues of Plato, Including the Letters. Bollingen Series 71. Eds. Edith Hamilton and Huntington Cairns. New York: Pantheon Books, 1966. 575-844.

23. *Purusa Sûkta. Srî Rudram and Purusasùktam*. Trans. and Ed. Swami Amritananda. Ed. Swami Amritananda. Chennai: Sri Ramakrishna Math, 1997.

24. Radhakrishnan, S. *The Hindu View of Life*. Books that matter. London: G. Allen & Unwin, 1961.

25. Radhakrishnan, S., and Charles Alexander Moore, eds. *A Source Book in Indian Philosophy*. Princeton, N.J.: Princeton University Press, 1967.

26. Râmânuja. Srî Râmânuja *Gîtâ Bhâsya*. Trans. and Ed. Swâmi Âdidevânada. Madras: Sri Ramakrishna Math, 1991.

27. Râmânuja. *Vedânta Sûtras with the commentary of Râmânuja (Râmânuja Brahma Sûtra Bhâsya; Srî Bhâsya)*. Trans. George Thibaut. Sacred Books of the East. Vol. 48. Delhi: Motilal Banarsidass, 1996.

28. Râmânuja. *Vedârthasangraha*. Trans. and Ed. S.S. Ragavachar. Mysore: Sri Ramakrishna Ashrama, 1968.

29. *Zg Veda. Vedic hymns*. Trans. Hermann Oldenberg. Sacred books of the East. Ed. F. Max Müller. Vol. 32, 46. 2 vols. Oxford: The Clarendon Press, 1891.

30. Sabara. *Sabara Bhâsya*. Trans. Ganganatha Jha. Gaekwad's Oriental Series. Vol. 66, 70, 73. Baroda: Oriental Institute, 1933.

31. *Samyutta Nikâya. The Connected Discourses of the Buddha : a New Translation of the Samyutta Nikâya; translated from the Pâli.* Trans. Bhikkhu Bodhi. 2 vols. Somerville, MA: Wisdom Publications, 2000.

32. Sankara (*âcârya*). *Bhagavad Gîtâ with the commentary of Sankarâcârya.* Trans. Swâmi Gambhirânanda. Calcutta: Advaita Ashrama, 1991.

33. Sankara (*âcârya*). "Taittitrîya *Upanisad* Bhâsya." Trans. Swami Gambirananda. *Eight Upanisads, With the Commentary of Sankarâcârya.* Vol. 1: Advaita Ashrama, 1977. 3-29.

34. Sankara (*âcârya*). *The Vedânta Sûtras (Brahma Sûtra Bhâsya).* Sacred books of the East, vol.38. Delhi: Motilal Banarsidass, 1994.

35. Sankara-Misra. *Vaisesika Sûtra Bhâsya.* Trans. Nandalal Sinha. Sacred Books of the Hindus. Ed. Nandal Sinha. 2nd rev. and enl. ed. Vol. 6. Allahabad: Sudhindra Nath Basu, Panini Office, 1923.

36. *Sûtrakrtânga*. Trans. Harmann Georg Jacobi. Jaina Sûtras. Ed. Harmann Georg Jacobi. Vol. 2. Delhi: AVF Books, 1987. 235–436.

37. Tapasyânanda, Swâmi. *Bhakti Schools of Vedânta.* Madras: Ramakrishna Math, 1990.

38. Udayanâcârya and Haridâsa Nyâyâlamkâra. *The Kusumâñjali: or, Hindu Proof of the Existence of a Supreme Being (10th Century).* (Udayanâcârya's *Nyâyausumâñjali* with Haridâsa's Nyâyâlamkâra's Vyâkhyâ). Trans. and Ed. E.B. Cowell. Varanasi: Bharat-Bharati, 1980.

39. Vivekânanda. *The Complete Works of Swami Vivekânanda.* Mayavati memorial ed. Calcutta: Advaita Ashrama, 1964.

b. Secondary Sources

1. Bharadwaja, V.K. "A Non-Ethical Concept of Ahimsâ." *Indian Philosophical Quarterly.* xi.2 (1984): 171-77.

2. Chaterjee, Satischandra, and Dhirendramohan Data. *An Introduction to Indian Philosophy.* Calcutta: University of Calcutta, 1960.

3. Dasgupta, Surendranath. *A History of Indian Philosophy.* 5 vols. Delhi: Motilal Banarsidas, 1975.

4. Deutsch, Eliot. *Advaita Vedânta: a Philosophical Reconstruction.* 1st ed. Honolulu: East-West Center Press, 1969.

5. Dundas, Paul. *The Jains.* New York: Routledge, 1992.

6. Flintoff, Everard. "Pyrrho and India." *Phronesis* 25 (1980): 88-106.

7. Fox, Michael W. *Bringing Life to Ethics: Global Bioethics for a Humane Society*. Albany: State University of New York Press, 2001.

8. Hacker, Paul. *Philology and Confrontation*. Ed. Wilhelm Halbfass. Albany: State Universisty of New York, 1995.

9. Halbfass, Wilhelm. *India and Europe: an Essay in Understanding. Indien und Europa: Perspektiven ihrer geistigen Begegnung*. Basel; Stuttgart: Schwabe, 1981. Albany, N.Y.: State University of New York Press, 1988.

10. Halbfass, Wilhelm. *Tradition and Reflection: Explorations in Indian Thought*. Albany, N.Y.: State University of New York Press, 1991.

11. Jha, Ganganatha. *Purva Mîmâmsâ in its Sources*. Trans. Jha, Ganganatha. Library of Indian Philosophy and Religion. Benares: Benares Hindu University, 1942.

12. Kane, Pandurạng Vaman. *History of Dharmasâstra: Ancient and Mediæval Religious and Civil Law in India*. Government Oriental Series. Class B. no. 6. 2nd rev. and enl. ed. 5 vols. Poona: Bhandarkar Oriental Research Institute, 1990.

13. Klostermaier, Klaus. "*Dharmamegha samâdhi*: Comments on *Yoga Sûtra* IV.29." *Philosophy East and West* 36.3 (1986:): 253-62.

14. Larson, Gerald James, and Ram Shankar Bhattacharya. *Samkhya: a Dualist Tradition in Indian Philosophy*. Encyclopedia of Indian Philosophies. Ed. Karl H. Potter. Vol. 4. Princeton, N.J.: Princeton University Press, 1987.

15. Monier-Williams, Monier. *A Sanskrit-English Dictionary: Etymologically and Philologically Arranged, with Special Reference to Cognate Indo-European Languages*. Oxford University Press 1872, enlarged 1899. "greatly enlarged and improved" ed. Delhi: Motilal Banarsidass Publishers, 1995.

16. Potter, Karl H., ed. *Encyclopedia of Indian Philosophies*. 5 vols. Princeton NJ; Delhi: Princeton University Press; Motilal Banarsidass, 1970–1995.

17. Potter, Karl H., ed. *Presuppositions of India's Philosophies*. Prentice-Hall Philosophy Series. Englewood Cliffs, N.J.: Prentice-Hall, 1963.

18. Potter, Karl H., and Sibajiban Bhattacharya. *Indian Metaphysics and Epistemology: The Tradition of Nyâya–Vaisesika up to Gangesa*. The

Encyclopedia of Indian Philosophies. Ed. Karl H. Potter. Vol. 2. Princeton NJ: Princeton University, 1977.

19. Sharma, B. N. Krsnamurti. *The Brahma Sûtras and their Principal Commentaries; a Critical Exposition*. 2nd ed. New Delhi: Munshiram Manoharlal, 1986.
20. Thapar, Romila. *A History of India*. Vol. 1. London: Penguin Books, 1990.
21. Whicher, Ian. *The Integrity of the Yoga Darsana*. Albany: State University of New York, 1998.

2

Lokayata/Carvaka – Indian Materialism

In its most generic sense, "Indian Materialism" refers to the school of thought within Indian philosophy that rejects supernaturalism. It is regarded as the most radical of the Indian philosophical systems. It rejects the existence of other worldly entities such an immaterial soul or god and the after-life. Its primary philosophical import comes by way of a scientific and naturalistic approach to metaphysics. Thus, it rejects ethical systems that are grounded in supernaturalistic cosmologies. The good, for the Indian materialist, is strictly associated with pleasure and the only ethical obligation forwarded by the system is the maximization of one's own pleasure.

The terms Lokâyata and Cârvâka have historically been used to denote the philosophical school of Indian Materialism. Literally, "Lokâyata" means philosophy of the people. The term was first used by the ancient Buddhists until around 500 B.C.E. to refer to both a common tribal philosophical view and a sort of this-worldly philosophy or nature lore. The term has evolved to signify a school of thought that has been scorned by religious leaders in India and remains on the periphery of Indian philosophical thought. After 500 B.C.E., the term acquired a more derogatory connotation and became synonymous with sophistry. It was not until between the 6th and 8th century C.E. that the term "Lokâyata" began to signify Materialist thought. Indian Materialism has also been named Cârvâka after one of the two founders of the school. Cârvâka and

Ajita Kesakambalin are said to have established Indian Materialism as a formal philosophical system, but some still hold that Brhaspati was its original founder. Brhaspati allegedly authored the classic work on Indian Materialism, the Brhaspati Sátra. There are some conflicting accounts of Brhaspati's life, but, at the least, he is regarded as the mythical authority on Indian Materialism and at most the actual author of the since-perished Brhaspati Sátra. Indian Materialism has for this reason also been named "Brhaspatya."

1. HISTORY

Traces of materialism appear in the earliest recordings of Indian thought. Initially, Indian Materialism or Lokâyata functioned as a sort of negative reaction to spiritualism and supernaturalism. During the 6th and 7th centuries C.E. it evolved into a formal school of thought and remains intact, though consistently marginalized.

a. Vedic Period

Vedic thought, in the most comprehensive sense, refers to the ideas contained within the Samhitas and the Brâhamanas, including the Upanisads. Historians have estimated that the Vedas were written and compiled between the years 1500 B.C.E. and 300 B.C.E. It is difficult to point to one philosophical view in the Upanisads, at least by Western standards; however they are considered by scholars to comprise all of the philosophical writing of the Vedas. The Vedas exemplify the speculative attitude of the ancient Indians, who had the extreme luxury of reflecting on the whence and whither of their existence. The ancient Indians, also called Aryans, flourished due to the bounty of food and resources provided by the land. Free from the burdens of political conflict and social upheaval, they were able to ponder the origin of the universe and the purpose of life. Their meditations on such subjects have been recorded in the literature of the Vedas.

The Vedic period marked the weakest stage of the development of Indian Materialism. In its most latent form, Materialism is evident in early Vedic references to a man who was known as Brhaspati and his followers. The literature suggests that Brhaspati did not attempt to forward a constructive system of philosophy but rather characteristically refuted the claims of others schools of thought. In this sense, followers of Brhaspati were not only skeptical but intentionally destructive of the orthodoxies of the time. It is thought that any mention of "unbelievers" or "scoffers" in the Vedas refers to those who identified with Brhaspati and his materialist views. Thus, Materialism in its original form was essentially anti-Vedic. One of Brhaspati's principal objections to orthodoxy was the practice of repeating verses of sacred texts without understanding their meaning. However, Brhaspati's ideas ("Brhaspatya") would not become a coherent philosophical view without any positive import. His followers eventually adopted the doctrine of "Svabhava," which at this point in history signified the rejection of 1) the theory of causation and 2) the notion that there are good and evil consequences of moral actions. "Svabhava" enhanced Brhaspatya by providing it with the beginnings of a metaphysical framework. In the concluding portions of the Vedas there are violent tales of the opposition of the Brhaspatya people to the spiritualism of the time. Interestingly, the following anecdote from the Taittiriya Brâhmana implies that the gods were impervious to the destructive efforts of Brhaspati:

Once upon a time Brhaspati struck the goddess Gâyatrî on the head. The head smashed into pieces and the brain split. But Gâyatrî is immortal. She did not die. Every bit of her brain was alive. (Dakshinaranjan, 12)

The term "Svabhava" in Sanskrit can be translated to "essence" or "nature." Brhaspati used the term to indicate a school of thought that rejected supernaturalism and the ethical teachings that followed from supernaturalist ideologies. Brhaspati and his followers were scorned and ridiculed for not believing in the eternal nature of reality and for not revering the gods and the truths they were supposed to have espoused. It is interesting to note that while other schools have incorporated the "Svabhava" as a doctrine of essences or continuity of the soul, the use of the term by Brhaspati was specifically meant to represent his association with the philosophical naturalism. Naturalism, in this sense, rejects a Platonicnotion of essences and the dualism that is exemplified in Platonic philosophy as well as some of the Indian spiritualistic schools. This brand of dualism is that which asserts that there are two categorically different realms of reality: the material and the immaterial. Supernaturalism in general embraces this doctrine and holds that the latter realm is not encompassed by "nature." In contrast to this, Naturalism rejects the existence of the immaterial realm and suggests that all of reality is encompassed by nature. Widely varying schools of Naturalism exist today and do not necessarily embrace the mechanistic materialism that was originally embraced by the Cârvâka.

b. Epic Period and Brâhmanical Systems

The major work of the Epic Period of Indian history (circa 200 B.C.E. to 200 C.E.) is the Mahâbhârata. The Great War between the Kurus and the Pandavas inspired a many-sided conversation about morality. Conversation developed into intellectual inquiry and religion began to be replaced by philosophy. It was around the beginning of this period that the Brhaspati school began to merge with the philosophical naturalism of the time. Naturalism rejected the existence of a spiritual realm and also rejected the notion that the morality of an action can cause either morally good or evil consequences. Naturalist underpinnings helped to further shape Indian Materialism into a free-standing philosophical system. The term Lokâyata replaced Brhaspatya and scholars have speculated that this was due to the desire for a distinction between the more evolved philosophical system and its weaker anti-Vedic beginnings. The Lokâyata remained oppositional to the religious thought of the time, namely, Jainism and Buddhism, but it was also positive in that it claimed the epistemological authority of perception. Furthermore, it attempted to explain existence in terms of the four elements (earth, air, fire, water). While there is little certainty about the formal development of the Lokâyata school during the Epic Period, it is suspected that its adoption of naturalistic metaphysics led to its eventual association with scientific inquiry and rationalistic philosophy. Materialism stood out as a doctrine because it rejected the theism of the Upanisadic teachings as well as the ethical teachings of Buddhism and Jainism. It stood for individuality and rejected the authority of scripture and testimony.

The Lokâyata adopted its hedonistic values during the development of the Brâhmanical systems of philosophy (circa 1000 C.E.). As a reaction against the ascetic and meditative practices of the religious devout, Indian Materialism celebrated the pleasures of the body. People began gratifying their senses with no restraint. Pleasure was asserted as the highest good and, according to the Lokâyata, was the only reasonable way to enjoy one's life. Some scholarship suggests that during this stage of its development Indian Materialism began to be referred to as "Cârvâka" in addition to the "Lokâyata." This is contrary to the more popular view that the school was named Cârvâka after its historical founder helped to establish the Lokâyata as a legitimate philosophy. The term Cârvâka literally means "entertaining speech" and is derived from the term charva, which means to chew or grind with one's teeth. It is possible that Cârvâka himself acquired the name due to his association with Indian Materialism, which then led to the school acquiring the name as well. This is one of many areas of the history of Indian Materialism that remains open to debate.

2. STATUS IS INDIAN THOUGHT

The perceived value of Lokâyata from within the Indian Philosophical community is as relevant a topic as its philosophical import. If nothing else, the etymology of the term Lokâyata is evidence of the consistent marginalization of Indian Materialism. Because of its association with hedonistic behaviour and heretical religious views, followers of the spiritualistic schools of Indian philosophy (Jainism, Buddhism, Hinduism) are reticent on the subject of the materialistic tendencies present in their own systems; however, some scholars, such as Daya Krishna, have suggested that materialism is, in varying degrees, present in all Indian philosophical schools. This is not to say that materialism replaces other ideologies – it is to say rather that notions about the priority of this-worldliness appear even in some spiritualistic schools. While matter does not take priority over the spiritual realm in every sense, its significance is elevated more so than in other major world religions. This observation, for some, carries little weight when examining the philosophical import of the various Indian schools of thought; however, it seems relevant when considering the evolution of Indian thought. The original meaning of Lokâyata as prevalent among the people has become true in the sense that it is pervasive in Indian philosophical thought at large. This is not to say that materialism is widely accepted or even that its presence is overtly acknowledged, but it is difficult to deny its far-reaching influence on Indian Philosophy as a whole.

a. Contributions to Science

The most significant influence that Materialism has had on Indian thought is in the field of science. The spread of Indian Materialism led to the mindset that matter can be of value in itself. Rather than a burden to our minds or souls, the Materialist view promoted the notion that the body itself can be regarded as wondrous and full of potential.

Evidence in this shift in perspective can be seen by the progress of science over the course of India's history. Materialist thought dignified the physical world and elevated the sciences to a respectable level. Moreover, the Materialist emphasis on empirical validation of truth became the golden rule of the Scientific Method. Indian Materialism pre-dated the British Empiricist movement by over a millennium. Whereas the authority of empirical evidence carried little weight in Ancient India, modern thought began to value the systematic and cautious epistemology that first appeared in the thought of the Lokâyata.

b. Materialism as Heresy

Regardless of its positive influence on Indian thought, the fact remains that Indian Materialism is often regarded as blatant heresy against the Spiritualistic schools. It rejects the theism of Hinduism as well as the moralism of Buddhist and Jain thought. The anti-orthodox claims of the Materialists are seen as heretical by the religious masses and fly in the face of the piety promoted by most religious sects. However, it is questionable whether the formal ethics of Materialism are truly practiced to their logical extent by those who claim to belong to the school. It is suspected by many scholars that Indian Materialism today stands for an atheistic view that values science in place of supernaturalism. More than anything,

Materialists have historically expressed a view that has not found favour among the established religious and social authorities.

3. DOCTRINE

There are no existing works that serve as the doctrinal texts for the Lokâyata. The available materials on the school of thought are incomplete and have suffered through centuries of deterioration. Mere fragments of the Brhaspati Sátra remain in existence and because of their obscure nature provide little insight into the doctrine and practices of ancient Indian Materialists. Clues about the history of Indian Materialism have been pieced together to formulate at best a sketchy portrayal of how the "philosophy of the people" originated and evolved over thousands of years.

a. Epistemology

Epistemological thought varies in Indian philosophy according to how each system addresses the question of "Pramânas" or the "sources and proofs of knowledge." (Mittal 41) The Lokâyata (Cârvâka) school recognized perception (pratkaysa) alone as a reliable source of knowledge. They therefore rejected two commonly held pramânas: 1) inference (anumana) and 2) testimony (sabda). Because of its outright rejection of such commonly held sources of knowledge, the Lokâyata was not taken seriously as a school of philosophy. The common view was that Cârvâkas merely rejected truth claims and forwarded none of their own. To be a mere skeptic during the time amounted to very low philosophical stature.

However, there are additional accounts of the Lokâyata that suggest that the epistemology was more advanced and positivistic than that of mere skepticism. In fact, it has been compared to the empiricism of John Locke and David Hume. The Cârvâkas denied philosophical claims that could not be verified through direct experience. Thus, the Lokâyata denied the validity of inferences that were made based upon truth claims that were not empirically verifiable. However, logical inferences that were made based on premises that were derived from direct experience were held as valid. It is believed that this characterization of the epistemology of the Lokâyata most accurately describes the epistemological position of contemporary Indian Materialism.

Cârvâkas were, in a sense, the first philosophical pragmatists. They realized that not *all* sorts of inference were problematic; in order to proceed through daily life inference is a necessary step. For practical purposes, the Lokâyata made a distinction between inferences made based on probability as opposed to certainty. The common example used to demonstrate the difference is the inference that if smoke is rising from a building it is *probably* an indication that there is a fire within the building. However, Cârvâkas were unwilling to accept anything beyond this sort of mundane use of inference, such as the mechanical inference forwarded by the Buddhists. The Lokâyata refused to accept inferences about what has never been perceived, namely god or the after-life.

b. Ontology

The ontology of the Lokâyata rests on the denial of the existence of non-perceivable entities such as God or spiritual realm. Critics of this school of thought point to the fallacy of moving from the premise "the soul cannot be known" to the conclusion "the soul does not exist." Again, there is a pragmatic tendency in this sort of thinking. It seems that followers of the Lokâyata were not concerned with truths that could not be verified; however they were not entirely skeptical. The Lokâyata posited that the world itself and all material objects of the world are real. They held that all of existence can be reduced to the four elements of air, water, fire and earth. All things come into existence through a mixture of these elements and will perish with their separation. Perhaps the most philosophically sophisticated position of Indian Materialism is the assertion that even human consciousness is a material construct. According to K. K. Mittal, the ontology of the Lokâyata is strictly set forth as follows:

1. Our observation does not bring forth any instance of a disincarnate consciousness. For the manifestation of life and consciousness, body is an inalienable factor.
2. That body is the substratum of consciousness can be seen

in the undoubted fact of the arising of sensation and perception only in so far as they are conditioned by the bodily mechanism.

3. The medicinal science by prescribing that certain foods and drinks (such as Brâhmighrta) have the properties conducive to the intellectual powers affords another proof and evidence of the relation of consciousness with body and the material ingredients (of food). (Mittal 47)

Mittal reports (*ibid.*), apparently two schools of thought within the Lokâyata arose out of these tenets. One forwarded the position that there can be no self or soul apart from the body; another posited that a soul can exist alongside a body as long as the body lives, but that the soul perishes with the body. The latter view adopted the position that the soul is pure air or breath, which is a form of matter. Therefore, the Lokâyata collectively rejects the existence of an other-worldly soul, while sometimes accepts the notion of a material soul.

c. Cosmology

To speculate as to why the universe exists would be an exercise in futility for an Indian Materialist. The purpose and origin of existence is not discoverable through scientific means. Furthermore, the speculation about such matters leads to anxiety and frustration, which reduce pleasure and overall contentment. There is no teleology implicit in Indian Materalism, which is evidenced in the school's position that the universe itself probably came into existence by chance. Although there can be no certainty about the origin of the universe, the most *probable* explanation is that it evolved as a result of a series of random events.

There is also no doctrine of Creation in the Lokâyata. The principles of karma (action) and niyati (fate) are rejected because they are derived from the notion that existence in itself is purposeful. The fundamental principle of Indian Materialism was and remains "Svabhava" or nature. This is not to suggest that nature itself has no internal laws or continuity. It would be a misinterpretation of Indian Materialism to suppose that it forwards a cosmology of chaos. Rather, it resembles most closely the naturalism forwarded by the American philosopher John Dewey. While it posits no "creator" or teleology, Indian Materialism regards nature itself as a force that thrives according to its own law.

4. ETHICS

The most common view among scholars regarding the ethic of Indian Materialism is that it generally forwards Egoism. In other words, it adopts the perspective that an individual's ends take priority over the ends of others. Materialists are critical of other ethical systems for being tied to notions of duty or virtue that are derived from false, supernaturalist cosmologies. Indian Materialism regards pleasure in itself and for itself as the only good and thus promotes hedonistic practices. Furthermore, it rejects a utilitarian approach to pleasure. Utilitarianism regards pleasure (both higher and lower) as the ultimate good and therefore promotes the maximization of the good (pleasure) on a collective level. Indian Materialism rejects this move away from pure egoism. The doctrine suggests that individuals have no obligation to promote the welfare of society and would only tend to do so if it were to ultimately benefit them as well.

It is interesting to note that the Cârvâka school has been maligned by virtually all schools of Indian philosophy not merely for its rejection of the supernatural but probably more so for its insistent rejection of anything beyond Egoistic ethics. In fact, some scholars hold that Indian Materialism is purely nihilistic. That is to say that an Egoistic or Hedonistic ethic are not even essential elements of the system, but certainly serve as accurate descriptions for the held values and practices of the Cârvâka people. This view holds that the axiology of the Cârvâka was purely negative. It claims nothing more than the rejection of both what we think of now as a Platonic notion of "The Good" along with any notion of "god" or "gods."

The term "nâstika" is used by almost all schools of Indian Philosophy as a critical term to refer to another school of thought that has severely breeched what is thought to be acceptable in terms of both religious beliefs and ethical values. The greatest recipient of this term is the Cârvâka school. Commonly degraded to the same degree, the term "Cârvâka" and the more general term "nâstika" are sometimes used interchangeably simply to denote a brand of thinking that does not fall in line with the classical schools of Indian thought. The chief insult that is imported by the term "nâstika" is that the recipient of the title has strayed dangerously away from a path toward enlightenment. Ethical practices and one's spiritual education in Indian culture are inextricably tied to one another. Those who identify with the Indian Materialist school are criticized by the prominent Indian philosophical schools of thought because they are viewed as largely ignorant of both metaphysical and moral truths. This sort of ignorance is not perceived as a grave threat to the greater good of society, but rather to the individual who is bereft of spiritual and moral knowledge. That Indian Philosophy as a whole shows concern for the individual beliefs and practices of its members is in stark contrast to the cultural and individual relativism that is largely embraced by the West.

REFERENCES :

a. Primary Sources

1.Gunaratna. *Tarkarahasyadîpika.* Cârvâka/Lokâyata: an Anthology of Source Materials and Some Recent Studies. Ed. Debiprasad Chattopadhyaya. New Delhi: Indian Council of Philosophical Research in association with Rddhi-India Calcutta, 1990.

2.*The Mahâbhârata.* Trans. and Ed. James L. Fitzgerald. Chicago: Chicago University Press, 2004.

3.*The Râmâyana of Vâlmîki : an Epic of Ancient India.* Ed. Robert Goldman and Sally J. Sutherland. Trans. Robert Goldman. Princeton: Princeton University Press, 1984.

4.*The Hymns of the Rgveda.* Ed. Jagdish L. Shastri. Trans. Ralph T. H. Griffith. New Revised Edition. Delhi: Motilal Banarsidass, 1973.

Secondary Sources

1.Chattopadhyaya, Debiprasad. *Lokâyata; a Study in Ancient Materialism.* Bombay: People's Publishing House, 1959.

2.Daksinaranjan, Sastri. *A Short History of Indian Materialism.* Calcutta: The Book Company, Ltd., 1957.

3.Dasgupta, Surendranath. A History of Indian Philosophy. Vol. V. Cambridge: Cambridge University Press, 1955.

4.Flint, Robert. *Anti-theistic theories: being the Baird lecture for 1877.* Edinburgh and London: W. Blackwood and Sons, 1879.

5.Garbe, Richard. *The Philosophy of Ancient India.* Chicago: Open Court Publishing Company, 1899.

6.Grimes, John A. *A Concise Dictionary of Indian Philosophy: Sanskrit Terms Defined in English.* New and Revised Edition. Albany: State University of New York Press, 1996.

7.Halbfass, Wilhelm. *Tradition and Reflection: Explorations in Indian Thought.* Albany, NY: State University of New York Press, 1991.

8.Hopkins, Edward Washburn. *Ethics of India.* New Haven: Yale University Press, 1924.

9.Mittal, Kewal Krishan. *Materialism in Indian Thought.* New Delhi: Munihiram Manoharlal Publishers Pvt. Ltd., 1974.

10.Radhakrishnan, Sri. *Indian Philosophy.* Vols. I & II. New York: Macmillan, 1927-1929.

11.Raju, P. T. *The Philosophical Traditions of India.* Pittsburgh: University of Pittsburgh Press, 1972.

12.Raju, P. T. *Structural Depths of Indian Thought.* Albany, NY: State University of New York Press, 1985.

13.Ranganathan, Shyam. *Ethics and The History of Indian Philosophy.* Delhi: Motilal Banarsidass Publishers Pvt. Ltd., 2007.

14.Sharma, Ishwar Chandra. *Ethical philosophies of India.* Lincol, NE: Johnsen Publishing Company, 1965.

15.Smart, Ninian. *Doctrine and Argument in Indian Philosophy.* London: Allen and Unwin, 1964.

16.Vanamamalai, N. "Materialist Thought in Early Tamil Literature." *Social Scientist,* 2.4 (1973): 25-41.

3

Jain Philosophy

Jainism is properly the name of one of the religious traditions that have their origin in the Indian subcontinent. According to its own traditions, the teachings of Jainism are eternal, and hence have no founder; however, the Jainism of this age can be traced back to Mahavira, a teacher of the sixth century BCE, a contemporary of the Buddha. Like those of the Buddha, Mahavira's doctrines were formulated as a reaction to and rejection of the Brahmanism (religion based on the Hindu scriptures, the Vedas and Upanisads) then taking shape. The brahmans taught the division of society into rigidly delineated castes, and a doctrine of reincarnation guided by karma, or merit brought about by the moral qualities of actions. Their schools of thought, since they respected the authority of the Vedas and Upanisads, were known as *orthodox darsanas* ('*darsanas*' means literally, 'views'). Jainism and Buddhism, along with a school of materialists called *Carvaka*, were regarded as the *unorthodox darsanas*, because they taught that the Vedas and Upanisads, and hence the brahman caste, had no authority.

1. METAPHYSICS

According to Jain thought, the basic constituents of reality are souls (*jiva*), matter (*pudgala*), motion (*dharma*), rest (*adharma*), space (*akasa*), and time (*kala*). Space is understood to be infinite in all directions, but not all of space is inhabitable. A finite region of space, usually described as taking the shape of a standing man with arms akimbo, is the only region of space that can contain anything. This is so because it is the only region of space that is pervaded with *dharma*, the principle of motion (*adharma*is not simply. the absence of *dharma*, but rather a principle that causes objects to stop moving). The physical world resides in the narrow part of the middle of inhabitable space. The rest of the inhabitable universe may contain gods or other spirits.

While Jainism is dualistic—that is, matter and souls are thought to be entirely different types of substance—it is frequently said to be atheistic. What is denied is a creator god above all. The universe is eternal, matter and souls being equally uncreated. The universe contains gods who may be worshipped for various reasons, but there is no being outside it exercising control over it. The gods and other superhuman beings are all just as subject to karma and rebirth as human beings are. By their actions, souls accumulate karma, which is understood to be a kind of matter, and that accumulation draws them back into a body after death. Hence, all souls have undergone an infinite number of previous lives, and—with the exception of those who win release from the bondage of karma—will continue to reincarnate, each new life determined by the kind and amount of karma accumulated. Release is achieved by purging the soul of all karma, good and bad.

Every living thing has a soul, so every living thing can be harmed or helped. For purposes of assessing the worth of actions (see Ethics, below), living things are classified in a hierarchy according to the kinds of senses they have; the more senses a being has, the more ways it can be harmed or helped. Plants, various one-celled animals, and 'elemental' beings (beings made of one of the four elements—earth, air, fire, or water) have only one sense, the sense of touch. Worms and many insects have the senses of touch and taste. Other insects, like ants and lice, have those two senses plus the sense of smell. Flies and bees, along with other higher insects, also have sight. Human beings, along with birds, fish, and most terrestrial animals, have all five senses. This complete set of senses (plus, according to some Jain thinkers, a separate faculty of consciousness) makes all kinds of knowledge available to human beings, including knowledge of the human condition and the need for liberation from rebirth.

2. EPISTEMOLOGY AND LOGIC

Underlying Jain epistemology is the idea that reality is multifaceted (*anekanta*, or 'non-one-sided'), such that no one view can capture it in its entirety; that is, no single statement or set of statements captures the complete truth about the objects they describe. This insight, illustrated by the famous story of the blind men trying to describe an elephant, grounds both a kind of fallibilism in epistemology and a sevenfold classification of statements in logic.

Every school of Indian thought includes some judgment about the valid sources of knowledge (*pramanas*). While their lists of *pramanas* differ, they share a concern to capture the common-sense view; no Indian school is skeptical. The Jain list of *pramanas* includes sense perception, valid testimony (including scriptures), extra-sensory perception, telepathy, and *kevala*, the state of omniscience of a perfected soul. Notably absent from the list is inference, which most other Indian schools include, but Jain discussion of the *pramanas* seem to indicate that inference is included by implication in the *pramana*that provides the premises for inference. That is, inference from things learned by the senses is itself knowledge gained from the senses; inference from knowledge gained by testimony is itself knowledge gained by testimony, etc. Later Jain thinkers would add inference as a separate category, along with memory and *tarka*, the faculty by which we recognize logical relations.

Since reality is multi-faceted, none of the *pramanas* gives absolute or perfect knowledge (except *kevala*, which is enjoyed only by the perfected soul, and cannot be expressed in language). As a result, any item of knowledge gained is only tentative and provisional. This is expressed in Jain philosophy in the doctrine of *naya*, or partial predication (sometimes called the doctrine of perspectives or viewpoints). According to this doctrine, any judgment is true only from the viewpoint or perspective of the judge, and ought to be so expressed. Given the multifaceted nature of reality, no one should take his or her own judgments as the final truth about the matter, excluding all other judgments. This insight generates a sevenfold classification of predications. The seven categories of claim can be schematized as follows, where 'a' represents any arbitrarily selected object, and 'F' represents some predicate assertible of it:

1. Perhaps a is F.
2. Perhaps a is not-F.
3. Perhaps a is both F and not-F.
4. Perhaps a is indescribable.
5. Perhaps a is indescribable and F.
6. Perhaps a is indescribable and not-F.
7. Perhaps a is indescribable, and both F and not-F.

Each predication is preceded by a marker of uncertainty (*syat*), which I have rendered here as 'perhaps.' Some render it as 'from a perspective,' or 'somehow.' However it is translated, it is intended to mark respect for the multifaceted nature of reality by showing a lack of conclusive certainty.

Early Jain philosophical works (especially the *Tattvartha Sutra*) indicate that for any object and any predicate, all seven of these predications are true. That is to say, for every object a and every predicate F, there is some circumstance in which, or perspective from which, it is correct to make claims of each of these forms. These seven categories of predication are not to be understood as seven truth-values, since they are all seven thought to be true. Historically, this view has been criticized (by Sankara, among others) on the obvious ground of inconsistency.

While both a proposition and its negation may well be assertible, it seems that the conjunction, being a contradiction, can never be even assertible, never mind true, and so the third and seventh forms of predication are never possible. This is precisely the kind of consideration that leads some commentators to understand the 'syat' operator to mean 'from a perspective.' Since it may well be that from one perspective, a is F, and from another, a is not-F, then one and the same person can appreciate those facts and assert them both together. Given the multifaceted nature of the real, every object is in one way F, and in another way not-F. An appreciation of the complexity of the real also can lead one to see that objects are, as they are in themselves, indescribable (as no description can capture their entirety). This yields the fourth form of predication, which can then be combined with other insights to yield the last three forms.

Perhaps the deepest problem with this doctrine is one that troubles all forms of skepticism and fallibilism to one degree or another; it seems to be self-defeating. After all, if reality is multifaceted, and that keeps us from making absolute judgments (since my judgment and its negation will both be equally true), the doctrines that underlie Jain epistemology are themselves equally tentative. For example, take the doctrine of *anekantevada.* According to that doctrine, reality is so complex that any claim about it will necessarily fall short of complete accuracy. The doctrine itself must then fall short of complete accuracy. Therefore, we should say, "Perhaps (or "from a perspective") reality is multifaceted." At the same time, we have to grant the propriety, in some circumstances, of saying, "Perhaps reality is not multifaceted." Jain epistemology gains assertibility for its own doctrine, but at the cost of being unable to deny contradictory doctrines. What begins as a laudable fallibilism ends as an untenable relativism.

3. ETHICS

Given that the proper goal for a Jain is release from death and rebirth, and rebirth is caused by the accumulation of karma, all Jain ethics aims at purging karma that has been accumulated, and ceasing to accumulate new karma. Like Buddhists and Hindus, Jains believe that good karma leads to better circumstances in the next life, and bad karma to worse. However, since they conceive karma to be a material substance that draws the soul back into the body, all karma, both good and bad, leads to rebirth in the body. No karma can help a person achieve liberation from rebirth. Karma comes in different kinds, according to the kind of actions and intentions that attract it. In particular, it comes from four basic sources: (1) attachment to worldly things, (2) the passions, such as anger, greed, fear, pride, etc., (3) sensual enjoyment, and (4) ignorance, or false belief. Only the first three have a directly ethical or moral upshot, since ignorance is cured by knowledge, not by moral action.

The moral life, then, is in part the life devoted to breaking attachments to the world, including attachments to sensual enjoyment. Hence, the moral ideal in Jainism is an ascetic ideal. Monks (who, as in Buddhism, live by stricter rules than laymen) are constrained by five cardinal rules, the "five vows": (1) *ahimsa*, frequently translated "non-violence," or "non-harming," *satya*, or truthfulness, *asteya*, not taking anything that is not given, *brahmacharya*, chastity, and *aparigraha*, detachment. This list differs from the rules binding on Buddhists only in that Buddhism requires abstention from intoxicants, and has no separate rule against attachment to the things of the world.

The cardinal rule of interaction with other *jivas* is the rule of *ahimsa*. This is because harming other *jivas* is caused by either passions like anger, or ignorance of their nature as living beings. Consequently, Jains are required to be vegetarians.

According to the earliest Jain documents, plants both are and contain living beings, although one-sensed beings, so even a vegetarian life does harm. This is why the ideal way to end one's life, for a Jain, is to sit motionless and starve to death. Mahavira himself, and other great Jain saints, are said to have died this way. That is the only way to be sure you are doing no harm to any living being.

While it may seem that this code of behaviour is not really moral, since it is aimed at a specific reward for the agent—and is therefore entirely self-interested—it should be noted that the same can be said of any religion-based moral code. Furthermore, like the Hindus and Buddhists, Jains believe that the only reason that personal advantage accrues to moral behaviour is that the very structure of the universe, in the form of the law of karma, makes it so.

REFERENCES :

1.Battacharya, Hari Mohan. *Jaina Logic and Epistemology*. Calcutta: K. P. Gagchi and Company, 1994. A full explanation and critical examination of Jain theory of knowledge.

2.Battacharya, Narendra Nath. *Jain Philosophy: Historical Outline*. Delhi: Munshiram Manoharlal Publishers. 1976.

3.Benesch, Walter. *An Introduction to Comparative Philosophy*. London: Macmillan Press, 1997.

4..A systematic comparison of Western philosophical systems with Asian, including Jain, systems.

5.Jacobi, Herman, trans. *Jaina Sutras*. Sacred Books of the East, vols 22 and 45. London: Oxford University Press, 1884. The only English translation of the Jain scriptures.

6.Sharma, Arvind. *A Jaina Perspective on the Philosophy of Religion*. Delhi: Motilal Banarsidas, 2001.

7.Tatia, Nathmal, trans. *That Which Is: Tattvartha Sutra*. San Francisco: HarperCollins Publishers, 1994.

4

Buddha (480 BCE-400BCE)

The historical Buddha, also known as Gotama Buddha, Siddhârtha Gautama, and Buddha Sâkyamuni, was born in Lumbini, in the Nepalese region of Terai, near the Indian border. He is one of the most important Asian thinkers and spiritual masters of all time, and he contributed to many areas of philosophy, including epistemology, metaphysics and ethics. The Buddha's teaching formed the foundation for Buddhist philosophy, initially developed in South Asia, then later in the rest of Asia. Buddhism and Buddhist philosophy now have a global following.

In epistemology, the Buddha seeks a middle way between the extremes of dogmatism and skepticism, emphasizing personal experience, a pragmatic attitude, and the use of critical thinking toward all types of knowledge. In ethics, the Buddha proposes a threefold understanding of action: mental, verbal, and bodily. In metaphysics, the Buddha argues that there are no self-caused entities, and that everything dependently arises from or upon something else. This allows the Buddha to provide a criticism of souls and personal identity; that criticism forms the foundation for his views about the reality of rebirth and an ultimate liberated state called "Nirvana." Nirvana is not primarily an absolute reality beyond or behind the universe but rather a special state of mind in which all the causes and conditions responsible for rebirth and suffering have been eliminated. In philosophical anthropology, the Buddha explains human identity without a permanent and substantial self. The doctrine of non-self, however, does not imply the absolute inexistence of any type of self whatsoever, but is compatible with a conventional self composed of five psycho-physical aggregates, although all of them are unsubstantial and impermanent. Selves are thus conceived as evolving processes causally constrained by their past.

1. INTERPRETING THE HISTORICAL BUDDHA

a. Dates

There is no complete agreement among scholars and Buddhist traditions regarding the dates of the historical Buddha. The most common dates among Buddhists are those of the Theravâda school, 623-543 B.C.E. From the middle of the 19th century until recently, Western scholars had believed the dates of the Buddha to be ca. 560-480 B.C.E. However, after the publication in 1991-2 of the proceedings of the international symposium on the date of the historical Buddha held in Göttingen in 1988, the original consensus on these dates no longer exists.

Although there is no conclusive evidence for any specific date, most current scholars locate the Buddha's life one hundred years earlier, around the fifth century B.C.E. Some of the new dates for the Buddha's "death" or more accurately, for his parinirvâna are: ca. 404 B.C.E. (R. Gombrich), between 410-390 B.C.E. (K.R. Norman), ca. 400 B.C.E. (R. Hikata), ca. 397 B.C.E. (K.T.S. Sarao), between ca.400-350 B.C.E. (H. Bechert), 383 B.C.E. (H. Nakamura), 368 B.C.E. (A. Hirakawa), between 420-380 B.C.E. (A. Bareau).

b. Sources

The historical Buddha did not write down any of his teachings, they were passed down orally from generation to generation for at least three centuries. Some scholars have attempted to distinguish the Buddha's original teachings from those developed by his early disciples. Unfortunately, the contradictory conclusions have led most scholars to be skeptical about the possibility of knowing what the Buddha really taught. This however, does not mean that all Buddhist texts that attribute teachings to the Buddha are equally valuable to reconstruct his thought. The early sûtras in Pâli and other Middle Indo-Aryan languages are historically and linguistically closer to the cultural context of the Buddha than

Mahâyâna sûtras in Sanskrit, Tibetan, and Chinese. This does not imply that later translations of the early sûtras in Chinese (there are no Tibetan translations of the early sûtras) are less authentic or useless in reconstructing the philosophy of the Buddha. On the contrary, the comparative study of Pâli and Chinese versions of the early sûtras can help to infer what might have been the Buddha's position on a number of issues.

Following what seems to be a growing scholarly tendency, I will reconstruct the philosophy of the historical Buddha by drawing on the Sutta Pimaka of the Pâli canon. More specifically, our main sources are the first four Pâli Nikâyas (Dîgha, Majjhima, Samyutta, Amguttara) and some texts of the fifth Pâli Nikâya (Dhammapada, Udâna, Itivuttaka, and Sutta Nipâta). I do not identify these sources with the Buddha's "*ipsissima verba*," that is, with "the very words" of the Buddha, even less with his "actual" thought. Whether these sources are faithful to the actual thought and teachings of the historical Buddha is an unanswerable question; I can only say that to my knowledge there are not better sources to reconstruct the philosophy of the Buddha.

According to the traditional Buddhist account, shortly after the Buddha's death five hundred disciples gathered to compile his teachings. The Buddha's personal assistant, Ânanda, recited the first part of the Buddhist canon, the Sûtra Pimaka, which contains discourses in dialogue form between the Buddha, his disciples, and his contemporaries on a variety of doctrinal and spiritual questions. Ânanda is reported to have recited the sutras just as he had heard them from the Buddha; that is why Buddhist sutras begin with the words "Thus have I heard." Another disciple, Upâli, recited the second part of the Buddhist canon, the Vinaya Pimaka, which also contains sutras, but primarily addresses the rules that govern a monastic community. After the recitation of Ânanda and Upâli, the other disciples approved what they had heard and communally recited the teachings as a sign of agreement. The third part of the Buddhist canon or Abhidharma Pimaka, was not recited at that moment. The Theravâda tradition claims that the Buddha taught the Abhidharma while visiting the heaven where his mother was residing.

From a scholarly perspective, the former account is questionable. It might be the case that a large collection of Buddhist texts was written down for the first time in Sri Lanka during the first century B.C.E. However, the extant Pâli canon shows clear signs of historical development in terms of both content and language. The three parts of the Pâli canon are not as contemporary as the traditional Buddhist account seems to suggest: the Sûtra Pimaka is older than the Vinaya Pimaka, and the Abhidharma Pimaka represents scholastic developments originated at least two centuries after the other two parts of the canon. The Vinaya Pimaka appears to have grown gradually as a commentary and justification of the monastic code (Prâtimoksa), which presupposes a transition from a community of wandering mendicants (the Sûtra Pimaka period) to a more sedentary monastic community (the Vinaya Pimaka period). Even within the Sûtra Pimaka it is possible to detect older and later texts.

Neither the Sûtra Pimaka nor the Vinaya Pimaka of the Pâli canon could have been recited at once by one person and repeated by the entire Buddhist community. Nevertheless, the Sûtra Pimaka of the Pâli canon is of particular importance in reconstructing the philosophy of Buddha for four main reasons. First, it contains the oldest texts of the only complete canon of early Indian Buddhism, which belong to the only surviving school of that period, namely, the Theravâda school, prevalent in Sri Lanka and Southeast Asia. Second, it has been preserved in a Middle Indo-Aryan language closely related to various Prakrit dialects spoken in North of India during the third century B.C.E., including the area where the Buddha spent most of his teaching years (Magadha). Third, it expresses a fairly consistent set of doctrines and practices. Fourth, it is strikingly similar to another version of the early Sûtra Pimaka extant in Chinese (Âgamas). This similarity seems to indicate that a great part of the Sûtra Pimaka in Pâli does not contain exclusively Theravâda texts, and belongs to a common textual tradition probably prior to the existence of Buddhist schools.

c. Life

Since the Pâli Nikâyas contain much more information about the teachings of the Buddha than about his life, it seems safe to postulate that the early disciples of the Buddha were more interested in preserving his teachings than in transmitting all the details of his life. The first complete biographies of the Buddha as well as the Jâtaka stories about his former lives appeared centuries later, even after, and arguably as a reaction against, the dry lists and categorizations of early Abhidharma literature. The first complete biography of the Buddha in Pâli is the Nidânakathâ, which serves as an introduction to the Jâtaka verses found in the fifth Pâli Nikâya. In Sanskrit, the most popular biographies of the Buddha are the Buddhacarita attributed to the Indian poet Asvaghosa (second century C.E), the Mahâvastu, and the Lalitavistara, both composed in the first century C.E.

The first four Pâli Nikâyas contain only fragmented information about the Buddha's life. Especially important are the Mahâpadâna-suttanta, the Ariyapariyesanâ-suttanta, the Mahâsaccaka-suttanta, and the Mahâparinibbâna-suttanta. According to the Mahâpadâna-suttanta, the lives of all Buddhas or perfectly enlightened beings follow a similar pattern. Like all Buddhas of the past, the Buddha of this cosmic era, also known as Gautama (Gotama in Pâli), was born into a noble family. The Buddha's parents were King Suddhodana and Queen Mâyâ. He was a member of the Sakya clan and his name was Siddhartha Gautama. Even though he was born in Lumbinî while his mother was travelling to her parents' home, he spent the first twenty-nine years of his life in the royal capital, Kapilavastu, in the Nepalese region of Terai, close to the Indian border.

Like all past Buddhas, the conception and birth of Gautama Buddha are considered miraculous events. For instance, when all Buddhas descend into their mothers' wombs from a heaven named Tusita, a splendid light shines forth and the entire universe quakes; their mothers are immaculate, healthy, and without pain of any sort during their ten months of pregnancy, but they die a week after giving birth. Buddha babies are born clean, though they are ritually bathed with two streams of water that fall from the sky; they all take seven steps toward the north and solemnly announce that this is their last rebirth.

Like former Buddhas, prince Siddhartha enjoyed all types of luxuries and sensual pleasures during his youth. Unsatisfied with this type of life, he had a crisis when he realized that everything was ephemeral and that his existence was subject to old age, sickness, and death. After seeing the serene joy of a monk and out of compassion for all living beings, he renounced his promising future as prince in order to start a long quest for a higher purpose, nirvâna (Pali nibbâna), which entails the cessation of old age, sickness and death. Later traditions speak of the Buddha as abandoning his wife Yasodharâ immediately after she gave birth to Râhula, the Buddha's only son. The Pâli Nikâyas, however, do not mention this story, and refer to Râhula only as a young monk.

According to the Ariyapariyesanâ-suttanta and the Mahâsaccaka-suttanta, the Buddha tried different spiritual paths for six years. First, he practiced yogic meditation under the guidance of Âlâra Kâlâma and Uddaka Râmaputta. After experiencing the states of concentration called base of nothingness and base of neither-perception-nor-non-perception, he realized that these lofty states did not lead to nirvana. Then the Buddha began to practice breathing exercises and fasting. The deterioration of his health led the Buddha to conclude that extreme asceticism was equally ineffective in attaining nirvana. He thus resumed eating solid food; after recovering his health, he began to practice a more moderate spiritual path, the middle path, which avoids the extremes of sensual self-indulgence and self-mortification. Soon after, the Buddha experienced enlightenment, or awakening, under a bodhi-tree. First he was inclined to inaction rather than to teaching what he had discovered. However, he changed his mind after the god Brahmâ Sahampati asked him to teach. Out of compassion for all living beings, he decided to start a successful teaching career that lasted forty-five years.

d. Significance

It would be simplistic to dismiss all supernatural aspects of the Buddha's life as false and consider historically true only those elements that are consistent with our contemporary scientific worldview. However, this approach towards the Buddha's life was prevalent in the nineteenth century and a great part of the twentieth century. Today it is seen as problematic because it imposes modern western ideals of rationality onto non-western texts. Here I set aside the question of historical truth and speak exclusively of significance. The significance of all the biographies of Buddha does not lie in their historical accuracy, but rather in their effectiveness to convey basic Buddhist ideas and values throughout history. Even today, narratives about the many deeds of Buddha are successfully used to introduce Buddhists of all latitudes into the main values and teachings of Buddhism.

The supernatural elements of the Buddha's life are as historically significant as the natural ones because they help to understand the way Buddhists conceived – and in many places continue to conceive – the Buddha. Like followers of other religious leaders, Buddhist scribes tended to glorify the sanctity of their foundational figure with extraordinary events and spectacular accomplishments. In this sense, the narratives of the Buddha are perhaps better understood as hagiographies rather than as biographies. The historical truth behind hagiographies is impossible to determine: how can we tell whether or not the Buddha was conceived without sexual intercourse; whether or not he was able to talk and walk right after his birth; whether or not he could walk over water, levitate, fly, and ascend into heaven at will? How do we know whether the Buddha was really tempted by Mâra the evil one; whether there was an earthquake at the moment of his birth and death? The answers to these questions are a matter of faith. If the interpreter does not believe in the supernatural, then many narratives will be dismissed as historically false. However, for some Buddhists the supernatural events that appear in the life of Buddha did take place and are historically true.

The significance of the hagiographies of the Buddha is primarily ethical and spiritual. In fact, even if the life of Buddha did not take place as the hagiographies claim, the ethical values and the spiritual path they illustrate remain significant. Unlike other religions, the truth of Buddhism does not depend on the historicity of certain events in the life of the Buddha. Rather, the truth of Buddhism depends on the efficacy of the Buddhist path exemplified by the life of the Buddha and his disciples. In other words, if the different Buddhist paths inspired by the Buddha are useful to overcome existential dissatisfaction and suffering, then Buddhism is true regardless of the existence of the historical Buddha.

The fundamental ethical and spiritual point behind the Buddha's life is that impermanent, conditioned, and contingent things such as wealth, social position, power, sensual pleasures, and even lofty meditative states, cannot generate a state of ultimate happiness. In order to overcome the profound existential dissatisfaction that all ephemeral and contingent things eventually generate, one needs to follow a comprehensive path of ethical and mental training conducive to the state of ultimate happiness called nirvana.

2. THE BUDDHA'S EPISTEMOLOGY

a. The Extremes of Dogmatism and Skepticism

While the Buddha's view of the spiritual path is traditionally described as a middle way between the extremes of self-indulgence and self-mortification, the Buddha's epistemology can be interpreted as a middle way between the extremes of dogmatism and skepticism.

The extreme of dogmatism is primarily represented in the Pâli Nikâyas by Brahmanism. Brahmanism was a ritualistic religion that believed in the divine revelation of the Vedas, thought that belonging to a caste was determined by birth, and focused on the performance of sacrifice. Sacrifices involved the recitation of hymns taken from the Vedas and in many cases the ritual killing of animals.

Ritual sacrifices were offered to the Gods (gods for Buddhism) in exchange for prosperity, health, protection, sons, long life, and immortality. Only the male members of the highest caste, the priestly caste of Brahmins, could afford the professional space to seriously study the three Vedas (the Atharva Veda did not exist, or if it existed, it was not part yet of the Brahmanic tradition). Since only Brahmins knew the three Vedas, only they could recite the hymns necessary to properly perform the ritual sacrifice. Both ritual sacrifice and the social ethics of the caste system were seen as an expression of the cosmic order (Dharma) and as necessary to preserve that order.

Epistemologically speaking, Brahmanism emphasized the

triple knowledge of the Vedas, and dogmatic faith in their content: "in regard to the ancient Brahmanic hymns that have come down through oral transmission and in the scriptural collections, the Brahmins come to the definite conclusion: 'Only this is true, anything else is wrong' " (M.II.169).

The extreme of skepticism is represented in the Pâli Nikâyas by some members of the Sramanic movement, which consisted of numerous groups of spiritual seekers and wandering philosophers. The Sanskrit word "*sramana*" means "those who make an effort," and probably refers to those who practice a spiritual discipline requiring individual effort, not just rituals performed by others. In order to become a sramana it was necessary to renounce one's life as householder and enter into an itinerant life, which entailed the observance of celibacy and a simple life devoted to spiritual cultivation. Most sramanas lived in forests or in secluded places wandering from village to village where they preached and received alms in exchange.

The Sramanic movement was extremely diverse in terms of doctrines and practices. Most sramanas believed in free will as well as the efficacy of moral conduct and spiritual practices in order to attain liberation from the cycle of reincarnations. However, there was a minority of sramanas who denied the existence of the after life, free will, and the usefulness of ethical conduct and other spiritual practices. Probably as a reaction to these two opposite standpoints, some sramanas adopted a skeptic attitude denying the possibility of knowledge about such matters. Skeptics are described by the Buddha as replying questions by evasion (D.I.58-9), and as engaging in verbal wriggling, in eel-wriggling (amarâvikkhepa): "I don't say it is like this. And I don't say it is like that. And I don't say it is otherwise. And I don't say it is not so. And I don't say it is not not so" (M.I. 521).

b. The Role of Personal Experience and the Buddha's Wager

In contrast to Brahmanic dogmatism, the Buddha of the Pâli Nikâyas did not claim to be omniscient (M.I.482); in fact, he proposed a critical attitude toward all sources of knowledge. In the *Majjhima Nikâya* (II.170-1), the Buddha challenges Brahmins who accept Vedic scriptures out of faith (saddhâ) and oral tradition (anussava); he compares those who blindly follow scripture and tradition without having direct knowledge of what they believe with "a file of blind men each in touch with the next: the first one does not see, the middle one does not see, and the last one does not see." The Buddha also warns Brahmins against knowledge based on likeability or emotional inclination (ruci), reflection on reasons (âkâraparivitakka), and consideration of theories (dimmhinijjhânakkhanti). These five sources of knowledge may be either true or false; that is, they do not provide conclusive grounds to claim dogmatically that "only this is true, anything else is wrong."

Dogmatic claims of truth were not the monopoly of Brahmins. In the *Majjhima Nikâya* (I.178), the Buddha uses the simile of the elephant footprint to question dogmatic statements about him, his teachings, and his disciples: he invites his followers to critically investigate all the available evidence (different types of elephant footprints and marks) until they know and see for themselves (direct perception of the elephant in the open). The Pâli Nikâyas also refer to many sramanas who hold dogmatic views and as a consequence are involved in heated doctrinal disputes. The conflict of dogmatic views is often described as "a thicket of views, a wilderness of views, a contortion of views, a vacillation of views, a fetter of views. It is beset by suffering, by vexation, by despair, and by fever, and it does not lead to disenchantment, to dispassion, to cessation, to peace, to higher knowledge, to enlightentment, to Nibbâna" (M.I.485).

Public debates were common and probably a good way to gain prestige and converts. Any reputed Brahmin or sramana had to have not only the ability to speak persuasively but also the capacity to argue well. Rational argument played an important role in justifying doctrines and avoiding defeat in debate, which implied conversion to the other's teaching. At the time of the Buddha many of these debates seem to have degenerated into dialectical battles that diverted from spiritual practice and led to disorientation, anger, and frustration. Although the Buddha of the Pâli Nikâyas utilizes reasoning to justify his positions in debates and conversations with others, he discourages dogmatic attachment to doctrines including his own (see the simile of the raft, M.I.135), and the use of his teachings for the sake of criticizing others and for winning debates (M.I.132).

Unlike the skepticism of some sramanas, the Buddha of the Pâli Nikâyas takes clear stances on ethical and spiritual issues, and rejects neither the existence of right views (M.I.46-63) nor the possibility of knowing certain things as they are (yathâbhûtam). In order to counteract skepticism, the Buddha advises to the Kâlâma people "not go by oral tradition, by succession of disciples, by hearsay, by the content of sacred scripture, by logical consistency, by inference, by reflection on reasons, by consideration of theories, by appearance, by respect to a teacher." Instead, the Buddha recommends knowing things for oneself as the ultimate criterion to adjudicate between conflicting claims of truth (A.I.189).

When personal experience is not available to someone, the Buddha of the Pâli Nikâyas proposes taking into account what is praised or censored by the wise, as well as a method to calculate the benefits of following certain opinions called the incontrovertible teaching (apannakadhamma), which, in some ways, resembles Pascal's wager. According to the incontrovertible teaching, it would be better to believe in certain doctrines because they produce more benefits than others. For instance, even if there is no life after death and if good actions do not produce good consequences, still a moral person is praised in this life by the wise, whereas the immoral person is censured by society. However, if there is life after death and good action produce happy consequences, a moral person is praised in this life, and after death he or she goes to heaven. On the contrary, the immoral person is censured in this life, and after death he or she goes to hell (M.I.403). Therefore, it is better to believe that moral actions produce good consequences even if we do not have personal experience of karma and rebirth.

c. Interpretations of the Buddha's Advice to the Kâlâma People

Some have interpreted the Buddha's advice to the Kâlâma people as an iconoclast rejection of tradition and faith. This, however, does little justice to the Pâli Nikâyas, where the Buddha is said to be part of a long and respectable tradition of past

Buddhas, and where the first Brahmins are sometimes commended by their holiness. The Buddha shows respect for many traditional beliefs and practices of his time, and rejects only those that are unjustified, useless, or conducive to suffering for oneself and others.

Faith in the Buddha, his teachings, and his disciples, is highly regarded in the Pâli Nikâyas: it is the first of the five factors of striving (M.II.95-6), and a necessary condition to practice the spiritual path (M.III.33). Buddhist faith, however, is not unconditional or an end in and of itself but rather a means towards direct knowledge that must be based on critical examination, supported by reasons, and eventually verified or rooted in vision (dassanamulikâ) (M.I.320).

Another common interpretation of the advice to the Kâlâmas is that for the Buddha of the Pâli Nikâyas only personal experience provides reliable knowledge. However, this is misleading because analogical and inferential reasoning are widely used by the Buddha and his disciples to teach others as well as in debates with non-Buddhists. Similarly, analytical or philosophical meditation is a common practice for the attainment of liberation through wisdom. Personal experience, like any other means of knowledge is to be critically examined. Except in the case of Buddhas and liberated beings, personal experience is always tainted by affective and cognitive prejudices.

The Pâli Nikâyas might give the first impression of endorsing a form of naïve or direct realism: that is, the Buddha and his disciples seem to think that the world is exactly as we perceive it to be. While it is true that the Pâli Nikâyas do not question the common sense connection between objects of knowledge and the external world, there are some texts that might support a phenomenalist reading. For instance, the Buddha defines the world as the six senses (five ordinary senses plus the mind) and their respective objects (S.IV.95), or as the six senses, the six objects, and the six types of consciousness that arise in dependence on them (S.IV.39-40).

Here, the epistemology of the Buddha is a special form of realism that allows both for the direct perception of reality and the constructions of those less realized. Only Buddhas and liberated beings perceive the world directly; that is, they see the Dharma, whose regularity and stability remains independent of the existence of Buddhas (S.II.25). Unenlightened beings, on the other hand, see the world indirectly through a veil of negative emotions and erroneous views. Some texts go so far as to suggest that the world is not simply seen indirectly, but rather that it is literally constructed by our emotional dispositions. For instance, in the *Majjhima Nikâya* (I.111), the Buddha explicitly states that "what one feels, one perceives" (Yam vedeti, tam sañjânâti). That is, our knowledge is formed by our feelings. The influence of feelings in our ways of knowing can also be inferred from the twelve-link chain of dependent arising, which explains the arising and cessation of suffering. The second link, sankhâra, or formations, conditions the arising of the third link, consciousness. The term sankhâra literally means "put together," connoting the constructive role of the mental factors that fall into this category, many of them affective in nature.

Similarly, the Buddha of the Pâli Nikâyas says that "with what one has mentally constructed as the root cause (Yam papañceti tato nidânan), perceptions, concepts, and [further] mental constructions (papañcasaññâsankhâ) beset a man with respect to past, future, and present forms...sounds...odours... flavors...tangibles...mind-objects cognizable by the eye...ear... nose...tongue...body...mind" (M.I.111-112). That is, the knowledge of unenlightened beings has papañca, or mental constructions, as its root cause. The word papañca is a technical term that literally means diversification or proliferation; it refers to the tendency of unenlightened minds to construct or fabricate concepts conducive to suffering, especially essentialist and ego-related concepts such as "I" and "mine," concepts which lead to a variety of negative mental states such as craving, conceit, and dogmatic views about the self (Ñânananda 1971).

It is precisely because our experiences are affectively and cognitively conditioned that the Buddha of the Pâli Nikâyas advocates a critical approach toward all sources of knowledge, including personal experience. Even the lofty experiences derived from meditation are to be analyzed carefully because they might lead to false opinions about the nature of the self, the world, and the after life. The epistemological ideal is to know things directly beyond mental constructions (papañca), which presupposes the "tranquilization of all mental formations" (sabbasankhârasamatha).

d. Higher Knowledge and the Question of Empiricism

Contemplative experiences are of two main types: meditative absorptions or abstractions (jhâna), and higher or direct knowledge (abhiññâ). There are six classes of higher or direct knowledge: the first one refers to a variety of supernatural powers including levitation and walking on water; in this sense, it is better understood as a know-how type of knowledge. The second higher knowledge is literally called "divine ear element" or clairaudience. The third higher knowledge is usually translated as telepathy, though it means simply the ability to know the underlying mental state of others, not the reading of their minds and thoughts.

The next three types of higher knowledge are especially important because they were experienced by the Buddha the night of his enlightenment, and because they are the Buddhist counterparts to the triple knowledge of the Vedas. The fourth higher knowledge is retrocognition or knowledge of past lives, which entails a direct experience of the process of rebirth. The fifth is the divine eye or clairvoyance; that is, direct experience of the process of karma, or as the texts put it, the passing away and reappearing of beings in accordance with their past actions. The sixth is knowledge of the destruction of taints, which implies experiential knowledge of the four noble truths and the process of liberation.

Some scholars have interpreted the Buddha's emphasis on direct experience and the verifiable nature of Buddhist faith as a form of radical empiricism (Kalupahana 1992), and logical empiricism (Jayatilleke 1963). According to the empiricist interpretation, Buddhist faith is always subsequent to critically verifying the available empirical evidence. All doctrines taught by the Buddha are empirically verifiable if one takes the time and effort to attain higher or direct knowledge, interpreted as extraordinary sense experience. For instance, the triple knowledge of enlightenment implies a direct experience of the processes of karma, rebirth, and the four noble truths. Critiques of the empiricist interpretation point out that, at least at the beginning of the path, Buddhist faith is not always based on empirical evidence, and that the purpose of extraordinary knowledge is not to verify the doctrines of karma, rebirth, and the four noble truths (Hoffman 1982, 1987).

Whether or not the Buddha's epistemology can be considered empiricist depends on what we mean by empiricism and experience. The opposition between rationalism and empiricism and the sharp distinction between senses and reason is foreign to Buddhism. Nowhere in the Pâli Nikâyas does the Buddha say that all knowledge begins in or is acquired from sense experience. In this sense, the Buddha is not an empiricist.

3. THE BUDDHA'S COSMOLOGY AND METAPHYSICS

a. The Universe and the Role of Gods

The Buddha of the Pâli Nikâyas accepts the cosmology characteristic of his cultural context: a universe with several realms of existence, where people are reborn and die again and again (samsâra) depending on their past actions (karma) until they attain salvation (moksa). However, the Buddha substantially modifies the cosmology of his time. Against the Brahmanic tendency to understand karma as ritual action, and the Jain claim that all activities including involuntary actions constitute karma, the Buddha defines karma in terms of volition, or free will, which is expressed through thoughts, words, and behaviour. That is, for the Buddha, only voluntary actions produce karma.

Another important modification is that for the Buddha of the Pâli Nikâyas, samsâra refers primarily to a psychophysical process that takes place within the physical universe. For instance, when the Buddha speaks about the end of the world, he says that it cannot be reached by travelling through the physical universe, but only by putting an end to suffering (samsâra), where "one is not born, does not age, does not die, does not pass away, and is not reborn" Accordingly, salvation is not understood in world-denying terms or as an escape from the physical universe, but rather as an inner transformation that takes place within one's own psychophysical organism: "It is, friend, in just this fathom-high carcass endowed with perception and mind that I make known the world, the origin of the world, the cessation of the world, and the way leading to the cessation of the world." (S.I.62; A.II.47-9).

There are five kinds of destinations within samsâra: hell, animal kingdom, realm of ghosts, humankind, and realm of devas or radiant beings, commonly translated as gods (M.I.73). There are many hells and heavens and life there is transitory, just as in other destinations. In some traditions there is another destination, the realm of asuras or demigods, who are jealous of the gods and who are always in conflict with them.

The Pâli Nikâyas further divide the universe of samsâra into three main planes of existence, each one subdivided into several realms. The three planes of existence are sensorial, fine-material, and immaterial (M.I.50). Most destinations belong to the sensorial realm. Only a minority of heavens belong to the fine-material and immaterial realms. Rebirth in a particular realm depends on past actions: good actions lead to good destinations and bad actions to bad rebirths. Rebirth as a human or in heaven is considered a good destination; rebirth in the realm of ghosts, hell, and the animal realm are bad. Human rebirth is extremely difficult to attain (S.V.455-6; M.III.169), and it is highly regarded because of its unique combination of pain and pleasure, as well as its unique conductivity for attaining enlightenment. In this last sense human rebirth is said to be even better than rebirth as a god.

Rebirth also depends on the prevalent mental states of a person during life, and especially at the moment of death. That is, there is a correlation between mental states and realms of rebirth, between cosmology and psychology. For instance, a mind where hatred and anger prevails is likely to be reborn in hell; deluded and uncultivated minds are headed toward the animal kingdom; someone obsessed with sex and food will probably become bound to earth as a ghost; loving and caring persons will be reborn in heaven; someone who frequently dwells in meditative absorptions will be reborn in the fine-material and immaterial realms. Human rebirth might be the consequence of any of the aforementioned mental states.

Perhaps the most important modification the Buddha introduces into the traditional cosmology of his time was a new view of Gods (gods within Buddhism). In the Pâli Nikâyas, gods do not play any significant cosmological role. For the Buddha, the universe has not been created by an all-knowing, all-powerful god that is the lord of the universe and father of all beings (M.I.326-7). Rather, the universe evolves following certain cyclic patterns of contraction and expansion (D.III.84-5).

Similarly, the cosmic order, or Dharma, does not depend on the will of gods, and there are many good deeds far more effective than ritual sacrifices offered to the gods (D.I144ff). Gods for the Buddha are unenlightened beings subject to birth and death that require further learning and spiritual practice in order to attain liberation; they are more powerful and spiritually more developed than humans and other living beings, but Buddhas excel them in all regards: spiritual development, wisdom, and power. Even the supreme type of god, Brahmâ, offers his respects to the Buddha, praises him, and asks him to preach the Dharma for those with little dust in their eyes (M.I.168-9).

Since the Buddha of the Pâli Nikâyas does not deny the existence of gods, only their cosmological and soteriological functions, it is inaccurate to define early Buddhism as atheistic or as non-theistic. The word atheistic is usually associated with anti-religious attitudes absent in the Buddha, and the term non-theistic seems to imply that rejecting the theistic concept of God is one of the main concerns of the Buddha, when in fact it is a marginal question in the Pâli Nikâyas.

b. The Four Noble Truths or Realities

One the most common frameworks to explain the basic teachings of early Buddhism is the four noble truths (ariyasacca, Sanskrit âryasatya). The word sacca means both truth and reality. The word ariya refers primarily to the ideal type of person the Buddhist path is supposed to generate, a noble person in the ethical and spiritual sense. Translating ariyasacca by 'noble truths' is somehow misleading because it gives the wrong impression of being a set of beliefs, a creed that Buddhists accept as noble and true. The four noble truths are primarily four realities whose contemplation leads to sainthood or the state of the noble ones (ariya). Other possible translations of ariyasacca are "ennobling truths" or "truths of the noble ones."

Each noble truth requires a particular practice from the disciple; in this sense the four noble truths can be understood as four types of practice. The first noble truth, or the reality of suffering, assigns to the disciple the practice of cultivating understanding. Such understanding takes place gradually through reflection, analytical meditation, and eventually direct experience. What needs to be understood is the nature of suffering, and the different types of suffering and happiness within samsâra.

A common misconception about the first noble truth is to think that it presupposes a pessimistic outlook on life. This interpretation would be correct only if the Buddha of the Pâli Nikâyas had not taught the existence of different types of happiness and the third noble truth, or cessation of suffering; that is, the good news about the reality of nirvana, defined as the highest happiness (Dhp.203; M.I.505). Since the Buddha of the Pâli Nikâyas teaches the reality of both suffering and the highest happiness, perhaps it is more accurate to speak of his attitude as realist: there is a problem but there is also a solution to that problem.

The second noble truth, or reality of the origin of suffering, calls for the practice of renunciation to all mental states that generate suffering for oneself and others. The mental state that appears in the second noble truth is tanhâ, literally "thirst." It was customary in the first Western translations of Buddhist texts (Burnouf, Fausboll, Muller, Oldenberg, Warren) to translate tanhâ by desire. This translation has misled many to think that the ultimate goal of Buddhists is the cessation of all desires. However, as Damien Keown puts it, "it is an oversimplification of the Buddhist position to assume that it seeks an end to all desire." (1992: 222).

In fact, there are many terms in the Pâli Nikâyas that can be translated as desire, not all of them related to mental states conducive to suffering. On the contrary, there are many texts in the Pâli Nikâyas that demonstrate the positive role of certain types of desire in the Buddha's path (Webster, 2005: 90-142). Nonetheless, the term tanhâ in the Pâli Nikâyas designates always a harmful type of desire that leads to "repeated existence" (ponobhavikâ), is "associated with delight and lust" (nandirâgasahagatâ), and "delights here and there" (tatra tatrâbhinandinî) (M.I.48; D.II.308; etc). There is only one text (Nettipakarana 87) that speaks about a wholesome type of tanhâ that leads to its own relinquishment, but this text is extra-canonical except in Myanmar.

The most common translation of tanhâ nowadays is craving. Unlike the loaded, vast, and ambivalent term desire, the term craving refers more specifically to a particular type of desire, and cannot be misinterpreted as conveying any want and aspiration whatsoever. Rather, like tanhâ in the Pâli Nikâyas, craving refers to intense (râga can be translated by both lust and passion), obsessive, and addictive desires (the idiom tatra tatra can also be interpreted as connoting the idea of repetition or tendency to repeat itself).

Since craving, or tanhâ, does not include all possible types of desires, there is no "paradox of desire" in the Pâli Nikâyas. In other words, the Buddha of the the Pâli Nikâyas does not teach that in order to attain liberation from suffering one has to paradoxically desire to stop all desires. There is no contradiction in willing the cessation of craving. That is, for the Buddha of the Pâli Nikâyas it is possible to want, like, or strive for something without simultaneously craving for it.

The Pâli Nikâyas distinguish between three kinds of tanhâ: craving for sensual pleasures (kâmatanhâ), craving for existence (bhavatanhâ), and craving for non-existence (vibhavatanhâ). Following Webster, I understand the last two types of craving as "predicated on two extreme (wrong) views, those of eternalism and annihilationism" (2005:130-1). In other words, craving for existence longs for continued existence of one's self within samsâra, and craving for non-existence is a reversed type of desire or aversion to one's own destruction at the moment of death.

The underlying root of all suffering, however, is not craving but spiritual ignorance (avijjâ). In the Pâli Nikâyas spiritual ignorance does not connote a mere lack of information but rather a misconception, a distorted perception of things under the influence of conceptual fabrications and affective prejudices. More specifically, ignorance refers to not knowing things as they are, the Dharma, and the four noble truths. The relinquishing of spiritual ignorance, craving, and the three roots of the unwholesome (greed or lobha, aversion or dosa, delusion or moha) entails the cultivation of many positive mental states, some of the most prominent in the Pâli Nikâyas being: wisdom or understanding (paññâ), letting go (anupâdâna), selflessness (alobha), love (avera, adosa, avyâpâda), friendliness (mettâ), compassion (karunâ), altruistic joy (muditâ), equanimity (upekkhâ), calm (samatha, passaddhi), mindfulness (sati), diligence (appamâda).

The third noble truth, or reality of the cessation of suffering, asks us to directly realize the destruction of suffering, usually expressed with a variety of cognitive and affective terms: peace, higher knowledge, the tranquilization of mental formations, the abandonment of all grasping, cessation, the destruction of craving, absence of lust, nirvana (Pali nibbâna). The most popular of all the terms that express the cessation of suffering and rebirth is nirvana, which literally means blowing out or extinguishing.

Metaphorically, the extinction of nirvana designates a mental event, namely, the extinguishing of the fires of craving, aversion, and delusion (S.IV.251). That nirvana primarily denotes a mental event, a psychological process, is also confirmed by many texts that describe the person who experiences nirvana with intransitive verbs such as to nirvanize (nibbâyati) or to parinirvanize (parinibbâyati). However, there are a few texts that seem to indicate that nirvana might also be a domain of perception (âyatana), element (dhâtu), or reality (dhamma) known at the moment of enlightenment, and in special meditative absorptions after enlightenment. This domain is usually defined as having the opposite qualities of samsâra (Ud 8.1), or with metaphoric expressions (S.IV.369ff).

What is important to point out is that the concern of the Pâli Nikâyas is not to describe nirvana, which, strictly speaking, is beyond logic and language (It 37), but rather to provide a systematic explanation of the arising and cessation of suffering. The goal of Buddhism as it appears in the Pâli Nikâyas does not consist in believing that suffering arises and ceases like the Buddha says, but in realizing that what he teaches about suffering and its cessation is the case; that is, the Buddha's teaching, or Dharma, is intended to be experienced by the wise for themselves (M.I.265).

The fourth noble truth, or reality of the path leading to the cessation of suffering, imposes on us the practice of developing the eightfold ennobling path. This path can be understood either as eight mental factors that are cultivated by ennobled disciples at the moment of liberation, or as different parts of the entire Buddhist path whose practice ennoble the disciple gradually. The eight parts of the Buddhist path are usually divided into three kinds of training: training in wisdom (right view and right intention), ethical training (right speech, right bodily conduct, and right livelihood), and training in concentration (right effort, right mindfulness and right concentration).

c. Ontology of Suffering: the Five Aggregates

A prominent concern of the Buddha in the Pâli Nikâyas is to provide a solution to the problem of suffering. When asked about his teachings, the Buddha answers that he only teaches suffering and its cessation (M.I.140). The first noble truth describes what the Buddha means by suffering: birth, aging, illness, death, union with what is displeasing, separation from what is pleasing, not getting what one wants, the five aggregates of grasping (S.V.421).

The original Pali term for suffering is dukkha, a word that ordinarily means physical and mental pain, but that in the first noble truth designates diverse kinds of frustration, and the existential angst generated by the impermanence of life and the unavoidability of old age, disease, and death. However, when the Buddha of the Pâli Nikâyas mentions birth and the five aggregates of grasping, he seems to be referring to the fact that our psychophysical components are conditioned by grasping, and consequently, within samsâra, the cycle of births and deaths. This interpretation is consistent with later Buddhist tradition, which speaks about three types of dukkha: ordinary suffering (mental and physical pain), suffering due to change (derived from the impermanence of things), and suffering due to conditions (derived from being part of samsâra).

When the Buddha of the Pâli Nikâyas speaks about personal identity and the human predicament, he uses the technical expression "five aggregates of grasping" (pañcupâdânakkhandhâ). That is, the Buddha describes human existence in terms of five groups of constituents. The five aggregates are: material form (rûpa), sensations (vedanâ), perceptions (saññâ), mental formations (samkhâra), consciousness (viññâna). While the first aggregate refers to material components, the other four designate a variety of mental functions.

The aggregate material form is explained as the four great elements and the shape or figure of our physical body. The four great elements are earth, water, fire, and air. The earth element is further defined as whatever is solid in our body, and water as whatever is liquid. The fire element refers to "that by which one is warmed, ages, and is consumed," and the process of digestion. The air element denotes the breathing process and movements of gas throughout the body (M.I.185ff).

The aggregate sensations denote pleasant, unpleasant and neutral feelings experienced after there is contact between the six sense organs (eye, ear, nose, tongue, body, and mind) and their six objects (forms, sounds, odors, tastes, tangible objects, and mental phenomena). The aggregate perceptions express the mental function by which someone is able to identify objects. There are six types of perceptions corresponding to the six objects of the senses. The aggregate formations express emotional and intellectual dispositions, literally volitions (sañcetanâ), towards the six objects of the senses. These dispositions are the result of past cognitive and affective conditioning, that is, past karma or past voluntary actions. The aggregate consciousness connotes the ability to know and to be aware of the six objects of the senses (S.III.59ff).

d. Arguments for the Doctrine of Non-self

The Buddha reiterates again and again throughout the Pâli Nikâyas that any of the five aggregates "whether past, future or present, internal or external, gross or subtle, inferior or superior, far or near, ought to be seen as it actually is with right wisdom thus: 'this is not mine, this I am not, this is not my self.' " When the disciple contemplates the five aggregates in this way, he or she becomes disenchanted (nibbindati), lust fades away (virajjati), and he or she attains liberation due to the absence of lust (virâgâ vimuccati) (M.I.138-9).

The Buddha of the Pâli Nikâyas justifies this view of the five aggregates as non-self with three main arguments, which are used as a method of analytical meditation, and in polemics with members of other schools. The assumption underlying the Buddha's arguments is that something might be considered a self only if it were permanent, not leading to suffering, not dependently arisen, and subject to one's own will. Since none of the five aggregates fulfill any of these conditions, it is wrong to see them as belonging to us or as our self.

In the first and most common argument for non-self the Buddha asks someone the following questions: "What do you think, monks, is material form permanent or impermanent?" – "Impermanent, venerable sir." – "Is what is impermanent suffering or happiness?" – "Suffering, venerable sir." –Is what is impermanent, suffering, and subject to change, fit to be regarded as: "this is mine, this I am, this is my self?" – "No, venerable sir" (M.I.138, etc). The same reasoning is applied to the other aggregates.

The first argument is also applied to the six sensual organs, the six objects, the six types of consciousness, perceptions, sensations, and formations that arise dependent on the contact between the senses and their objects (M.III.278ff). Sometimes the first argument for non-self is applied to the six senses and their objects without questions and answers: "Monks, the visual organ is impermanent. What is impermanent is suffering. What is suffering is non-self. What is non-self ought to be seen as it really is with right wisdom thus: 'this is not mine, this I am not, this is not my self' " (S.IV.1ff).

The second argument for non-self is much less frequent: "Monks, material form is non-self. If it were self, it would not lead to affliction. It would be possible [to say] with regard to material form: 'Let my material form be thus. Let my material form not be thus.' But precisely because it is non-self, it leads to affliction. And it is not possible [to say] with regard to material form: 'Let my material form be thus. Let my material form not be thus' "(S.III.66-7). The same reasoning is applied to the other four aggregates.

The third argument deduces non-self from that fact that physical and mental phenomena depend on certain causes to exist. For instance, in (M.III.280ff), the Buddha first analyzes the dependent arising of physical and mental phenomena. Then he argues: "If anyone says: 'the visual organ is self,' that is unacceptable. The rising and falling of the visual organ are fully known (paññâyati). Since the rising and falling of the visual organ are fully known, it would follow that: 'my self arises and falls.' Therefore, it is unacceptable to say: 'the visual organ is self.' Thus the visual organ is non-self." The same reasoning is applied to the other senses, their objects, and the six types of consciousness, contacts (meeting of sense, object and consciousness), sensations, and cravings derived from them.

The third argument also appears combined with the first one without questions and answers. For instance, in (A.V.188), it is said that "whatever becomes, that is conditioned, volitionally formed, dependently arisen, that is impermanent. What is impermanent, that is suffering. What is suffering, that is [to be regarded thus]: 'this is not mine, this I am not, this is not my self.' "

If something can be inferred from these three arguments, it is that the target of the doctrine of non-self is not all concepts of self but specifically views of the self as permanent and not dependently arisen. That is, the doctrine of non-self opposes what is technically called "views of personal identity" or more commonly translated "personality views" (sakkâyadimmhi). Views of personal identity relate the five aggregates to a permanent and independent self in four ways: as being identical, as being possession of the self, as being in the self, or as the self being in them (M.I.300ff). All these views of personal identity are said to be the product of spiritual ignorance, that is, of not seeing with right wisdom the true nature of the five aggregates, their origin, their cessation, and the way leading to their cessation.

e. Human Identity and the Meaning of Non-self

Since the Pâli Nikâyas accept the common sense usages of the word "self" (attan, Skt. âtman), primarily in idiomatic expressions and as a reflexive pronoun meaning "oneself," the doctrine of non-self does not imply a literal negation of the self. Similarly, since the Buddha explicitly criticizes views that reject karma and moral responsibility (M.I.404ff), the doctrine of non-self should not be understood as the absolute rejection of moral agency and any concept of personal identity. In fact, the Buddha explicitly defines "personal identity" (sakkâya) as the five aggregates (M.I.299).

Since the sixth sense, or mind, includes the four mental aggregates, and since the ordinary five senses and their objects fall under the aggregate of material form, it can be said that for the Buddha of the Pâli Nikâyas personal identity is defined not only in terms of the five aggregates, but also in terms of the six senses and their six objects.

If the meaning of non-self were that there is literally no self whatsoever, no personal identity and no moral agency whatsoever, then the only logical conclusion would be to state that the Buddha taught nonsense and that the Pâli Nikâyas are contradictory, sometimes accepting the existence of a self and other times rejecting it. Even though no current scholar of Buddhism would endorse such an interpretation of non-self, it is still popular in some missionary circles and apologetic literature.

A more sympathetic interpretation of non-self distinguishes between two main levels of discourse (Collins 1982). The first level of discourse does not question the concept of self and freely uses personal terms and expressions in accordance with ordinary language and social conventions. The second level of discourse is philosophically more sophisticated and rejects views of self and personal identity as permanent and not dependently arisen. Behind the second level of discourse there is a technical understanding of the self and personal identity as the five aggregates, that is, as a combination of psychophysical processes, all of them impermanent and dependently originated.

This concept of the self as permanent and not dependently arisen is problematic because it is based on a misperception of the aggregates. This misperception of the five aggregates is associated with what is technically called "the conceit I am" (asmimâna) and "the underlying tendency to the conceits 'I' and 'mine' " (ahamkâra-mamankâra-mânânusaya).

This combination of conceit and ignorance fosters different types of cravings, especially craving for immortal existence, and subsequently, speculations about the past, present, and future nature of the self and personal identity. For instance, in (D.I.30ff), the Buddha speaks of different ascetics and Brahmins who claim that the self after death is "material, immaterial, both material and immaterial, neither material nor immaterial, finite, infinite, both, neither, of uniform perception, of varied perception, of limited perception, of unlimited perception, wholly happy, wholly miserable, both, neither."

The doctrine of non-self is primarily intended to counteract views of the self and personal identity rooted in ignorance regarding the nature of the five aggregates, the conceit "I am," and craving for immortal existence.

A minority of scholars reject the notion that the Buddha's doctrine of non-self implies the negation of the true self, which for them is permanent and independent of causes and conditions. Accordingly, the purpose of the doctrine of non-self is simply to deny that the five aggregates are the true self.

The main reason for this interpretation is that the Buddha does not say anywhere in the Pâli Nikâyas that the self does not exist; he only states that a self and what belongs to a self are not apprehended (M.I.138). Therefore, for these interpreters the Buddha of the Pâli Nikâyas only claims that impermanent and conditioned things like the five aggregates are not the true self. For these scholars, the Buddha does talk about the true self when he speaks about the consciousness of liberated beings (M.I.140), and the unconditioned, unborn and deathless nirvana (Bhattacarya 1973; Pérez Remón 1981).

However, the majority of Buddhist scholars agree with the traditional Buddhist self-understanding: they think that the doctrine of non-self is incompatible with any doctrine about a permanent and independent self, not just with views that mistakenly identify an alleged true self with the five aggregates. The main reason for this interpretation relates to the doctrine of dependent arising.

f. Causality and the Principle of Dependent Arising

The importance of dependent arising (pamiccasamuppâda) cannot be underestimated: the Buddha realized its workings during the night of his enlightenment (M.I.167). Preaching the doctrine of dependent arising amounts to preaching the Dharma (M.II.32), and whoever sees it sees the Dharma (M.I.191). The Dharma of dependent arising remains valid whether or not there are Buddhas in the world (S.II.25), and it is through not understanding it that people are trapped into the cycle of birth and death (D.II.55).

The doctrine of dependent arising can be formulated in two ways that usually appear together: as a general principle or as a chain of causal links to explain the arising and ceasing of suffering and the process of rebirth. The general principle of dependent arising states that "when this exists, that comes to be; with the arising of this, that arises. When this does not exist, that does not come to be; with the cessation of this, that ceases" (M.II.32; S.II.28).

Unlike the logical principle of conditionality, the principle of dependent arising does not designate a connection between two ideas but rather an ontological relationship between two things or events within a particular timeframe. Dependent arising expresses not only the Buddha's understanding of causality but also his view of things as interrelated. The point behind dependent arising is that things are dependent on specific conditions (pamicca), and that they arise together with other things (samuppâda). In other words, the principle of dependent arising conveys both ontological conditionality and the constitutive relativity of things. This relativity, however, does not mean that for the Buddha of the Pâli Nikâyas everything is interdependent or that something is related to everything else. This is a later development of Buddhist thought, not a characteristic of early Indian Buddhism.

The most comprehensive chain of dependent arising contains twelve causal links: (1) ignorance, (2) formations, (3) consciousness, (4) mentality-materiality, (5) the six senses, (6) contact, (7) sensations, (8) craving (9) grasping, (10) becoming, (11) birth, (12) old age and death. The most common formulation is as follows: with 1 as a condition 2 [comes to be]; with 2 as a condition 3 [comes to be], and so forth. Conversely, with the cessation of 1 comes the cessation of 2; with the cessation of 2 comes the cessation of 3, and so forth.

It is important to keep in mind that this chain does not imply a linear understanding of causality where the antecedent link disappears once the subsequent link has come to be. Similarly, each of the causal links is not to be understood as the one and only cause that produces the next link but rather as the most necessary condition for its arising. For instance, ignorance, the first link, is not the only cause of the process of suffering but rather the cause most necessary for the continuation of such a process. For the Buddha of the Pâli Nikâyas, as well as for later Buddhist tradition, there is always a multiplicity of causes and conditions at play.

The traditional interpretation divides the twelve link chain of dependent arising into three lives. The first two links (ignorance and formations) belong to the past life: due to a misperception of the nature of the five aggregates, a person (the five aggregates) performs voluntary actions: mental, verbal, and bodily actions, with wholesome, unwholesome, and neutral karmic effects. The next ten factors correspond to the present life: the karmic effects of past voluntary formations are stored in consciousness and transferred to the next life. Consciousness together with the other mental aggregates combines with a new physical body to constitute a new psychophysical organism (mentality-materiality). This new stage of the five aggregates develops the six senses and the ability to establish contact with their six objects. Contacts with objects of the senses produce pleasant, unpleasant and neutral sensations. If the sensations are pleasant, the person usually responds with cravings for more pleasant experiences, and if the sensations are unpleasant, with aversion. Craving and aversion, as well as the underlying ignorance of the nature of the five aggregates are fundamental causes of suffering and rebirth: the three roots of the unwholesome according to the Pâli Nikâyas, or the three mental poisons according to later Buddhist traditions.

By repeating the affective responses of craving and aversion, the person becomes more and more dependent on whatever leads to more pleasant sensations and less unpleasant ones. This creates a variety of emotional dependencies and a tendency to grasp or hold onto what causes pleasure and avoids pain. The Buddha of the Pâli Nikâyas speaks about four types of grasping: towards sensual pleasures, views, rites-and-observances, and especially towards doctrines of a [permanent and independent] self (D.II.57-8).

The original term for grasping is upâdâna, which also designates the fuel or supply necessary to maintain a fire. In this sense, grasping is the psychological fuel that maintains the fires of craving, aversion, and delusion, the fires whose extinction is called nirvana. The Buddha's ideal of letting go and detachment should not be misunderstood as the absence of any emotions whatsoever including love and compassion, but specifically as the absence of emotions associated with craving, aversion, and delusion. Motivated by grasping and the three mental fires, the five aggregates perform further voluntary actions, whose karmic effects perpetuate existence within the cycle of rebirth and subsequent suffering. The last two links (birth, aging and death) refer to the future life. At the end of this present existence, a new birth of the five aggregates will take place followed by old age, death, and other kinds of suffering.

The twelve-link chain of dependent arising explains the processes of rebirth and suffering without presupposing a permanent and independent self. The Buddha of the Pâli Nikâyas makes this point explicit in his passionate rebuttal of the monk Sâti, who claimed that it is the same consciousness that wanders through the cycle of rebirth. For the Buddha, consciousness, like the other eleven causal links, is dependent on specific conditions (M.I.258ff), which entails that consciousness is impermanent, suffering, and non-self.

Instead of a permanent and independent self behind suffering and the cycle of rebirth, the Buddha of the Pâli Nikâyas presupposes five psychophysical sets of processes, namely, the five aggregates, which imply an impermanent and dependently-arisen concept of 'self' and 'personal identity.' In other words, the Buddha rejects substance-selves but accepts process-selves (Gowans 2003). Yet, the Buddha of the Pâli Nikâyas explicitly refuses to use personal terms such as 'self' in technical explanations of rebirth and suffering, and he prefers to speak in terms of causes and conditions that produce other causes and conditions (S.II.13-4; S.II.62; M.III.19). But what happens to consciousness and the other aggregates when grasping no longer exists and the three mental fires have been extinguished? What happens when suffering ceases and the cycle of rebirth stops?

4. NIRVANA AND THE SILENCE OF THE BUDDHA

a. Two Kinds of Nirvana and the Undetermined Questions

When the fires of craving, aversion, and ignorance are extinguished at the moment of enlightenment, the aggregates are liberated due to the lack of grasping. This is technically called nirvana with remainder of grasping (saupâdisesa-nibbâna), or as later tradition puts it, nirvana of mental defilements (kilesa-parinibbâna). The expression 'remainder of grasping' refers to the five aggregates of liberated beings, which continue to live after enlightenment but without negative mental states.

The aggregates of the liberated beings perform their respective functions and, like the aggregates of anybody else, they grow old, get sick, and are subject to pleasant and unpleasant sensations until death. The difference between unenlightened and enlightened beings is that enlightened beings respond to sensations without craving or aversion, and with higher knowledge of the true nature of the five aggregates.

The definition of nirvana without remainder (anupâdisesa-nibbâna) that appears in (It 38) only says that for the liberated being "all that is experienced here and now, without enchantment [another term for grasping], will be cooled (sîta)." Since "all" is defined in the Pâli Nikâyas as the six senses and their six objects (S.IV.15), which is another way of describing the individual psychophysical experience or the five aggregates, the expression "all that is experienced" refers to what happens to the aggregates of liberated beings. Since (It 38) explicitly uses the expression "here and now" (idheva), it seems impossible to conclude that the definition of nirvana without remainder is intended to say anything about nirvana or the aggregates beyond death. Rather (It 38) describes nirvana and the aggregates at the moment of death: they will be no longer subject to rebirth and they will become cooled, tranquil, at peace. The question is: what does this peace or coolness entail? What happens after the nirvana of the aggregates? Does the mind of enlightened beings survive happily ever after? Does the liberated being exist beyond death or not?

These questions are left undetermined (avyâkata) by the Buddha of the the Pâli Nikâyas. The ten questions in the the Pâli Nikâyas ask whether (1) The world is eternal; (2) The world is not eternal; (3) The world is infinite; (4) The world is finite; (5) Body and soul are one thing; (6) Body and soul are two different things; (7) A liberated being (tathâgata) exists after death; (8) A liberated being (tathâgata) does not exist after death; (9) A liberated being (tathâgata) both exists and does not exist after death; (10) A liberated being (tathâgata) neither exists nor does not exist after death. In Sanskrit Buddhist texts the ten views become fourteen by adding the last two possibilities of the tetralema (both A and B, neither A nor B) to the questions about the world.

Unfortunately for those looking for quick answers, the Buddha of the Pâli Nikâyas does not provide a straightforward yes or no response to any of these questions. When the Buddha is asked whether the liberated being exists, does not exist, both, or neither, he sets aside these questions by saying that (1) he does not hold such views, (2) he has left the questions undetermined, and (3) the questions do not apply (na upeti). The first two answers are also used to respond to questions about the temporal and spatial finitude or infinitude of the world, and the identity or difference between the soul and the body. Only the third type of answer is given to the questions about liberated beings after death.

Most presentations of early Buddhism interpret these three answers of the Buddha as an eloquent silence about metaphysical questions due primarily to pragmatic reasons, namely, the questions divert from spiritual practice and are not conducive to liberation from suffering. While the pragmatic reasons for the answers of the Buddha are undeniable, it is inaccurate to understand them as silence about metaphysical questions. In fact, the Buddha of the

Pâli Nikâyas does address many metaphysical issues with his teachings of non-self and dependent arising.

The answers of the Buddha to the undetermined questions are due not only to pragmatic reasons but also to metaphysical reasons: the questions are inconsistent with the doctrines of non-self and dependent arising because they assume the existence of a permanent and independent self, a self that is either finite or infinite, identical or different from the body, existing or not existing after death. Besides pragmatic and metaphysical reasons, there are cognitive and affective reasons for the answers of the Buddha: the undetermined questions are based on ignorance about the nature of the five aggregates and craving for either immortal existence or inexistence. The questions are expressions of 'identity views,' that is, they are part of the problem of suffering. Answering the questions directly would have not done any good: a yes answer would have fostered more craving for immortal existence and led to eternalist views, and a no answer would have fostered further confusion and led to nihilist views (S.IV.400-1).

In the case of the undetermined questions about the liberated being, there are also apophatic reasons for answering "it does not apply." The Buddha of the Pâli Nikâyas illustrates the inapplicability of the questions with the simile of the fire extinct: just as it does not make sense to ask about the direction in which an extinct fire has gone, it is inappropriate to ask about the status of the liberated being beyond death: "The fire burned in dependence on its fuel of grass and sticks. When that is used up, if it does not get any more fuel, being without fuel, it is reckoned as extinguished. Similarly, the enlightened being has abandoned the five aggregates by which one might describe him...he is liberated from reckoning in terms of the five aggregates, he is profound, immeasurable, unfathomable like the ocean" (M.I.487-8).

b. Eternalism, Nihilism, and the Middle Way

There are three possible interpretations of the simile of the extinct fire: (1) liberated beings no longer exist beyond death (2) liberated beings exist in a mysterious unfathomable way beyond death (3) the Buddha is silent about both the liberated being and nirvana after death. The first interpretation seems the most logical conclusion given the Buddha's ontology of suffering and the doctrine of non-self. However, the nihilist interpretation makes Buddhist practice meaningless and contradicts texts where the Buddha criticizes teachings not conducive to spiritual practice such as materialism and determinism (M.I.401ff). But more importantly, the nihilist interpretation is vehemently rejected in the Pâli Nikâyas: "As I am not, as I do not proclaim, so have I been baselessly, vainly, falsely, and wrongly misrepresented by some ascetics and brahmins thus: 'the ascetic Gotama [Buddha] is one who leads astray; he teaches the annihilation, the destruction, the extermination of an existing being' "(M.I.140).

The second interpretation appears to some as following from the Buddha's incontrovertible response to the nihilist reading of his teachings: since the Buddha rejects nihilism, he must somehow accept the eternal existence of liberated beings, or at least the eternal existence of nirvana. For eternalist interpreters, the texts in the Pâli Nikâyas that speak about the transcendence and ineffability of liberated beings and nirvana can be understood as implying their existence after or beyond death.

There are several eternalist readings of the Buddha's thought. We have already mentioned the most common: the doctrine of non-self merely states that the five aggregates are not the true self, which is the transcendent and ineffable domain of nirvana. However, there are eternalist interpretations within Buddhism too. That is, interpretations that are nominally consistent with the doctrine of non-self but that nevertheless speak of something as eternally existing: either the mind of liberated beings or nirvana. For instance, Theravâda Buddhists usually see nirvana as non-self, but at the same time as an unconditioned (asamkhata) and deathless (amata) reality. The assumption, though rarely stated, is that liberated beings dwell eternally in nirvana without a sense of "I" and "mine," which is a transcendent state beyond the comprehension of unenlightened beings. Another eternalist interpretation is that of the Dalai Lama who, following the standard interpretation of Tibetan Buddhists, claims that the Buddha did not teach the cessation of all aggregates but only of contaminated aggregates. That is, the uncontaminated aggregates of liberated beings continue to exist individually beyond death, though they are seen as impermanent, dependently arisen, non-self, and empty of inherent existence (Dalai Lama 1975:27). Similarly, Peter Harvey understands nirvana as a selfless and objectless state of consciousness different from the five aggregates that exists temporarily during life and eternally beyond death (1995: 186-7).

The problem with eternalist interpretations is that they contradict what the Pâli Nikâyas say explicitly about the way to consider liberated beings, the limits of language, the content of the Buddha's teachings, and dependent arising as a middle way between the extremes of eternalism and annihilationism. In (S.III.110ff), Sâriputta, the Buddha's leading disciple in doctrinal matters, explains that liberated beings should be considered neither as annihilated after death nor as existing without the five aggregates.

In (D.II.63-4) the Buddha makes clear that consciousness and mentality-materiality, that is, the five aggregates, are the limits of designation (adhivacana), language (nirutti), cognitions (viññatti), and understanding (paññâ). Accordingly, in (D.II.68) the Buddha says it is inadequate to state that the liberated being exists after death, does not exist, both, or neither. This reading is confirmed by (Sn 1076): "There is not measure (pamâna) of one who has gone out, that by which [others] might speak (vajju) of him does not exist. When all things have been removed, then all ways of speech (vâdapathâ) are also removed."

Given the Buddha's understanding of the limits of language and understanding in the Pâli Nikâyas, it is not surprising that he responded to the accusation of teaching the annihilation of beings, by saying that "formerly and now I only teach suffering and the cessation of suffering." Since the Buddha does not teach anything beyond the cessation of suffering at the moment of death, that is, beyond the limits of language and understanding, it is inaccurate to accuse him of teaching the annihilation of beings. Similarly, stating that liberated beings exist after death in a mysterious way beyond the four logical possibilities of existence, non-existence, both or neither, is explicitly rejected in (S.III.118-9) and (S.IV.384), where once again the Buddha concludes that he only makes known suffering and the cessation of suffering.

If the eternalist interpretation were correct, it would have been unnecessary for the Buddha of the Pâli Nikâyas to put so much emphasis on the teaching of dependent arising. Why would dependent arising be defined in (S.II.17) as right view and as the middle way between the extremes of eternalism and annihilationism if the truth were that the consciousness of liberated beings or the unconditioned nirvana exist eternally? If knowing and seeing dependent arising precludes someone from speculating about a permanent self in the past and the future (M.I.265), why would the Buddha teach anything about the eternal existence of liberated beings and nirvana?

In order to avoid the aforementioned contradictions entailed by eternalist readings of the Pâli Nikâyas, all texts about nirvana and the consciousness of liberated beings are to be understood as referring to this life or the moment of death, never to some mysterious consciousness or domain that exists beyond death. Since none of the texts about nirvana and liberated beings found in the Pâli Nikâyas refer unambiguously to their eternal existence beyond death, I interpret the Buddha as being absolutely silent about nirvana and liberated beings beyond death (Vélez de Cea 2004a). In other words, nothing of what the Pâli Nikâyas say goes beyond the limits of language and understanding, beyond the content of the Buddha's teachings, and beyond dependent arising as the middle way between eternalism and annihilationism.

Instead of focusing on nirvana and liberated beings beyond death, the Buddha of the Pâli Nikâyas emphasizes dependent arising and the practice of the four foundations of mindfulness. Dependent arising is intended to avoid views about a permanent and independent self in the past and the future (M.I.265; M.III.196ff), and the four foundations of mindfulness are said to be taught precisely to destroy such views (D.III.141). That is, the Buddha's fundamental concern is to address the problem of suffering in the present without being distracted by views about the past or the future: "Let not a person revive the past, or on the future build his hopes; for the past has been left behind and the future has not been reached. Instead with insight let him see each presently arising state (paccuppannañca yo dhammam tattha tattha vipassati); let him know that and be sure of it, invincibly, unshakeably. Today the effort must be made, tomorrow death may come, who knows?" (Bhikkhu Bodhi's translation. M.III.193).

5.Buddhist Ethics

Early Buddhist ethics includes more than lists of precepts and more than the section on ethical training of the eightfold noble path; that is, Buddhist ethics cannot be reduced to right action (abstaining from killing, stealing, lying), right speech (abstaining from false, divisive, harsh, and useless speech), and right livelihood (abstaining from professions that harm living beings). Besides bodily and verbal actions, the Pâli Nikâyas discuss a variety of mental actions including thoughts, motivations, emotions, and perspectives. In fact, it is the ethics of mental actions that constitutes the main concern of the Buddha's teaching.

Early Buddhist ethics encompasses the entire spiritual path, that is, bodily, verbal, and mental actions. The factors of the eightfold noble path dealing with wisdom and concentration (right view, right intentions, rights effort, right concentration, right mindfulness) relate to different types of mental actions. The term "right" (sammâ) in this context does not mean the opposite of "wrong," but rather "perfect" or "complete;" that is, it denotes the best or the most effective actions to attain liberation. This, however, does not imply that the Buddha advocates the most perfect form of ethical conduct for all his disciples.

Early Buddhist ethics is gradualist in the sense that there are diverse ways of practicing the path with several degrees of commitment; not all disciples are expected to practice Buddhist ethics with the same intensity. Monks and nuns take more precepts and are supposed to devote more time to spiritual practices than householders. However, a complete monastic code (prâtimoka) like those found in later Vinaya literature does not appear in the Pâli Nikâyas. The most comprehensive formulation of early Buddhist ethics, probably common to monastic disciples and lay people, is the list of ten dark or unwholesome actions and their opposite, the ten bright or wholesome actions: three bodily actions (abstaining from killing, stealing, sexual misconduct), four verbal actions (abstaining from false, divisive, harsh, and useless speech), and tree mental actions (abstaining from covetousness, ill-will, and dogmatic views).

The Buddha of the Pâli Nikâyas defines action in terms of intention or choice (cetanâ): "It is intention, monks, what I call action. Having intended, someone acts through body, speech, and mind" (A.III.415). The Pâli Nikâyas define the roots of unwholesome (akusala) actions as greed (lobha), aversion (dosa), and delusion (moha). Conversely, the roots of wholesome actions are defined as the opposite mental states (M.I.47). Some scholars infer from these two definitions that Buddhist ethics is an ethics of intention or an agent-based form of virtue ethics. That is, according to these scholars, for the Buddha of the the Pâli Nikâyas, only the agent's intention or motivation determine the goodness of actions. This interpretation, however, is disproved by many texts of the Pâli Nikâyas where good and evil actions are discussed without any reference to the underlying intention or motivation of the agent. Consequently, the more comprehensive account understands intention not as the only factor that determines the goodness of actions, but rather as the condition of possibility, the necessary condition for speaking about action in the moral sense. Without intention or choice, there is no ethical action. Similarly, motivation, while a central moral factor in Buddhist ethics, is neither the only factor nor always the most important factor to determine the goodness of actions. Understanding Buddhist ethics as concerned exclusively with the three roots of the wholesome does not fully capture the breath of moral concern of the Pâli Nikâyas (Vélez de Cea 2004b).

The fundamental moral law of the universe according to early Buddhism is what is popularly called the "law of karma": good actions produce good consequences, and bad actions lead to bad consequences. The consequences of volitional actions can be experienced in this life or in subsequent lives. Although not everything we experience is due to past actions, physical appearance, character, lifespan, prosperity, and rebirth destination are believed to be influenced by past actions. This influence however, is not to be confused with fatalism, a position rejected in the Pâli Nikâyas. There is always room for mitigating and even eradicating the negative consequences of past actions with new volitions in the present. That is, past karma does not dictate our situation: the existence of freewill and the possibility of changing our predicament is always assumed. There is conditioning of the will and other mental factors, but no hard determinism.

A common objection to early Buddhist ethics is how there can be freewill and responsibility without a permanent self that transmigrates through lives. If there is no self, who is the agent of actions? Who experiences the consequences of actions? Is the person who performs an action in this life the same person that experiences the consequences of that action in a future life? Is it a different person? The Buddha considers these questions improper of his disciples, who are trained to explain things in terms of causes and condition (S.II.61ff; S.II.13ff)). In other words, since the Buddha's disciples explain processes with the doctrine of dependent arising, they should avoid explanations that use personal terms and presuppose the extremes of eternalism and nihilism. The moral agent is not a substance-self but rather the five aggregates, a dynamic and dependently-arisen process-self who, like a flame or the water of a river, changes all the time and yet has some degree of continuity.

The most common interpretations of early Buddhist ethics view its nature as either a form of agent-based virtue ethics or as a sophisticated kind of consequentialism. The concern for virtue cultivation is certainly prevalent in early Buddhism, and evidently the internal mental state or motivation underlying actions is extremely important to determine the overall goodness of actions, which is the most important factor for advanced practitioners. Similarly, the concern for the consequences of actions, whether or not they lead to the happiness or the suffering of oneself and others, also pervades the Pâli Nikâyas. However, the goodness of actions in the Pâli Nikâyas does not depend exclusively on either the goodness of motivations or the goodness of consequences. Respect to status and duty, observance of rules and precepts, as well as the intrinsic goodness of certain external bodily and verbal actions are equally necessary to assess the goodness of at least certain actions. Since the foundations of right action in the Pâli Nikâyas are irreducible to one overarching principle, value or criterion of goodness, early Buddhist ethics is pluralistic in a metaethical sense. Given the unique combination of deontological, consequentialist, and virtue ethical trends found in the Pâli Nikâyas, early Buddhist ethics should be understood in its own terms as a sui generis normative theory inassimilable to Western ethical traditions.

6. REFERENCES AND FURTHER READING

a. Primary Sources

All references to the Pâli Nikâyas are to the edition of The Pâli Text Society, Oxford. References to the Anguttara, Dîgha, Majjhima, and Samyutta Nikâyas are to the volume and page number. References to Udâna and Itivuttaka are to the page number and to Dhammapada and Sutta Nipâta to the verse number.

A. Anguttara Nikâya

D. Dîgha Nikâya

M. Majjhima Nikâya

S. Samyutta Nikâya

Ud. Udâna

It. Itivuttaka

Dhp. Dhammapada

Sn. Sutta Nipâta

b. Secondary Sources

1.Bechert, H. (Ed) 1995. *When Did the Buddha Live? The Controversy on the Dating of the Historical Buddha. Selected Papers Based on a Symposium Held under the Auspices of the Academy of Sciences in Göttingen.* Delhi: Sri Satguru Publications. 1995.

2.Bhattacharya, K. 1973. *L'Âtman-Brahman dans le Bouddhisme Ancien.* París: EFEO.

3.Bhikkhu Ñânamoli and Bhikkhu Bodhi. 1995. *The Middle Length*

Discourses of the Buddha. A New Translation of the Majjhima Nikâya. Kandy: Buddhist Publication Society.

4.Bhikkhu Ñânananda. 1971. *Concept and Reality in Early Buddhist Thought.* Kandy: Buddhist Publication Society.

5.Cousins, L.S. 1996. "Good or Skillful? Kusala in Canon and Commentary." *Journal of Buddhist Ethics.*Vol. 3: 133-164.

6.Collins, S. 1982. *Selfless Persons.* Cambridge: Cambridge University Press.

7.Collins, S. 1994. "What are Buddhists Doing When They Deny the Self?" In *Religion and Practical Reason,* edited by Frank E. Reynolds and David Tracy. Albany: SUNY.

8Collins, S. 1998. *Nirvana and other Buddhist Felicities.* Cambridge: Cambridge University Press

9.Dalai Lama. 1994. *The Way to Freedom.* San Francisco: Harper.

10.Dharmasiri, G. 1996. *Fundamentals of Buddhist Ethics.* Singapore: Buddhist Research Society.

11.Fuller, P. 2005. *The Notion of Dimmhi in Theravâda Buddhism.* London: RoutledgeCurzon.

12.Gombrich, R. 1988. *Theravâda Buddhism: A Social History from Ancient Benares to Modern Colombo.* London: Routledge.

13.Gombrich, R. 1996. *How Buddhism Began.* London: Athlone.

14.Gethin, R. 2001. *The Buddhist Path to Awakening.* Richmon Surrey: Curzon Press.

15.Gowans, C. W. 2003. *Philosophy of the Buddha.* London: Routledge.

16.Hallisey, C. 1996. "Ethical Particularism in Theravâda Buddhism." *Journal of Buddhist Ethics.* Vol. 3: 32-34.

17.Hamilton, S. 2000. *Early Buddhism: A New Approach.* Richmon Surrey: Curzon Press.

18.Harvey, P. 1995. *The Selfless Mind: Personality, Consciousness, and Nirvana in Early Buddhism.* Richmon Surrey: Curzon Press.

19.Harvey, P. 1995. "Criteria for Judging the Unwholesomeness of Actions in the Texts of Theravâda Buddhism." *Journal of Buddhist Ethics.* Vol. 2: 140-151.

20.Harvey, P. 2000. *An Introduction to Buddhist Ethics.* Cambridge: Cambridge University Press.

21.Hoffman, F. J. 1987. *Rationality and Mind in Early Buddhism*. New Delhi: Motilal Banarsidass.

22.Hwang, S. 2006. *Metaphor and Literalism in Buddhism: The Doctrinal History of Nirvana*. London: RoutledgeCurzon.

23.Jayatilleke, K. N. 1963. *Early Buddhist Theory of Knowledge*. London: Allen & Unwin.

24.Johansson, R. 1969. *The Psychology of Nirvana*. London: Allen and Unwin Ltd.

25.Kalupahana, D. 1976. *Buddhist Philosophy: A Historical Analysis*. Honolulu: University Press of Hawai'i.

26.Kalupahana, D. 1992. *A History of Buddhist Philosophy: Continuities and Discontinuities*. Honolulu: University Press of Hawai'i.

27.Keown, D. 1992. *The Nature of Buddhist Ethics*. New York: Palgrave.

28.Norman, K. R. 1983. *Pâli Literature: Including the Canonical Literature in Prakrit and Sanskrit of all the Hînayâna schools of Buddhism*. Wiesbaden: Otto Harrassowitz.

29.Norman, K. R. 1990-6. *Collected Papers*. Oxford: The Pâli Text Society.

30.Pande, G.C. 1995. *Studies in the Origins of Buddhism*. New Delhi: Motilal Banarsidass.

31.Pérez-Remón, J. 1980. *Self and Non-Self in Early Buddhism*. New York: Mouton.

32.Perret, R. 1986. "Egoism, Altruism, and Intentionalism in Buddhist Ethics." *Journal of IndianPhilosophy*. Vol. 15: 71-85.

33.Premasiri, P. D. 1987. "Early Buddhist Concept of Ethical Knowledge: A Philosophical Analysis." Kalupahana, D.J. and Weeraratne, W.G. eds. *Buddhist Philosophy and Culture: Essays in Honor of N.A. Jayawickrema*. Colombo: N.A. Jayawickrema Felicitation Volume Committee. Pp. 37-70.

5

Sankhya Philosophy

Sânkhya (often spelled Sâmkhya) is one of the major "orthodox" (or Hindu) Indian philosophies. Two millennia ago it was the representative Hindu philosophy. Its classical formulation is found in ÎsvaraKrsna's *Sânkhya-Kârikâ* (ca. 350 CE), a condensed account in seventy-two verses. It is a strong Indian example of metaphysical dualism, but unlike many Western counterparts it is atheistic. The two types of entities of Sânkhya are *Prakrti* and *Purusa*-s, namely Nature and persons.

Nature is singular, and persons are numerous. Both are eternal and independent of each other. Persons (*Purusa*-s) are essentially unchangeable, inactive, conscious entities, who nonetheless gain something from contact with Nature. Creation as we know it comes about by a conjunction of Nature and persons. *Prakrti*, or Nature, is comprised of three *guna*-s or qualities.

The highest of the three is *sattva* (essence), the principle of light, goodness and intelligence. *Rajas* (dust) is the principle of change, energy and passion, while *tamas* (darkness) appears as inactivity, dullness, heaviness and despair. Nature, though unconscious, is purposeful and is said to function for the purpose of the individual *Purusa*-s. Aside from comprising the physical universe, it comprises the gross body and "sign-body" of a *Purusa*. The latter contains among other things the epistemological apparati of embodied beings (such as the mind, intellect, and senses). The sign body of a *Purusa* transmigrates: after the death of the gross body, the sign-body is reborn into another gross body according to past merit, and the *Purusa* continues to be a witness through its various bodies. An escape from this endless circle is possible only through the realization of the fundamental difference between Nature and persons, whereby an individual *Purusa* loses interest in Nature and is thereby liberated forever from all bodies, subtle and gross. Much of the Sânkhya system became widely accepted in India: especially the theory of the three *guna*-s; and it was incorporated into much latter Indian philosophy, especially Vedânta.

1. HISTORY

The word "Sânkhya" is derived from the Sanskrit noun sankhyâ (number) based on the verbal root *khyâ* (make known, name) with the preverb *sam*(together). "Sânkhya" thus denotes the system of enumeration or taking account. The first meaning is acceptable, as Sânkhya is very fond of sets, often naming them as "triad," "the group of eleven," and so forth; but the second meaning is more fitting, as the aim of Sânkhya is to take into account all the important factors of the whole world, especially of the human condition.

Sânkhya has a very long history. Its roots go deeper than textual traditions allow us to see. The last major figure in the tradition, Vijñâna Bhiksu, thrived as late as 1575 CE. Despite its long history, Sânkhya is essentially a one-book school: the earliest extant complete text, the *Sânkhya-Kârikâ*, is the unquestioned classic of the tradition. Not only are its formal statements accepted by all subsequent representatives, but also its ordering of the topics and its arguments are definitive – very little is added in the course of the centuries.

Besides its own author, ÎsvaraKrsna, the *Sânkhya-Kârikâ* itself names several ancient adherents of the school plus a standard work, the *sasti-Tantra* (the book of sixty [topics]). The ancient Buddhist Asvaghosa (in his Buddha-Carita) describes Arâa Kâlâma, the teacher of the young Buddha (ca. 420 BCE) as following an archaic form of Sânkhya. The great Indian epic, the *Mahâbhârata*, represents the Sânkhya system as already quite old at the time of the great war of the Bharata clan , which occurred during the first half of the first millennium BCE. Such textual evidence confirms that by the beginning of our era, Indian common opinion considered

Sânkhya as very ancient. Moreover, Sânkhya concepts and terminology frequently appear in the portion of the Vedas known as the Upanisads, notably in the *Katha* and the *Svetâsvatara*. The older (6th cent. BCE?) *Chândogya Upanisad* presents an important forerunner of the *guna*-theory, although the terminology is different. And before that, in the Creation-hymn of the Zg-Veda (X. 129) we find ideas of the evolution of a material principle and of cosmic dualism, in the company of words that later became the names of the *guna*-s.

Sânkhya likely grew out of speculations rooted in cosmic dualism and introspective meditational practice. The agriculturally-rooted concept of the productive union of the sky-god (or sun-god or rain-god) and the earth goddess appears in India typically as the connection of the spiritual, immaterial, lordly, immobile fertilizer (represented as the *Siva-lingam,* or phallus) and of the active, fertile, powerful but subservient material principle (Sakti or Power, often as the horrible Dark Lady, Kâlî). The ascetic and meditative yoga practice, in contrast, aimed at overcoming the limitations of the natural body and achieving perfect stillness of the mind. A combination of these views may have resulted in the concept of the *Purusa,* the unchanging immaterial conscious essence, contrasted with *Prakrti,* the material principle that produces not only the external world and the body but also the changing and externally determined aspects of the human mind (such as the intellect, ego, internal and external perceptual organs).

Both the agrarian theology of Siva-Sakti/Sky-Earth and the tradition of yoga (meditation) do not appear to be rooted in the Vedas. Not surprisingly, classical Sânkhya is remarkably independent of orthodox Brahmanic traditions, including the Vedas. Sânkhya is silent about the Vedas, about their guardians (the Brahmins) and for that matter about the whole caste system, and about the Vedic gods; and it is slightly inimical towards the animal sacrifices that characterized the ancient Vedic religion. But all our early sources for the history of Sânkhya belong to the Vedic tradition, and it is thus reasonable to suppose that we do not see in them the full development of the Sânkhya system, but rather occasional glimpses of its development as it gained gradual acceptance in the Brahmanic fold.

From these and also from some quotations in later literature commenting on the tradition (first of all in the *Yukti-dîpikâ*), a variety of minor variations and differing opinions have been collected that point to the existence of many branches of the school. The most significant divergence is perhaps the development of a theistic school of Orthodox Hindu philosophy, called Yoga, which absorbs the basic dualism of Sânkhya, but is theistic, and thus regards one *Purusa* as a special *Purusa,* called the Lord (Îsvara).

According to the Indian tradition, the first masters of Sânkhya are Kapila and his disciple Âsuri. They belong to antiquity (and sometimes, prehistory) and are known only through ancient legends. Another putative ancient master of Sânkhya, Pañcaœikha, seems to be more historical, and may have been the author of the original *sasti-Tantra*. Other important figures in the tradition, frequently referred to and also quoted in the commentaries, include Vârsaganya, and Vindhyavâsin, who may have been an older contemporary of ÎsvaraKrsna.

Around the beginning of our era, Sânkhya became the representative philosophy of Hindu thought in Hindu circles, and this probably explains why we find it everywhere – not only in the epics and the Upanisads but also in other important texts of the Hindu tradition, such as the *Dharmasâstra-s* (law-books), medical treatises (*âyurveda*) and the basic texts of the meditational Yoga school. And in fact much of the philosophy of Yoga (as formulated by Patañjali ca. 300 CE) is considered by several modern scholars as a version of Sânkhya.

Of ÎsvaraKrsna we know nothing; he may have lived around 350 CE, in any case after the composition of the foundational text of the Nyâya school of Indian philosophy, known as the *Nyâya-Sûtra,* and before the famous Buddhist philosopher, Vasubandhu. ÎsvaraKrsna's work, the *Sânkhya-Kârikâ* consists of 72 stanzas in the *âryâ* meter. Perhaps some of the verses were added by a student, but most of the work clearly tells of a single, philosophically and poetically ingenious hand. Unlike the (older) sûtras (aphorisms) of other systems, which are often cryptic and ambiguous, the *Sânkhya-Kârikâ* is a clear composition that is well ordered and argued. It is stated in the last stanza that it is a condensation of the whole *sasti-Tantra,* leaving out only stories and debates. And in fact ÎsvaraKrsna never refers to the theses of other systems, nor to differences within the school. He purposefully avoids all points of conflict: he is either silent about them or uses ambivalent expressions. It is perfectly clear that he wanted to write the common standard for the whole school, acceptable to all adherents to the philosophy; and he succeeded. The *Kârikâ* ousted all previous Sânkhya writings, of which only stray quotations remain. The presentation given below will thus follow this work very closely.

Many commentaries were written on the *Kârikâ,* mostly simple explanations of the text, and very similar to each other (the better known are Gauapâda's *Bhâsya,* Mâmhara's *Vrtti* and Sankarâcârya's *Jaya-Mangalâ* — this Gauapâda and Sankarâcârya are generally thought to be different from the famous Advaitins of the same name). By far the most important and also longest commentary is the *Yukti-dîpikâ,* "Light on the arguments" written perhaps by Râjan or Râjâna around 700 CE. This commentary discusses different positions within the school (and is therefore our most important historical source for old Sânkhya) and debates with other schools over many fundamental points of doctrine. It follows the polemical style of writing in the early classical schools, with heavy emphasis on epistemological issues. Unfortunately this text received very little response in classical times; in fact it was hardly known outside Kashmir. One of the reasons for this may be the extreme popularity of another commentary, Vâcaspati Misra's *Sânkhya-Tattva-Kaumudî,* or "Moonlight of the Principles of Sânkhya," (circa 980 CE). This commentary, although incomparably simpler, still follows mature classical philosophical style, and was written by a master of all philosophies, respected for his works on all major schools. It was the starting point of a tradition of sub-comments continuing to the present day.

Besides the *Kârikâ* there are two other important foundational texts of Sânkhya. The cryptic, half page long *Tattva-Samâsa-Sûtra* (Summary of the Principles) is very old at least in some parts, but no Sânkhya author mentions it before the 14th century. It is only a list of topics, but a list quite different from the categories of the *Kârikâ;* it has several commentaries, the best known is the *Krama-*

Dîpikâ, "Light on the Succession." The other text is the well-known, longish *Sânkhya-Sûtra,* which plainly follows the *Kârikâ* in most respects but adds many more illustrative stories and polemics with later philosophic positions. It is markedly atheistic and makes arguments against the existence of God. It appears first in the 15th century and is probably not very much older. It has attracted a commentary by Vijñâna Bhiksu, the eminent Vedântist of the 16th century, entitled *Sânkhya-Pravacana-Bhâsya* or "Commentary expounding Sânkhya." He also authored a small systematic treatise, the *Sânkhya-Sâra* (The Essence of Sânkhya). He introduced several innovations into the system, notably the idea that the number of the qualities is not three but infinite and that the *guna*-s are substances, not qualities.

2. SÂNKHYA'S EXISTENTIAL QUANDARY AND SOLUTION

The first premise of Sânkhya is the universal fact of suffering. There are many practical ways to ward off the darker side of life: such as self-defence, pleasures, medicine, and meditation. But, according to Sânkhya, all of them are of limited efficacy and at best can offer only temporary relief. The refuge offered by traditional Vedic religion is similarly unsatisfactory—it does not lead to complete purification (mainly because it involves bloody animal sacrifices), and the rewards it promises are all temporary: even after a happy and prolonged stay in heaven one will be reborn on Earth for more suffering.

Therefore the solution offered by Sânkhya is arguably superior: it analyzes the fundamental metaphysical structure of the world and the human condition, and finds the ultimate source of suffering, thereby making it possible to fight it effectively. Cutting the root of rebirth is the only way to final emancipation from suffering, according to Sânkhya.

Sânkhya analyzes the cosmos into a dualistic, and atheistic scheme. The two types of entities that exist, on Sânkhya's account, are *Prakrti* or Nature and *Purusa*-s or persons. Nature is singular, but persons are numerous. Both are eternal and independent of each other.

Creation as we know it comes about by a conjunction of these two categories. Nature, though unconscious, is purposeful and is said to function for the purpose of the individual *Purusa*-s. Aside from comprising the physical universe, it comprises the gross body and "sign body" (or "subtle body") of a *Purusa*. The sign body of a *Purusa* transmigrates: after the death of the gross body, the sign body is reborn in another gross body according to past merit. An escape from this endless circle is possible only through the realization of the fundamental difference between Nature and persons, whereby an individual *Purusa* loses interest in Nature and is thereby liberated forever from all bodies, subtle and gross. Characteristic of Sânkhya is a metaphorical but consistent presentation of the *Purusa* as a conscious, unchangeable, male principle that is inactive, while Nature is the unconscious, forever changing, female principle that is active, yet subservient to the ends of the *Purusa*. This is reminiscent of the cosmic dualism in Indian religions such as Tantrism, where the spiritual supreme male God mates with his female Sakti (Power) resulting in creation.

Prakrti, or Nature, is comprised of three *guna*-s or qualities. The highest of the three is *sattva* (essence), the principle of light, goodness and intelligence. *Rajas* (dust) is the principle of change, energy and passion, while *tamas* (darkness) appears as inactivity, dullness, heaviness and despair. *Prakrti* as unmanifest, pure potentiality is the substrate of the whole world, while in her manifest form she has twenty-three interdependent structures (*tattva*-s). Of the latter the highest is intellect or *buddhi*: it is not conscious, but through its closeness to *Purusa* it appears to be so. The others are egoism, mind, senses, biological abilities, the sensibilia like colour and the elements (earth etc.).

3. EPISTEMOLOGY

Sânkhya recognizes only three valid sources of information: perception, inference and reliable tradition. The ordering is important: we use inference only when perception is impossible, and only if both are silent do we accept tradition. A valid source of information (*pramâna*) is veridical, yielding knowledge of its object. Perception is the direct cognition of sensible qualities (such as colour and sound), which mediate cognition of the elements (such as earth and water). Perception, on the Sânkhya account, is a complex process: the senses (such as sight) cognize their respective objects (colour and shape) through the physical organs (such as the eye). And these senses are themselves the objects of cognition of the psyche (which in turn is comprised of three faculties—the mind (*manas*), the intellect (*buddhi*), and the ego (*ahamkâra*). The mind for its part internally constructs a representation of objects of the external world with the data supplied by the senses. The ego contributes personal perspective to knowledge claims. The intellect contributes understanding to knowledge. The *Purusa* adds consciousness to the result: it is the mere witness of the intellectual processes. According to a simile, the *Purusa* is the lord of the house, the tripartite psyche is the door-keeper and the senses are the doors.

For Sânkhya , perception is reliable and supplies most of the practical information needed in everyday life, but for this very reason it cannot supply philosophically interesting data. Things that can be seen are not objects of philosophical inquiry. There are many possible reasons why an existent material object is not (or cannot be) perceived: it may be too far (or near), or it is too minute or subtle; there may be something that obstructs perception; it may be indistinguishable from other surrounding objects or the sensation produced by another object may be so strong as to overweigh it. A fault of the sense-organs or an inattentive mind can also cause a failure of perception.

For philosophy, the central source of information is inference, and this is clearly emphasized in Sânkhya. ÎsvaraKrsna appears to recognize three kinds of inference (SK 5b) (as evidenced by his clear reference to the *Nyâya-Sûtra* 1.1.5): cause to effect, effect to cause and analogical reasoning. The first two types are based on the previous observation of causal connections. Therefore they cannot lead us to the sphere of the essentially imperceptible. Thus all metaphysical statements are based on analogical inference—such as: the body is a complex structure; complex structures, like a bed, serve somebody else's purpose; so there must be somebody else (the *Purusa*) that the body serves. Of course the analogies utilized are themselves analogies of the causal relation; so it would be a little more appropriate to say that they are analogical reasonings from the effect to the cause, but traditionally the three classes of inference are considered mutually exclusive.

The two members of an inference are the *linga,* 'sign' (the given or premise) and the *lingin,* 'having the sign', i.e. the thing of which the linga is the sign (the inferred or conclusion).

The last valid source of information, *âpta-vacana,* literally means reliable speech, but in the context of Sânkhya it is understood as referring to scriptures (the Vedas) only. While the validity of scriptural authority is affirmed, its importance is downplayed: they are never used to derive or confirm philosophical theses.

4. METAPHYSICS

Sânkhya is very fond of numbers, and in its classical form it is the system of 25 realities (*tattva*-s). In standard categories it is a dualism of *Purusa* (person) and *Prakrti* (nature); but *Prakrti* has two basic forms, *vyakta,* "manifest," and *avyakta,* "unmanifest," so there are three basic principles. *Purusa* and the *avyakta* are the first two *tattva*-s; the remaining twenty-three from intellect to the elements belong to the manifest nature.

The relation of the unmanifest and manifest nature is somewhat vague, perhaps because there were conflicting opinions on this question. Later authors understand it as a cosmogonical relation: the unmanifest was the initial state of *Prakrti,* where the *guna*-s were in equilibrium. Due to the effect of the *Purusa*-s this changed and evolved the manifold universe that we see, the manifest. This view nicely conforms to the standard Hindu image of cosmic cycles of creation and destruction; but it is problematic logically (without supposing God) and ÎsvaraKrsna – without directly opposing it – does not seem to accept it. He says that we do not grasp the unmanifest because it is subtle, not because it does not exist; and that implies that it exists also at present, as an imperceptible homogenous substrate of the world.

It is a notable feature of Sânkhya that its dualism is somewhat unbalanced: if we dropped *Purusa* from the picture, we would still have a fairly complete picture of the world, as *Prakrti* is not inert, mechanical matter but is a living, creative principle that has all the resources to produce from itself the human mind and intellect. Sânkhya thus looks like a full materialist account of the world, with the passive, unchanging principle of consciousness added almost as an afterthought.

a. Causality

According to Sânkhya, causality is the external, objective counterpart of the intellectual process of inference. As Sânkhya understands itself as the school of thought that understands reality through inference, causality plays a central role in the Sânkhya philosophy. According to Sânkhya, the world as we see it is the effect of its fundamental causes, which are only known through their effects and in conjunction with a proper understanding of causation.

The Indian tradition conceives of causality differently from the recent European tradition, where it is typically regarded as a relation between events. In the Indian tradition it rather consists in the origin of a thing. The standard example of the causal relationship is that of the potter making a pot from clay, where the cause *par excellence* is taken to be the clay. The Sânkhya analysis of causation is called *sat-kârya-vâda,* or literally the "existent effect theory," which opposes the view taken by the Nyâya philosophy. Perhaps sat-kârya is better rendered as "the effect of existent [causes]"; it stands for a moderate form of determinism. In the commentaries it is normally explained as the view that the effect already exists in its cause prior to its production. Understood literally, this is not tenable—if the cause existed, why was it not perceived prior to the point called its production? Rather the theory states that there is nothing absolutely new in the product: everything in it was determined by its causes.

The following five considerations are used in an argument for the *sat-kârya-vâda*: (a) the nonexistent cannot produce anything (given the assumed definition of "existence" as the ability to have some effect); (b) when producing a specific thing, we always need a specific substance as material cause (such as the clay for a pot, or milk for curds); (c) otherwise everything (or at least anything) would come into being from anything; (d) the creative agent (the efficient cause) produces only what it can, not anything (a potter cannot make jewellery); (e) the effect is essentially identical with its material cause, and so it has many of its qualities (a pot is still clay, and thus consists of the primary attributes of clay). This last argument is utilized to determine the basic attributes of the imperceptible metaphysical causes of the empirical world: the substrate must have the same fundamental attributes and abilities as the manifest world.

b. *Prakrti* and the three *guna*-s

The term *"Prakrti"* (meaning nature and productive substance) is actually used in three related but different senses. (1) Sometimes it is a synonym for the second *tattva,* called *"mûla-Prakrti"* (root-nature), *"avyakta"* (the unmanifest) or *"pradhâna"* (the principal). (2) Sometimes it is paired with *"vikrti"* (modification); *"Prakrti"* in this sense could be rendered as "source." Then the unmanifest is *Prakrti*-only; and the intellect, the ego and the five sense qualities are both *Prakrti*-s and *vikrti*-s – thus producing the set of *eight Prakrti*-s. (The remaining sixteen *tattva*-s are *vikrtis*-only, while the first *tattva,* the unchanging, eternal *Purusa* is neither *Prakrti* nor *vikrti.*) (3) And in most cases, *"Prakrti"* means both the manifest and the unmanifest nature (which consists of the twenty-four *tattva*-s starting from the second).

"Prakrti" is female gendered in Sanskrit, and its anaphora in Sânkhya is "she," but this usage seems to be consistently metaphorical only. *Prakrti,* in its various forms, contrasts with *Purusa* in being productive, unconscious, objective (knowable as an object), not irreducibly atomic, and comprised of three *guna*-s.

The unmanifest form of *Prakrti* contrasts with the manifest form in being single, uncaused, eternal, all-pervasive, partless, self-sustaining, independent and inactive; it is alingin (known from inference only). Ironically, all these attributes with the exception of singleness also characterize the *Purusa,* thus some ancient Sânkhya masters did call the *Purusa* also *avyakta* (unmanifest).

Sânkhya analyzes manifest *Prakrti*—the world, both physical and mental—into three omnipresent aspects, the *guna*-s. This is one of Sânkhya's main contributions to Indian thought. "*Guna*" variously means 'a thread, subordinate component, quality or virtue. Here it is not just any simple quality but rather a quite complex side or aspect of anything materially existent. (The *Purusa* has no *guna*-s.) The *guna*-s cannot be understood as ordinary qualities: their names are nouns, not adjectives; they are not simple, and they don't have degrees; they themselves have qualities and activity; they interact with each other; they do not have a substrate or a substance distinct from themselves to inhere in. But neither are they substances: they cannot exist separately (in every phenomenon all the three *guna*-s are present), they are not spatially or temporally delimited, they do not have separate individuality, and they can increase or decrease gradually in an object.

They are generally characterized as the real actors, even in mental phenomena such as cognition; they are the substrata for each other and they are interrelated in various ways. They "subdue, give birth to and copulate with" each other. In other words, they compete but also combine with each other, and they can even produce each other. They cooperate for an external purpose (the *Purusa*'s aim) like the parts of a lamp – the wick, the oil and the flame.

Their names are quite obscure, perhaps intentionally: they resist any facile simplistic interpretation, forcing us to understand them from their description instead of the literal meaning. The name of the first *guna*, "*sattva*," means *sat*-ness, where the participle "sat" means being, existent, real, proper, good. "*Sattva*" is additionally often used for entity, existence, essence and intelligence. *Sattva* is light (not heavy). Its essence is affection, its purpose and activity is illuminating. "*Rajas*," the name of the second *guna*, means atmosphere, mist, and dust. *Rajas* is supportive like a column but also mobile like water. Its essence is aversion, its purpose is bringing into motion and its activity is seizing. The name of the third *guna*, "*tamas*," means darkness. *Tamas* is heavy and covering. Its essence is despair, its purpose is holding back, and its activity is preservation.

In more modern terms, these three *guna*-s may be paraphrased as coherence / structure / information / intelligence (*sattva*); energy / movement / impulse / change (*rajas*); and inertia / mass / passivity / conservation (*tamas*). The depth of this analysis is the extent to which it grasps the structure of both the external and the internal world.

c. *Purusa*

"*Purusa*," the name of the first *tattva* (reality) literally means "man" in Sanskrit (though it often is used for the wider concept of person in Sanskrit and the Sânkhya system, as the Sânkhya system holds that all sentient beings are embodied *Purusa*-s: not simply male humans). In the Sânkhya philosophy, "*Purusa*" is metaphorically considered to be masculine, but unlike our concept of virility it is absolutely inactive. It is pure consciousness: it enjoys and witnesses *Prakrti*'s activities, but does not cause them. It is characterized as the conscious subject: it is uncaused, eternal, all-pervasive, partless, self-sustaining, independent. It is devoid of the *guna*-s, and therefore inactive and sterile (unable to produce). It can be known from inference only. As *Purusa* is essentially private for every sentient being, being their true self, there are many irreducibly distinct *Purusa*-s. If *Prakrti* is equated with Matter, *Purusa* may be equated with the soul. If *Prakrti* is equated with the World, *Purusa* may be equated with the (true) self. If *Prakrti* is understood as Nature, *Purusa* can be understood as the person.

As the immaterial soul, *Purusa* is not known through direct perception. Five arguments are given to prove its existence. (1) All complex structures serve an external purpose, for instance, a bed is for somebody to lie on; so the whole of nature, or more specifically the body – a very complex system – must also serve something different from it, which is the *Purusa*. (2) The three *guna*-s give an exhaustive explanation of material phenomena, but in sentient beings we find features that are the direct opposites of the *guna*-s (such as consciousness or being strictly private), and thus they need a non-material cause, which is the *Purusa*. (3) The coordinated activity of all the parts of a human being prove that there is something supervising it; without it, it would fall apart, as we see in a dead body, hence the *Purusa* must exist. (4) Although we cannot perceive ourselves as *Purusa*-s with the senses, we have immediate awareness of ourselves as conscious beings: the "enjoyer," the experiencing self is the *Purusa*. (5) Liberation, or the separation of soul and matter, would be impossible without their being separate *Purusa*-s to be liberated, thus *Purusa*-s must exist.

An important difference between schools of Indian philosophy that recognize *moksa* (liberation) as an end is the accepted number of souls. In Buddhism there is no separate soul to be liberated. In Advaita Vedânta, there is one common world-soul, and individuality is a function of the material world only. Sânkhya adduces three arguments to prove that there is a separate *Purusa* for each individual: (1) Birth, death and the personal history of everybody is different (it is determined by the law of karma, according to our merits collected in previous lives). If there were one *Purusa* only, all bodies should be identical or at least indistinguishable for the function of the self or *Purusa* is to be a supervisor of the body. But this is clearly not so. Hence, there must be a plurality of distinct *Purusa*-s. (2) If there were only one *Purusa*, everyone would act simultaneously alike, for the *Purusa* is the supervisor of the body. But this is clearly not so. Hence, there must be a plurality of distinct *Purusa*-s. (3) If there were only one *Purusa*, we would all experience the same things. However, it is evident that the opposite is true: our experiences are inherently diverse and private, and they cannot be directly shared. Hence, there must be a separate *Purusa* for us all.

In time, it became difficult to follow most of the arguments given above: if *Purusa* is really inactive, it cannot supervise anything, and cannot be the source of our individual actions. Also if *Purusa* has no *guna*-s (qualities), one *Purusa* cannot be specifically different from another. These problems perhaps grew under the influence of the concept of the absolutely unchanging and quality-less spiritual essence elaborated in Vedânta philosophy and were thus, arguably, not part of the original Sânkhya philosophy. The influence of Advaita Vedanta on Sânkhya seems to involve a reinterpretation of two attributes of *Purusa*: in activty came to be understood as unchangingness, while having no *guna*-s was taken to mean that it has no qualities at all.

The problem appears to have been first formulated by opponents in the Nyâya and Vedânta schools, and the author of the *Yukti-dîpikâ* is also aware of it. The answer emerging, first in Vâcaspati Misra and then more elaborately in Vijñâna Bhiksu, involves the innovation of the theory of "reflection": as the image in the mirror has no effect on the object reflected and the mirror remains unchanged, but the image can be seen – so the unchanging *Purusa* can reflect the external world, and the material psyche can react to this reflection. In responding to the problems brought about by the influence of Advaita Vedanta on Sânkhya, these authors appear to have responded by formulating a version of Sânkhya that comes fairly close to the superimposition theory of Advaita Vedânta, according to which an individual person is a cognitive construction that comes about by the error of mixing up the qualities of objects upon the quality of pure subjectivity. (For more on this issue, see Shiv Kumar pp. 39–43, 102–109, 250–253 and Shikan Murakami in *Asiatische Studien* 53, pp.645–665, who give insightful analyses of the problem in the classical schools.)

In ÎsvaraKrsna's *Sânkhya-Kârikâ,* however, the inactivity of the *Purusa* does not seem to involve absolute incapability for change: the same word (*a-kriya,* "without activity") is used also for the unmanifest nature, the substrate of all material manifestations. Arguably, it means only inability to move in space or to have mechanical effect. As it is clear from the above arguments, *Purusa* is the determinative factor of our actions – and that presupposes that it changes in time (otherwise we would always do the same thing). So it must be the locus either of volition or of some hidden motivation underlying it. And although it is "a lonely, uninterested spectator, a witness unable to act," it does like or dislike what it sees: it can suffer (this is, after all, the existential starting point for Sânkhya). It cannot be the locus of our whole emotional life (passions are explicitly said to reside in the intellect), but it must be considered the final source of our conscious feelings.

This is a controversial issue. Many modern scholars understand *Purusa* as strictly unchanging; some of them (for example, A.B. Keith) are led by the inconsistencies following from this to consider Sânkhya as a hopeless bundle of contradictions. Larson (in Larson and Bhattacharya, pp. 79–83) translates "*Purusa*" as "contentless consciousness;" it is not only unchanging but also timeless and outside the realm of causality (a somewhat Kantian concept). He tries to solve some of the difficulties by proposing that the multiplicity of *Purusa*-s be understood as essentially epistemological in nature— and ontologically irrelevant.

d. Evolution, Humanity and the World

For Sânkhya, creation consists in the conjunction of the two categories of *Prakrti* and *Purusa(s)*. How this comes about is left somewhat of a mystery. As a result of this conjunction, the *Purusa* is embodied in the world and appears to be the agent, and moreover *Prakrti* seems to be conscious as it is animated by *Purusa*-s. The relation between a *Purusa* and *Prakrti*, according to the *Sânkhya-Kârika* are like two men, a lame man and a blind man, lost in the wilderness; the one without the power of sight (active *Prakrti*) carrying the cripple (conscious *Purusa*) that can navigate the wild. Their purpose is twofold: the *Purusa* desires experience—without blind nature, it would be unable to have experiences; and both *Prakrti* and *Purusa* desire liberation (in keeping with the simile, both nature and the person, the blind and the lame, desire to make their way home and part ways). Liberation is forestalled, on the Sânkhya account, because *Purusa* becomes enamoured with the beautiful woman, *Prakrti*, and refuses to part ways with her.

The nature of the *Purusa–Prakrti* connection is *prima facie* problematic. How can the inactive soul influence matter, and how could an unintelligent substance, nature, serve anybody's purpose? *Purusa* is unable to move *Prakrti*, but *Prakrti* is able to respond to *Purusa's* presence and intentions. *Prakrti*, although unconscious, possesses the capability to respond in a specific, structured way because of it *ssattva guna*, the information–intelligence aspect of nature. The standard simile in the early Sânkhya tradition explains that as milk (an unconscious substance) starts to flow in order to nurture the calf, *Prakrti* flows to nurture *Purusa*. In later texts, illumination and reflection are the standard models for this connection (*Purusa* is said to illuminate *Prakrti*, and *Prakrti* reflects the nature of *Purusa*), thus solving the problem of how *Prakrti* and

Purusa can seemingly borrow each others properties without affecting eachothers essential state.

In consequence of *Prakrti*'s connection with the soul, *Prakrti* evolves many forms: the twenty-three *tattva*-s (realities) of manifest *Prakrti*. The character of this evolution (*parinâma*) is somewhat vague. Is this an account of the origin of the cosmos, or of a single being? The cosmogenic understanding is probably older, and it seems to predominate in later accounts as well. In a pantheistic account the two accounts could be harmonized, but pantheism is alien from classical Sânkhya. ÎsvaraKrsna is again probably intentionally silent on this conflicting issue, but he seems to be inclined to the microcosmic interpretation: otherwise either a single super-*Purusa*'s influence would be needed (that is, God's influence) to account for how the universe on the whole comes about, or a coordinated effect of all the *Purusa*-s together would be required—and there seems to be no foundation for either of these views Sânkhya.

The central mechanism of evolution is the complicated interaction of the *guna*-s, which is sensitive to the environment, the substrate or locus of the current process. Just as water in different places behaves differently (on the top of the Himalaya mountain as ice, in a hill creek, in the ocean, or as the juice of a fruit) so do the *guna*-s. In the various manifestations of nature the dominance of the *guna*-s varies—in the highest forms *sattva* rules, in the lowest *tamas* covers everything.

The actual order of evolution is as follows: from root-nature first appears intellect (*buddhi*); from it, ego (*ahamkâra*); from it the eleven powers (*indriya*) and the five sensibilia (*tanmâtra*); and from the *tanmâtras* the elements (*bhûta*).

The function of the *buddhi* (intellect) is specified as *adhyavasâya* (determination); it can be understood as definite conceptual knowledge. It has eight forms: virtue, knowledge, dispassion and command, and their opposites. So it seems that on the material plane, *buddhi* is the locus of cognition, emotion, moral judgment and volition. All these may be thought to belong also to consciousness, or the *Purusa*. However, on the Sânkhya account, *Purusa* is connected directly only to the intellect, and the latter does all cognitions, mediates all experiences for it. The view of Sânkhya appears to be that when *sattva* (quality of goodness, or illumination) predominates in *buddhi* (the intellect), it can act acceptably for *Purusa,* when there is a predominance of *tamas,* it will be weak and insufficient.

The ego or *ahamkâra* (making the I) is explained as abhimâna—thinking of as [mine]. It delineates that part of the world that we consider to be or to belong to ourselves: mind, body, perhaps family, property, rank... It individuates and identifies parts of *Prakrti*: by itself nature is one, continuous and unseparated. It communicates the individuality inherent in the *Purusa*-s to the essentially common *Prakrti* that comprises the psyche of the individual. So it has a purely cognitive and a material function as well—like so many principles of Sânkhya.

The eleven powers (*indriya*) are mind (*manas*), the senses and the "powers of action" (*karmendriya*), the biological faculties. The senses (powers of cognition, *buddhîndriya*) are sight, hearing, smelling, tasting, and touching—they are the abilities, not the physical organs themselves through which they operate. The crude names of the powers of action are speech, hand, foot, anus and lap. They symbolize the fundamental biological abilities to communicate, to take in or consume, to move, to excrete and to generate.

"*Manas*" (often translated as "mind," though this may be misleading), designates the lowest, almost vegetative part of the central information-processing structure. Its function is *sankalpa*—arranging (literally 'fitting together') or coordinating the *indriya*-s. It functions partly to make a unified picture from sense data, provided by the senses, and partly to translate the commands from the intellect to actual, separate actions of the organs. So, it is both a cognitive power and a power of action. (Later authors take "*manas*" to also designate the will, for *sankalpa* also has this meaning.)

Intellect, ego and mind together constitute the *antah-karana* (internal organ), or the material psyche, while the other *indriya*-s (powers) collectively are called the external organ. The internal organ as an inseparable unit is the principle of life (*prâna*). In cognition the internal organ's activity follows upon that of the external, but they are continuously active, so their activity is also simultaneous. The external organ is strictly bound to the present tense, while the psyche is active in the past and future as well (memory, planning, and the grasping of timeless truths).

The material elements are derived from the gross, *tamas*-ic aspect of the ego, which yields what Sânkhya calls *tanmâtra*-s (only-that, that is, unmixed). These in turn yield the elements (*bhûta, mahâ-bhûta*). The elements are ether (*âkâsa*), air, fire, water and earth.

The *tanmâtra*-s seem to be uncompounded sensibilia; perhaps subtle elements or substances, each having only one sensible quality: sound, touch, visibility, taste and smell. The gross elements are probably fixed compounds of the *tanmâtra*-s: ether has only sound, air also touch, fire is also visible, water has in addition taste and earth has all the five qualities.

Human beings are a compound of all these. At death we lose the body made up of the five gross elements; the rest (from intellect down to the *tanmâtra*-s) make up the transmigrating entity, called *lingaor linga-sarîra* (sign-body), often known in English translations as the "subtle body." The *Purusa* itself does not transmigrate; it only watches. Transmigration is compared to an actor putting on different clothes and taking up many roles; it is determined by the law of (efficient) cause and effect, known also as the law of karma (action).

The world, "from the creator god Brahmâ down to a blade of glass" is just a compound of such embodied *linga-sarîra*-s. The gods are of eight kinds; animals are of five kinds – and humans, significantly, belongs to one group only (suggesting an egalitarianism with respect to humans). Of course, the gods of Sânkhya are not classical Judeo-Christian-Muslim God; they are just extra-long-lived, perhaps very powerful beings within the empirical world, themselves compounds of matter and soul.

5. LIBERATION

Because *Prakrti* is essentially changing, nothing is constant in the material world: everything decays and meets its destruction in the end. Therefore as long as the transmigrating entity persists, the suffering of old age and death is unavoidable.

The only way to fight suffering is to leave the circle of transmigration (*samsâra*) for ever. This is the liberation of *Purusa,* in Sânkhya, normally called *kaivalya* (isolation). It comes about through loosening the bond between *Purusa* and *Prakrti.* This bond was originally produced by the curiosity of the soul, and it is extremely strong because the ego identifies our selves with our empirical state: the body and the more subtle organs, including the material psyche. Although *Purusa* is not actually bound by any external force, it is an enchanted observer that cannot take his eyes off from the performance.

As all cognition is performed by the intellect for the soul, it is also the intellect that can recognize the very subtle distinction between *Prakrti* and *Purusa.* But first the effect of the ego must be neutralized, and this is done by a special kid of meditational praxis. Step by step, starting from the lowest *tattva*-s, the material elements, and gradually reaching the intellect itself, the follower of Sânkhya must practice as follows: "this constituent is not me; it is not mine; I am not this." When this has been fully interiorized with regard to all forms of *Prakrti,* then arises the absolutely pure knowledge of the metaphysical solitude of *Purusa*: it is *kevala,* (alone), without anything external-material belonging to it.

And as a dancer, after having performed, stops dancing, so does *Prakrti* cease to perform for an individual *Purusa* when its task is accomplished. She has always acted for the *Purusa,* and as he is no longer interested in her ("I have seen her"), she stops forever ("I have already been seen")—the given subtle body gets dissolved into the root-*Prakrti.* This happens only at death, for the gross body (like a potter's wheel still turning although no longer impelled) due to causally determined karmic tendencies (*sanskâra*-s) goes on to operate for a little while.

Purusa enters into liberation, forever. Although *Purusa* and *Prakrti* are physically as much in contact as before—both seem to be all-pervading in extension—there is no purpose of a new start: *Purusa* has experienced all that it wanted.

REFERENCES :

1.*Asiatische Studien / Studes Asiatiques 53* (1999): 457–798..Papers of an 1998 conference; allows a glimpse at the state of current researches.

2.Chakravarti, Pulinbihari: *Origin and Development of the Sâmkhya System of Thought*. Calcutta: Metropolitan Printing and Publishing House, 1951..A detailed account giving due weight to the *Yukti-dîpikâ*.

3.Chattopadhyaya, Debiprasad: *Lokâyata. A Study in Ancient Indian Materialism*. Delhi: People's Publishing House, 1959.A highly unorthodox approach utilizing anthropological and even archeological sources to understand the origins of philosophical thought.

4.Kumar, Shiv: *Sâmkhya Thought in the Brahmanical Systems of Indian Philosophy*. Delhi: Eastern Book Linkers, 1983.Looks at Sânkhya tradition from the outside, especially as it appears in Nyâya and Vedânta.

5.Larson, Gerald James. *Classical Sâmkhya. An Interpretation of its History and Meaning*.Delhi: Motilal Banarsidass, 1979.The standard book on the *Kârikâ* and a useful summary of its antecedents.

6.Larson, Gerald James, and Ram Shankar Bhattacharya, eds. *Sâmkhya. A Dualist Tradition in Indian Philosophy*. Princeton: Princeton University Press, 1987. (Vol. IV. in*Encyclopedia of Indian Philosophies.*)

6

The Yoga Sutras of Patanjali

The tradition of Patañjali in the oral and textual tradition of the Yoga Sûtras is accepted by traditional Vedic schools as the authoritative source on Yoga, and it retains this status in Hindu circles into the present day. In contrast to its modern Western transplanted forms, Yoga essentially consists of meditative practices culminating in attaining a state of consciousness free from all modes of active or discursive thought, and of eventually attaining a state where consciousness is unaware of any object external to itself, that is, is only aware of its own nature as consciousness unmixed with any other object. This state is not only desirable in its own right, but its attainment guarantees the practitioner freedom from every kind of material pain or suffering, and, indeed, is the primary classical means of attaining liberation from the cycle of birth and death in the Indic soteriological traditions, that is, in the theological study of salvation in India. The Yoga Sûtras were thus seen by all schools, not only as the orthodox manual for guidance in the techniques and practices of meditation, but also for the classical Indian position on the nature and function of mind and consciousness, for the mechanisms of action in the world and consequent rebirth, and for the metaphysical underpinnings and description of the attainment of mystical powers.

1. BACKGROUND AND AUTHOR

In terms of literary sources, there is evidence as early as the oldest Vedic text, the Zg Veda (c. 1200 – c. 1500 B.C.E.), that there were *yogî*-like ascetics on the margins of the Vedic world. In terms of the archaeological record, seals found in Indus Valley sites (c. 3000 – c. 1500 B.C.E.) with representations of figures seated in a clear *yogic* posture (the most famous figure is seated in *padmâsana,* lotus pose, with arms extended and resting on the knees in a classical meditative posture), suggest that, irrespective of its literary origins, Yoga has been practiced on the Indian subcontinent for well over 4000 years. However, it is in the late Vedic age, marked by the fertile speculations expressed in a genre of texts called the Upanisads (c. 800 – c. 600 B.C.E.), that practices that can be clearly related to classical Yoga are first articulated in literary sources.

While the Upanisads are especially concerned with *jñâna,* or understanding *Brahman,* the Absolute Truth, through the cultivation of knowledge, there are also several unmistakable references to a technique for realizing *Brahman* (in its localized aspect of *âtman*) called Yoga. As with the Upanisads in general, we do not find a systematic philosophy here, but mystico-poetic utterances, albeit profound in content (Katha Upanisad VI.11–18; Svetâsvatara Upanisad II.8–15; Maitrî Upanisad VI.18). The Mahâbhârata Epic, which is the largest literary epic in the world, also preserves significant material representing the evolution of Yoga, indeed, the term "yoga" and "yogî" occur about 900 times throughout the Epic. Usually dated somewhere between the 9th–4th centuries C.E., the Epic exhibits the transition between the origins of Yoga in the Upanisadic period and its expression in the systematized traditions of Yoga as represented in the classical period by Patañjali. Nestled in the middle of the Epic, the well-known Bhagavad Gîtâ (c. 4thcentury B.C.E.), devotes a good portion of its bulk to the practices of Yoga, which it considers to be "ancient" (IV.3).

This, of course, indicates that practices associated with Yoga had gained wide currency in the centuries prior to the common era, with a clearly identifiable set of basic techniques and generic practices, and we will here simply allude to the fact that scholars have long pointed out a commonality of vocabulary, and concepts between the Yoga Sûtras (YS) and Buddhist texts. All this underscores the fact that there was a cluster of numerous interconnected and cross-fertilizing variants of meditational Yoga – Buddhist and Jain as well as Hindu – prior to Patañjali, all drawn from a common but variegated pool of terminologies, practices and concepts (and, indeed, many strains continue to the present day). Of closer relevance to the Sûtras is the fact that the history of Yoga is inextricable from that of the Sâmkhya tradition. Sâmkhya provides the metaphysical infrastructure for Yoga (discussed in the section on metaphysics), and thus is indispensable to an understanding of Yoga. While both Yoga and Sâmkhya share the same metaphysics and the common goal of liberating *Purusa* from its encapsulation, their methods differ.

Sâmkhya occupies itself with the path of reasoning to attain liberation, specifically concerning itself with the analysis of the manifold ingredients of *Prakrti* from which the *Purusa* was to be extricated, and Yoga more with the path of meditation, focusing its attention on the nature of mind and consciousness, and the techniques of concentration in order to provide a practical method through which the *Purusa* can be isolated and extricated. Sâmkhya seems to have been perhaps the earliest philosophical system to have taken shape in the late Vedic period, and has permeated almost all subsequent Hindu traditions; indeed the classical Yoga of Patañjali has been seen as a type of neo-Sâmkhya, updating the old Sâmkhya tradition to bring it into conversation with the more technical philosophical traditions that had emerged by the 3–5th centuries C.E., particularly Buddhist thought. In fact, Sâmkhya and Yoga should not be considered different schools until a very late date: the first reference to Yoga itself as a distinct school seems to be in the writings of Sankara in the 9th century C.E. Yoga and Sâmkhya in the Upanisads and Epic simply refer to the two distinct paths of salvation by meditation and salvation by knowledge, respectively.

One might add, as an aside, that from the 900-odd references to Yoga in the Mahâbhârata, there are only two mentions of *âsana*, posture, the third limb of Patañjali's system. Neither the Upanisads nor the Gîtâ mention posture in the sense of stretching exercises and bodily poses (the term is used as "seat" rather than bodily postures), and Patañjali himself only dedicates three brief *sûtras* from his text to this aspect of the practice. The reconfiguring, presentation and perception of Yoga as primarily or even exclusively *âsana* in the sense of bodily poses, then, is essentially a modern Western phenomenon and finds no precedent in the premodern Yoga tradition. From this rich and fertile post-Vedic context, then, emerged an individual called Patañjali whose systematization of the heterogeneous practices of Yoga came to be authoritative for all subsequent practitioners and his system eventually reified into one of the six schools of classical Indian philosophy. It is important to stress here that Patañjali is not the founder or inventor of Yoga, the origins of which, as noted above, had long preceded him in primordial and mythic times. Patañjali systematized the preexisting traditions and authored what came to be the seminal text for Yoga discipline. There was never one uniform school of Yoga, or Ur-Yoga (or of any Indic school of thought for that matter): there was a plurality of variants, and certainly different conceptualizations of meditative practices that were termed Yoga. For example, while Patañjali organizes his system into eight limbs, and the Mahâbhârata, too, speaks of Yoga as having eight "qualities" (*astagunita*, XII.304.7), as early as in the Maitrî Upanisad of the 2nd century B.C.E., there is reference to a six-limbed Yoga (VI.18), as there is in the Visnu Purâna (VI.7.91). Along similar lines, there are various references to the twelve *yogas* and seven *dhâranâs* (*dhâranâ* is considered the sixth of Patañjali's limbs) found in the Epic Mahâbhârata. Yoga is thus best understood as a cluster of techniques, some more and some less systematized, that pervaded the landscape of ancient India. These overlapped and were incorporated into the various traditions of the day such as the *jñâna*, knowledge-based traditions, providing these systems with a practical method and technique for attaining an experienced-based transformation of consciousness. Patañjali's particular systematization of these techniques was in time to emerge as the most dominant, but by no means exclusive, version.

Indeed, internal to his own text, in his very first *sûtra, atha yoga anusâsanam*, Patañjali indicates that he is continuing the teachings of Yoga (the verbal prefix *anu* indicates the continuation of the action denoted by the verb), and the traditional commentators certainly perceive him in this light. In point of fact, the tradition itself ascribes the actual origins of Yoga to the legendary figure Hiranyagarbha. Moreover, evidence that Patañjali was addressing an audience already familiar with the tenets of Yoga can be deduced from the Yoga Sûtras themselves. For example, on occasion, Patañjali will mention one member of a list of items followed by "etc.,", thereby assuming his audience to be familiar with the remainder of the list. But, in short, because he produced the first systematized treatise on the subject, Patañjali was to become the prime or seminal figure for the Yoga tradition after his times, and was accepted as such by other schools. To all intents and purposes, his Yoga Sûtras were to become the canon for the mechanics of generic Yoga, so to speak, that other systems tinkered with, and flavoured with their own theological trappings.

As with the reputed founders of the other schools of thought, very little is known about Patañjali himself. Tradition, first evidenced in the commentary of Bhoja Râja in the 11th century C.E., considers him to be the same Patañjali who wrote the primary commentary on the famous grammar by Pânini, and also ascribes to him authorship of a treatise on medicine. There is an ongoing discussion amongst scholars as to whether this was likely or not, but there is not much to be gained by challenging the evidence of traditional accounts in the absence of alternative evidence to the contrary that is uncontroversial or at least adequately compelling.

Patañjali's date can only be inferred from the content of the text itself. Unfortunately, as with most classical Sanskrit texts from the ancient period, early Sanskrit texts tend to be impossible to date with accuracy, and there are always dissenters against whatever dates become standard in academic circles. Most scholars seem to date the text shortly after the turn of the common era, (c. 1st – c. 2nd century C.E.), but it has been placed as early as several centuries before the common era. Other than the fact that the text does not postdate the 5th century C.E., the date of the Yoga Sûtras cannot be determined with exactitude.

The Sûtra writing style is that used by the philosophical schools of ancient India (thus we have Vedânta Sûtras, Nyâya Sûtraṣ, etc.). The term "sûtra," (from the Sanskrit root *sû*, cognate with "sew") literally means a thread, and essentially refers to a terse and pithy philosophical statement in which the maximum amount of information is packed into the minimum amount of words. Knowledge systems were handed down orally in ancient India, and thus source material was kept minimal partly with a view to facilitating memorization. Being composed for oral transmission and memorization, the Yoga Sûtras, and sûtra traditions in general, allowed the student to "thread together" in memory the key ingredients of the more extensive body of material with which the student would become thoroughly acquainted. Thus, each sûtra served as a mnemonic device to structure the teachings and facilitate memorization, almost like a bullet point that would then be elaborated upon.

This very succinctness – the Yoga Sûtras contain about 1200 words in 195 sûtras – and the fact that the sûtras are in places cryptic, esoteric and incomprehensible in their own terms points to the fact that they served as manuals to be used in conjunction with a teacher. Therefore, it is an unrealistic (if not impossible) task to attempt to bypass commentary in the hope of retrieving some original pure, pre-commentarial set of Ur-interpretations

Knowledge systems in ancient Indian were transmitted orally, from master to disciple, with an enormous emphasis on fidelity towards the original set of Sûtras upon which the system is founded, the master unpacking the dense and truncated aphorisms to the students. Periodically, teachers of particular prominence wrote commentaries on the primary texts of many of these knowledge systems. Some of these gained wide currency to the point that the primary text was always studied in conjunction with a commentary, particularly since texts such as the Yoga Sûtras were designed to be unpacked because they contain numerous sûtras that are incomprehensible without further elaboration. One cannot overstress, therefore, that our understanding of Patañjali's text is completely dependent on the interpretations of later commentators: it is incomprehensible, in places, in its own terms.

In terms of the overall accuracy of the commentaries there is an *a priori* likelihood that the interpretations of the *Sûtras* were faithfully preserved and transmitted orally through the few generations from Patañjali until the first commentary by Vyâsa in the 5th Century C.E. Certainly, the commentators from Vyâsa onwards are remarkably consistent in their interpretations of the essential metaphysics of the system for over fifteen hundred years, which is in marked contrast with the radical differences in essential metaphysical understanding distinguishing commentators of the Vedânta school (a Râmânuja or a Madhva from a Sankara, for example). While the 15th century commentator VijñânaBhiksu, for example, may not infrequently quibble with the 9th century commentator Vâcaspati Misra, the differences generally are in detail, not essential metaphysical elements. And while VijñânaBhiksu may inject a good deal of Vedântic concepts into the basic dualism of the Yoga system, this is generally an addition (conspicuous and identifiable) to the system rather than a reinterpretation of it. There is thus a remarkably consistent body of knowledge associated with the Yoga school for the best part of a millennium and a half, and consequently one can speak of "the traditional understanding" of the Sûtras in the premodern period without overly generalizing or essentializing.

The first extant commentary by the legendary Vyâsa, typically dated to around the 4–5th century C.E., was to attain a status almost as canonical as the primary text by Patañjali himself. Consequently, the study of the Yoga Sûtras has always been embedded in the commentary that tradition attributes to this greatest of literary figures. Practically speaking, when we speak of the philosophy of Patañjali, what we really mean (or should mean) is the understanding of Patañjali according to Vyâsa: it is Vyâsa who determined what Patañjali's abstruse Sûtras meant, and all subsequent commentators elaborated on Vyâsa. The Vyâsa Bhâsya (commentary) becomes inseparable from the Sûtras; an extension of it. From one *sûtra* of a few words, Vyâsa might write several lines of comment without which the *sûtra* remains incomprehensible. Vyâsa's commentary, the Bhâsya, thus attains the status of canon, and is almost never questioned by any subsequent commentator. Subsequent commentators base their commentaries on unpacking Vyâsa's Bhâsya – rarely critiquing it, but rather expanding or elaborating upon it. It is this point of reference that produces a marked uniformity in the interpretation of the Sûtras in the pre-modern period.

The next commentary is called the Vivarana, attributed to the great Vedântin Sankara in the 8th – 9th century C.E. It has remained unresolved since it was first questioned in 1927 whether the commentary on the Yoga Sûtras assigned to Sankara is authentically penned by him. The next best known commentator is Vâcaspati Misra, whose commentary, the Tattvavai Sâradî, can be dated with more security to the 9th century C.E. Vâcaspati Misra was a prolific intellectual, penning important commentaries on the Vedânta, Sâmkhya, Nyâya and Mîmâmsâ schools in addition to his commentary on the Yoga Sûtras, and was noteworthy for his ability to present each tradition in its own terms, without displaying any overt personal predilection.

A fascinating Arabic translation of Patañjali's Sûtras was undertaken by the famous Arab traveller and historian al-Bîrunî (973–1050 C.E.), the manuscript of which was discovered in Istanbul in the 1920's. Roughly contemporaneous with al-Bîrunî is the 11th century King Bhoja, poet, scholar and patron of the arts, sciences and esoteric traditions, in whose commentary, called the Râjamârtanda, there are on occasion very valuable insights to be found. In the 15th century, VijñânaBhiksu wrote a most insightful and useful commentary after that of Vyâsa's, the Yogavârttika. VijñânaBhiksu was another prolific scholar, noteworthy for his attempt to harmonize Vedânta and Sâmkhya concepts. In the 16th century C.E., another Vedântin, Râmânanda Sarasvatî, wrote his commentary, called Yogamaniprabhâ, which also adds little to the previous commentaries. But there are valuable insights contained in the Bhâsvatî by Hariharânanda Âranya, written in Bengali, from a context nearer our own times, a standpoint exposed to Western thought, but still thoroughly grounded in tradition. While many other commentaries have been written, these are the primary commentaries written in the pre-modern era. The commentaries written in the modern period, many of which have made massive adjustments to modernity or the sensitivities of the Western market, are beyond the scope of this discussion, which limits itself to classical Yoga philosophy.

The Yoga Sûtras is divided into four *padas,* chapters. The first, *samâdhi pâda,* defines Yoga as the complete cessation of all active states of mind, and outlines various stages of insight that stem from this. The chapter points to the ultimate goal of Yoga, which is content-less awareness, beyond even the most supreme stages of insight. The second, *sâdhana pâda,* outlines the various practices, and moral and ethical observances that are preliminary requirements to serious meditative practice. The third, *vibhûti pada,* primarily deals with various super-normal powers that can accrue to the practitioner when the mind is in extreme states of concentration. There seems to have been a widespread culture in ancient India of engaging in Yoga-like practices but not in pursuit of the real goal of Yoga as defined by Patañjali, but rather in quest of such super-normal powers; this chapter can be read as Patañjali's warning against being side-tracked in this way. The fourth, *kaivalya pâda* deals with liberation, and, amongst other things, contains Patañjali's response to the Buddhist challenge.

2. METAPHYSICS

As noted, Yoga is not to be considered as a school distinct from Sâmkhya until well after Patañjali's time, but rather as a different approach or method towards enlightenment, although there are minor differences. Sâmkhya provides the metaphysical or theoretical basis for the realization of *Purusa,* and Yoga the technique or practice itself. While the Yoga tradition does not agree with the Sâmkhya view that metaphysical analysis, that is, *jñâna,* knowledge, constitutes a sufficient path towards enlightenment in and of itself the metaphysical presuppositions of the Yoga system assume those of Sâmkhya. Leaving aside the numerous variants of Sâmkhya (the Chinese Buddhist pilgrim Hsöen Tsang's disciple in the 7th century C.E. reports 18 schools, and the loss of the earlier material, the later *Sâmkhya Kârikâ* of Isvarakrsna (4th–5th century C.E.), has by default become the seminal text of the tradition, just as Patañjali's Yoga Sûtras has for the Yoga tradition.

In the generic Sâmkhya (literally "numeration") system, the universe of animate and inanimate entities is perceived as ultimately the product of two ontologically distinct categories; hence this system is quintessentially *dvaita,* or dualistic in presupposition.

These two categories are *Prakrti,* or the primordial material matrix of the physical universe, and *Purusa,* the innumerable conscious selves embedded within it. As a result of the interaction between these two entities, the material universe evolves in a series of stages. The actual catalysts in this evolutionary process are the three *gunas,* literally "strands" or "qualities," which are inherent in *Prakrti.* These are: *sattva,* "lucidity;" *rajas,* "action;" and *tamas,* "inertia." These *gunas* are sometimes compared to the threads which underpin the existence of a rope; just as a rope is actually a combination of threads, so all manifest reality actually consists of a combination of the *gunas.*

Given the meditative focus of the text, the *gunas* are especially significant to Yoga in terms of their psychological manifestation; in Yoga, the mind and therefore all psychological dispositions, are *Prakrti,* and therefore also comprised of the *gunas* – the only difference between mind and matter being that the former has a larger preponderance of *sattva,* and the latter of *tamas.* Therefore, according to the specific intermixture and proportionality of the *gunas,* living beings exhibit different types of mindsets and psychological dispositions. Thus, when *sattva* is predominant in an individual, the qualities of lucidity, tranquility, wisdom, discrimination, detachment, happiness, and peacefulness manifest; when *rajas* is predominant, hankering, attachment, energetic endeavour, passion, power, restlessness and creative activity; and when *tamas,* the *guna* least favourable for *yoga,* is predominant, ignorance, delusion, disinterest, lethargy, sleep, and disinclination towards constructive activity.

The *gunas* are continually interacting and competing with each other, one *guna* becoming prominent for a while and overpowering the others, only to be eventually dominated in turn by the increase of one of the other *gunas.* They are compared to the wick, fire and oil of the lamp which, while opposed to each other in their nature, come together to produce light. Just as there are an unlimited variety of colours stemming from the intermixture of the three primary colours, different hues being simply expressions of the specific proportionality of red, yellow and blue, so the unlimited psychological dispositions of living creatures (and of physical forms) stem from the intermixture of the *gunas;* specific states of mind being reflections of the particular proportionality of the intermixture of the three *gunas.*

The *gunas* not only underpin the philosophy of mind in Yoga, but the activation and interaction of these *guna* qualities result in the production of the entirety of physical forms that also evolve from the primordial material matrix, *Prakrti,* under the same principle. Thus the physical composition of objects like air, water, stone, fire, etc. differs because of their constitutional makeup of specific *gunas*: air contains more of the buoyancy of *sattva,* stones more of the sluggishness of the *tamas* element, and fire, of *rajas.* The *gunas* allow for the infinite plasticity of *Prakrti* and the objects of the world.

The process by which the universe evolves from *Prakrti* is usefully compared to the churning of milk: when milk receives a citric catalyst, yogurt, curds, or butter emerge. These immediate products, in turn, can be further manipulated to produce a further series of products – milk desserts, cheese, etc. Similarly, according to classical Sâmkhya, the first evolute emerging from *Prakrti* when it is churned by the *gunas* (*sattva* specifically) is *buddhi,* intelligence. Intelligence is characterized by the functions of judgment, discrimination, knowledge, ascertainment, will, virtue and detachment, and *sattva* is predominant in it. This means that in its purest state, when the potential of *rajas* and *tamas* are minimized, *buddhi* is primarily lucid, peaceful, happy, tranquil and discriminatory, all qualities of *sattva.* It is the interface between *Purusa* and all other *Prakrtic* evolutes. From this vantage point, it can direct awareness out into the objects and embroilments of the world, or, in its highest potential, it can become aware of the presence of *Purusa* and consequently redirect itself towards complete realization of the true source of consciousness that pervades it.

From *buddhi, ahamkâra,* or ego is produced (*aham* "I" + *kâra* "doing;" referred to as *asmiṭâ* in this text). This is characterized by the function of self-awareness and self-identity. It is the discursive aspect that processes and appropriates external reality from the perspective of an individualized sense of self or ego –

the notion of "I" and "mine" in human awareness. *Ahamkâra* also limits the range of awareness to fit within and identify with the contours of the particular psychophysical organism within which it finds itself in any one embodiment, as opposed to another. In other words, the *ahamkâra* of a typical, unenlightened, bug acts almost like a concave screen, which refracts consciousness to pervade and appropriate the contours of the bug. If the bug dies and becomes, say, a typical, unenlightened dog and then a typical human in subsequent lives, the *ahamkâra* aspect of the *citta* adjusts to accommodate and absorb consciousness into these new environments. Thus the bug thinks it is a bug, the dog thinks it is a dog, and the human thinks he or she is a human.

When ego in turn is "churned" by the *guna* of *sattva* inherent in it, *manas*, the mind, is produced. The mind is the seat of the emotions, of like and dislike, and is characterized by controlling the senses – filtering and processing the potentially enormous amount of data accessible to the senses. It primarily receives, sorts, categorizes and then transmits. It serves as the liaison between the activities of the senses transmitting data from the external world, and *buddhi*, intelligence. It therefore partakes both of internal and external functioning: internally, it is characterized by reflective synthesis, while simultaneously being a sense because it acts similar to the senses. The *Purusa*, or self, is cloaked in these psychic layers prior to receiving a gross body and senses. The Yoga school, while using the terminology of (especially) *buddhi*, but also *ahamkâra* and *manas*, differs somewhat from that of Sâmkhya in conceiving these three as interacting functions of the one *citta*, mind, rather than as three distinct metaphysical layers. *Citta*, then, as the term used by Patañjali and the commentators to refer to all three of these cognitive functionscombined, is one of the most important terms in the Yoga Sûtras.

3. PHILOSOPHY AND PSYCHOLOGY OF MIND

Yoga is defined by Patañjali as "*citta vrtti nirodha*" (YS I.2), the stilling of all states of the *citta*. There are five *vrttis*, a term used frequently throughout the Yoga Sûtras to essentially refer to any sensual impression, thought, idea, or cognition, psychic activity or conscious mental state whatsoever. These five *vrttis* are: right knowledge, error, metaphor, deep sleep and memory (YS I.5-11). They are either *klista,* detrimental to the goal of Yoga, or *aklista,* conducive to it. The *klista vrttis* are those stemming from the mind when it is subject to the five *klesas,* obstacles – ignorance, ego, desire, aversion, clinging to life – discussed below, and the *aklista vrttis* are those stemming from their opposites – knowledge of the true self and freedom from desire, etc. Put simply, *aklista vrttis are* the mental activities of a *jivanmukta,* a being who is liberated while still embodied.

The first of these five *vrttis* is epistemological, *pramâna,* that is, the sources that constitute the production of valid knowledge of an object – the methods of attaining accurate information about reality. This is discussed in the section on epistemology, and we will simply note here that the first *vrtti* is when the mind is in a state of right knowledge, that is, is accurately reflecting external reality (Yoga would not disagree with the basics of the Nyâya tradition as to what constitutes *right* knowledge, nor with the criteria that produce it). The second *vrtti* is error, which can be produced from the same sources as knowledge, and is defined as considering something to be what it is not, a state that can be subsequently removed by true knowledge of what the nature of the thing in question is (such as the perception of two moons when in an intoxicated state).

The third type of *vrtti* is, loosely speaking, imagination or metaphor, or, more precisely, the usage of words or expressions that do not correspond to any actual physical reality, but that are understood in common parlance. An example given in the commentaries is the statement that "the arrow stands still, stood still, will stand still." What this actually means in the mind of the listener is that the arrow has ceased (or will cease) to move, that is, "standing still," the absence of motion, is really an imagined state of affairs dependent on the idea of motion, but it is then projected as an actual characteristic of the arrow. A more straightforward example from English usage might be: "the sun rises and sets" or "time flies;" common usage has assigned meaning to these imaginary states of affairs, and no one bats an eyelid when such expressions are uttered. In fact, metaphors and similes, which, if dissected to their literal meanings do not correspond to actual objective reality, are normal everyday expressions and ubiquitous in human language, since language is largely figurative.

The fourth *vrtti* is deep sleep defined as a state of mind which is based on an absence [of any content]. There is some difference between schools but (in contrast to e.g. Vedânta), the Yoga tradition views deep sleep as a type of *vrtti* on the grounds that when one awakes, one remembers that one has either slept well, or slept restlessly, or slept in a stupor. One would not be able to do so if these impressions did not relate back to a state of mind that existed during deep sleep. This is because, in Yoga psychology, memory is the product of *samskâra,* and *samskâra* is caused by experience. Therefore, the memory of having slept well must relate to a state of mind experienced during deep sleep, which is recorded in the *citta* as memory (the topic of the next *sûtra*) and remembered upon awakening. This state of mind according to this line of reasoning must therefore pertain to a category of *vrtti* distinct from others.

Finally, the fifth *vrtti* is memory, defined as the retention of images of sense objects that have been experienced. Any *vrtti* leaves its copy on the *citta* before fading away. Memories are generated from and thus depend on the other types of *vrttis*. As noted earlier, every object that has ever been experienced forms a *samskâra,* an imprint, in the *citta* mind, like a sound is imprinted on a tape recorder, or an image on film. The mind forms an impression of an object through the sense organs, which is called a *pratyaya*. Once this *pratyaya* or active image of this object is no longer of active interest to the mind, it becomes an inactive, or latent, *samskâra*. Thus *vrttis,* and their *pratyaya* content, are retained as *Samskâras* when they fade. Memory consists of the retrieval of these *Samskâras;* memories are the reactivation of the imprints of sense objects that one has experienced and recognized in the past that are not too covered by forgetfulness (*tamas*). However, it is important to note that these *Samskâras* are not just passive imprints but vibrant latent impulses that can get activated under conducive circumstances and can exert influence on a person's thoughts and behaviours.

The notion of the subconscious in Western psychology corresponds to other less retrievable *Samskâras*, primarily from previous lives, which remain latent as subliminal impressions. The mind is thus a storehouse of these recorded *Samskâras*, deposited and accumulated in the *citta* over countless lifetimes. *Samskâras* also account for such things as personality traits, habits, compulsive and addictive behaviours, etc. The stronger or more dominant a cluster of *Samskâras* becomes, the more it activates and imposes itself upon the consciousness of the individual, demanding indulgence and perpetuating a vicious cycle that can be very hard to break (the reverse, of course, also holds true with the benevolent *aklista vrttis* discussed below: one can become "addicted," so to speak, to benevolent *yogic* activities and lifestyle by dint of constant repetition).

Any other states of mind that one might conceive of would be considered by the Yoga tradition as a subset of one of these five essential categories. Since the mind is never static but always active and changing, *vrttis* are constantly being produced, and thus constantly absorb the consciousness of *Purusa* away from its own pure nature, channelling it out into the realm of subtle or gross *Prakrti*.

As noted above, these five categories of *vrttis* can be either *aklista*, conducive (at least initially) to the ultimate goal of Yoga, or *klista*, detrimental. These participial terms assume an awareness of their nominal form, *klesa*; there are five *klesas*: ignorance, ego, desire, aversion and clinging to life (YS II.3-9). These *klesas* are deeper elements of the psyche than their surface level manifestations as *vrttis*. In resonance with all Indic soteriological thought, the first *klesa*, ignorance, is the foundation of all the other *klesas*, and hence of *samsâra*, so when ignorance is dispelled, the other *klesas*, which may exist in latent unconscious form, or in various stages of consciousness, disappear. It is defined as follows: "Ignorance is the notion which takes the self, which is joyful, pure and eternal, to be the non-self, which is painful, unclean and temporary." The "non-self," *an-âtman*, consists not only of the body, which is the locus for enjoyment; and the mind, which is an instrument through which the awareness of *Purusa* can contact the world; but also the accessories or paraphernalia of the body, whether animate (such as spouse, animals, and offspring), or inanimate (such as furniture or food).

Ego is to consider the nature of the seer and the nature of the instrumental power of seeing to be the same thing. In other words, ego is the specific aspect of ignorance which identifies the non-self – specifically the intelligence – with the true self, *Purusa* (*âtman*). Ego and ignorance are to some extent the same thing, but there is a difference in degree. Ignorance initially involves a not-as-yet specific notion of "I-ness," a sense of self as being something other than *Purusa* as yet undefined, a partial identification of the real self with *buddhi*, the intelligence, while ego involves a more developed or complete identity between the *Purusa* self and *buddhi*. The difference is one of degree; ego evolves out of ignorance, and makes the misidentification of non-self with self more concrete and specific.

Moving on to the third *klesa*: the hankering, desire or craving for pleasure or the means to attain pleasure by one who remembers past experiences of pleasure, is attachment, *râga*. The key ingredient in this process is memory. In other words, one who has experienced pleasure in the past recollects it and hankers to repeat the experience in the present or future, or to attain the means of repeating the experience. It is this dwelling on past experiences that constitutes "attachment." When a new means of pleasure is perceived, it is memory that infers that the new means of pleasure is the same as or similar to something that produced pleasure in the past, and therefore promises to provide the same or similar pleasure in the present or future.

The fourth *klesa* can be understood in a parallel manner to the previous *klesa* of attachment: the feeling of resistance, anger, frustration and resentment towards pain and its causes by one who remembers past experiences of similar pain, is aversion. The tendency of clinging-to-life is the fifth *klesa* which is taken to be a synonym for the fear of death. Just as the previous *sûtras* indicated that attachment or aversion to something is caused by positive or negative memories of that thing, aversion to death likewise indicates that one's memory retains unpleasant recollections of past deaths, although these are latent or subconscious in the present life.

When under the influence of the detrimental *vrttis* stemming from the *klesas*, the mind becomes attracted or repelled by sense objects drawing its attention. In its attempt to attain that which attracts it, that is, to fulfill desires, and avoid that which repels it, avoid aversions, the mind provokes action, *karma*, which initiates a vicious reactive cycle. *Karma*, from the root *kr*, to "do" or "make," literally means "work," but inherent in the Indic concept of work, or any type of activity, is the notion that every action breeds a reaction. Thus *karma* refers not only to an initial act, whether benevolent or malicious, but also to the reaction it produces (pleasant or unpleasant in accordance with the original act) which ripens for the actor either in this life or a future one. Hence people are born into different socio-economic situations, and pleasant or unpleasant things happen to them throughout life in accordance with their own previous actions.

This cycle of action and reaction, or *samsâra*, is potentially eternal and unlimited since not only does any one single act breed a reaction, but the actor must then react to this reaction causing a re-reaction, which in turn fructifies and provokes re-re-reactions, and so on *ad infinitum*. Since these reactions and re-reactions, etc., cannot possibly be fitted into one life, they spill over from one lifetime to the next. It is in an attempt to portray the sheer unlimited and eternal productive power of *karma* that Indic thinkers, both Hindu and Buddhist, use such metaphors as "the ocean" of birth and death. Thus, *karma*, which keeps consciousness bound to the external world and forgetful of its own nature, is generated by the *vrttis*, and the *vrttis*, in turn, are produced by the *klesas*. There is thus a cycle of *klesas*, *vrttis* and *Samskâras:vrttis*, that is thoughts, etc. stemming form sense experience, (and their consequent actions) are recorded in the *citta* as *Samskâras*, and these *Samskâras* eventually activate consciously or subliminally, producing further *vrttis*. These *vrttis* then provoke action with their corresponding reactions noted above, which in turn are recorded as *Samskâras*, and the cycle continues. *Klesas*, *vrttis*, *Samskâras* and *karma* are thus all interconnected links in the chain of *samsâra*.

The *aklista* non-detrimental mental *vrttis*, on the other hand, are produced by the *sâttvic* faculty of discrimination that seeks to control the influence of *rajas* and *tamas* and thereby the detrimental *vrttis* that they produce. Through the practice of yoga, the *yogî* attempts to supplant all the *râjasic* and *tâmasic Samskâras* with *sâttvic* ones until these, too, are restricted in the higher states of meditative concentration — the notions of detrimental and non-detrimental are from the relative perspective of *samsâra*; the detrimental (*râjasic* and *tâmasic*) *vrttis* cause pain, and the non-detrimental (*sâttvic*) ones at least lead in the direction of liberation, even though they too must eventually be given up. But these latter do point to the possibility of acting in the world, in one's *Prakrtic* body and mind, from an enlightened perspective free from ignorance. This points to the notion of the *jîvanmukta*: someone who is still embodied and thus functioning with a *citta*, but a *citta* that generates *vrttis* that are not subject to ignorance, ego, and attachment, etc.

4. SOTERIOLOGY AND PRAXIS

We have discussed that ignorance is the cause of suffering and *samsâra*, and that when this is removed by discrimination, liberation is attained. The core project of the Sûtras, then, is to outline how to accomplish this. The second chapter, *kriyâ yoga*, is dedicated to this effect, featuring the eight limbs of *yoga*, that is, to the means of achieving discriminative discernment. The eight limbs are: *yamas*, abstentions; *niyamas*, observances; *âsana*, posture; *prânâyâma*, breath control; *pratyahâra* disengagement of the senses; *dharanâ*, concentration, *dhyâna*, meditation and *samâdhi*, absorption.

The *yamas* are: non-violence, truthfulness; refrainment from stealing; celibacy; and renunciation of [unnecessary] possessions. The first of these, *ahimsâ*, non-violence, is the *yama* singled out by the commentators on Patañjali for special attention, indeed, as the root of the other *yamas*. Patañjali's goal is to achieve *ahimsâ* and enhance it. *Ahimsâ* is defined as not injuring any living creature anywhere at any time. Truth, the second *yama*, is defined as one's words and thoughts being in exact correspondence to fact. "Refrainment from stealing", the third *yama*, is described as not taking things belonging to others, and not even harbouring the desire to do so. Celibacy is the control of the sexual organs, a definition further refined as not seeing, speaking with, embracing, or otherwise interacting with members of the opposite sex as objects of desire. Renunciation of possessions is the ability to see the problems caused by the acquisition, preservation and destruction of things, since these only provoke attachment and injury. These *yamas* are considered the great vow. They are not exempted by one's class, place, time or circumstance. They are universal.

The *niyamas*, observances, are: cleanliness, contentment, austerity, study [of scripture], and devotion to God. Cleanliness is external and internal; the former pertains to the body, and the latter to purifying the mind of all contamination (jealousy, pride, vanity, hatred and attachment.) "Contentment," *santoca*, the second *niyama*, manifests as disinterest in accumulating more than one's immediate needs of life. "Austerity," *tapas*, is the ability to tolerate the urge to eat and drink, as well as the urge for the dualities of life – hot and cold, etc., to avoid useless talk, and to perform fasts. "Study," *svâdhyâya*, refers to reading sacred scriptures whose subject matter is liberation, and also includes the repetition of the *om* syllable. The last item on Patañjali's list, "devotion to God," *Isvara-pranidhâna*, includes offering all one's activities to *Isvara*, the "original teacher," (YS I.26), without desire for the fruit. This last *niyama* will be discussed further in the section on theism.

With regards to the third limb of Yoga, the term "*âsana*" is hardly found in the older texts, except on occasion in the sense of a "seat." Although the entirety of Yoga is typically understood and presented as*âsana*, physical posture, in the popular representations of the term in the West, it is actually only the third limb of Yoga, not an end or goal unto itself. Indeed, given that he dedicated 20 *sûtras* to the *yamas* and*niyamas*, Patañjali has relatively little to say about *âsana*, leaving us with only three *sûtras* to the topic consisting of a total of nine words – less than 1% of the text.

Vyâsa, the main commentator, knew of a range of *âsanas* in the 5th century C.E. (listing 12 followed by "etc.", suggesting a well known tradition of variants). Nonetheless, essentially, posture is a limb of the actual goal of Yoga to the extent that it allows the meditator to sit "firmly," *sthira*, and "comfortably," *sukha*, for meditation. Indeed, as noted, *âsana* in fact literally means "seat." The point is that *yogic* postures are useful only to the extent to which they facilitate fixing the mind completely by training the body not to be a source of distraction. *Prânâyâma*, breath control, consists of the regulation of the incoming and outgoing breaths. It is defined as the external, internal and restrained movements [of breath], which are drawn out and subtle in accordance to place, time and number. *Pratyâhâra*, the fifth limb, is defined as withdrawal from sense objects.

This process of consecutive stages of internalization seen in these first five limbs, then, continues throughout the remaining three limbs. The fifth limb, *dhâranâ*, concentration, involves fixing the mind on one place. Although Patañjali allows that any object can be used as the support of the mind in *dhâranâ*, theistic meditation comes highly recommended (see section on Theism). The seventh limb, meditation, is the one-pointedness of the mind on one image. More specifically, it consists of the continuous flow of the same thought or image of the object of meditation, without being distracted by any other thought. When the image of the object of meditation "flows" uninterrupted in the mind, that is to say when the mind can focus exclusively on that object without any other distraction, the seventh limb of Yoga, *dhyâna*, has been achieved. The sixth and seventh limbs of Yoga, as well as the eighth, are not different practices as is the case with the previous five limbs, but a continuation and deepening of the same practice.

Samâdhi, the final limb, is when that same *dhyâna* shines forth as the object alone and the mind is devoid of its own reflective nature. When the mind is so fully absorbed in the object of meditation that it loses all notions of itself as a self-conscious, reflective mind, one has reached the state of *samâdhi*. In this state, the mind is no longer aware of itself as meditating on something external to itself; all distinctions between the *yogî* as the subjective meditator, the act of meditation, and the object of meditation have disappeared. Like a pure crystal which, when placed next to a red flower, appears to completely lose its own character by reflecting the form and colour of the flower exclusively, the *yogî* is no longer self-aware, and is conscious only of the object of meditation, and it is in this level of intensity that *samâdhi* differs from *dhyâna*. There is thus a progression of concentrative absorption on the object of meditation from *dharanâ*, through *dhyâna*, to *samâdhi*, the state of consciousness ensuing when all thought has, in fact, been stilled. This is the final goal of Yoga.

There are four stages of *samprajñâta samâdhi*, all of which have an *âlambana*, "a support". This means that the consciousness of the *Purusa* is still flowing through the *Prakrtic citta* to connect with or be supported by an object of meditational focus (albeit in progressively more subtle ways). In this state, the mind is fixed on one *pratyaya*, image, or undeviating *vrtti*, that of the object of concentration, and resists all change into other states. The object of concentration, whatever it might be, is the *âlambana*, that is, the unwavering image the object produces on the concentrated mind.

The first level of *samprajñâta samâdhi*, *vitarka samâdhi*, is taken to be contemplation on a gross physical object, that is to say, meditating on an object which one experiences as a manifestation or construct of the gross physical or material atomic elements. It is thus the first level of experiencing an object in *samâdhi*.

This first stage is further refined by Patañjali, and subdivided into two subdivisions: *sa-* "with" *vitarka*, and *nir-* "without" *vitarka*. When the *yogî* uses an object such as, say, a cow, as the meditational support, or object of concentration (*âlambana*), but the *yogî's* awareness of this object is conflated with the word for and the concept of a cow, this absorption is known as *savitarka samâdhi* (*samâpatti*), "absorption with physical awareness." In other words, the *yogî's* experience of the object is still subtly tinged with awareness of what the object is called, and with the memory or idea corresponding to that object. Direct experience of the object in its own right and on its own ground of being is tainted by the imposition of conceptual thought upon it.

When, in contrast, the object stands out in its own right without being conflated with the conventional terminologies of language that might refer to it, or with any idea or meaning it might generate, *nirvitarkasamâdhi* has been attained. This non-conceptual, or, perhaps more accurately, super-conceptual stage occurs when the *yogî's citta* has been purged of any memory awareness of what the object is and what it is called. In other words, no *samskâric* imprints pertaining to "cow" are activated on any subconscious or intuitive level whatsoever. In this state there is no recognition of what the object of meditation is, or what its name or function are; recognition is coloured exclusively by the object of focus itself without any discursive analysis of the object's place in the greater scheme of things and without the normal instinctive impulsion to identify it. Moreover, the mind has also given up its own nature of being an organ of knowledge. In other words, awareness is not even aware of the mind as being an instrument channelling awareness onto an object. In a sense, all "knowledge" of the object as conventionally understood has been suspended, and the mind has completely transformed itself into the object, free from any discursive identification or self-awareness. The object can now shine forth in its own right as an object with its own inherent existence, free from labels, categorizations or situatedness in the grand scheme of things. We can note that the object has in effect become the *yogi's* entire universe, since awareness is focused on it exclusively and is thus unaware of anything else, even the discursive process itself.

Keeping the metaphysics of Sâmkhya in mind, we know that the five gross elements which constitute gross physical objects evolve from elements that are more subtle still. That is to say, they are actually evolutes from the *tanmâtras*, the five subtle elements. The second level of *samâdhi* concentration, *vicâra samâdhi*, involves absorption into this more subtle aspect of the object of meditation, that is to say, perceiving the object as actually consisting of these more subtle ingredients. In fact, the subtle substructure of external reality can refer to any of the evolutes from *Prakrti*, as the *tanmâtras* themselves evolve from *ahamkâra* which, in turn, evolves from *buddhi*. Thus, the latter can also be considered *sûksma*, subtle. As a new archer first aims at large objects, and then progressively smaller ones, so the neophyte *yogî* first experiences the gross nature of the object in meditation, and then its progressively more subtle nature. Thus, instead of experiencing the object as comprised of compact quantum masses, the *bhûtâdi* gross elements, as in the first state of *vitarka*, in *vicâra*, the *yogî* experiences them as vibratory, radiant potential, subtle energy, (a sublevel of reality normally imperceptible to the senses).

Vicâra samâdhi, like *vitarka*, is also subdivided into two subdivisions of *sa-* "with," and *nir-* "without." When the intensity of focus on the object of meditation deepens such that the *yogî* penetrates its gross externalization and experiences the object as consisting of subtle elements, the *tanmâtras*, but subtle elements circumscribed as existing in time and space, then the ensuing concentrative state of awareness is known as *savicâra*. In other words, in *savicâra* meditation, an object is perceived as consisting of subtle elements, but the object is still experienced as existing in the present time, rather than in the past or future, and is still bounded by space, that is, it is taking up some distinct physical space in the presence of the meditator rather than being situated anywhere else. Briefly put, at this stage, the *yogî* still has some level of awareness of space and time.

When, on the other hand, the *yogî* can focus on the object unconditioned by such dimensionality; in other words when he or she cannot just focus on the subtle nature of an object, but transcends space and time and perceives that these subtle essences pervade and underpin all things at all times, then the *yogî* has attained the state of *nirvicâra*. In this state, the *yogî* is no longer aware of dimensionality and temporality – the here and now. The object is no longer a distinct object taking up extension in a portion of space different from other spatial objects and existing in the present, rather than any other time, because the *yogî* experiences the subtle elements of the object as underpinning all objects at all times. In other words, the form of the object dissolves as it were under the power of the *yogî's* focus, and the *yogî* now is simply experiencing vibrant subtle energies pervading all reality everywhere and eternally.

There is no consensus amongst the commentators as to the exact nature of the last two stages of *samâdhi*, *ânanda* and *asmitâ*, underscoring the fact that such states are experiential and do not lend themselves to scholastic categorization and analysis. The version that surfaces most commonly utilizes the three components of knowledge identified in Hindu philosophical discourse to demarcate the differences between these four stages of *samâdhi*. In any act of knowledge, there is the "knower," or subject of knowledge; the instruments of knowledge (mind and senses, etc.); and the object of knowledge. These are termed "*grhit[*," "*grahana*," and "*grâhya*" respectively (literally: the "grasper," the "instrument of grasping," and "that which is grasped"). In the first two stages of *samâdhi* outlined above, *vitarka* and *vicâra*, the object upon which the mind is fixed, whether perceived as its grosser outer form or subtler inner constituents, is an external one and therefore considered *grâhya* ("that which is grasped"). Now, in the third stage, *ânanda samâdhi*, the *yogî* transfers awareness from the objects of the senses, *grâhya*, to the organs of the senses themselves, *grahana* (the instruments of grasping), or more precisely, the powers (*Sakti*) behind the sensual abilities of seeing, touching, smelling, tasting and hearing, (rather than the gross physical organs of eye, ear, nose, etc.). The *citta* now becomes aware of the mechanisms of cognition, the instruments of the senses. It becomes aware of the internal organ through which external objects are "grasped," rather than the external objects themselves, whether experienced in their gross or subtle constitutions.

Since, in Sâmkhya, the *grahana* includes the internal organ, *manas*, *buddhi* and *ahamkâra*, the support of the mind in *ânanda samâdhî* is the *citta* itself, specifically in its aspect as *ahamkâra*. Thus, in this third stage, awareness becomes aware of the *citta* itself in its capacity of acquiring knowledge, as an 'instrument' which 'grasps' the objects of the senses. In other words, the mind focuses on its own cognizing nature. Since the *guna* of *sattva* predominates in *ahamkâra* and *buddhi*, and *sattva* is the source of bliss, Patañjali calls this stage *ânanda samâdhi*, the "blissful absorption."

Finally, by involuting awareness further still and penetrating the internal organ of meditation to its still more essential nature, one transcends even the instruments of knowledge and arrives at *buddhi*, to the closest *Prakrtic* coverings, to the *Purusa* itself. Relentless in the pursuit of true and ultimate knowledge, at this point the *yogî* attains the fourth and final stage of *samprajñâta samâdhi*. Having penetrated the constituents of the external object of meditation through its gross and subtle elements, consecutively in the first two stages of *samâdhi,* and having withdrawn itself from external cognition and into a state of contemplating the powers behind the very organs of cognition in the third, awareness penetrates the *citta* further still, absorbing itself in the *citta's* feature of *buddhi,* the *grahitr,* "the grasper," the closest *Prakrtic* covering to the *Purusa* itself.

One final step now remains where this ultimate uncoupling of *Purusa* from all connection with *Prakrti* and all involvement with the *citta* occurs. This is *asamprajñâta samâdhi, samâdhi* without support. This all results in a total of six stages of *samprajñâta samâdhi,* before the final stage of *asamprajñâta samâdhi.* Therefore, including the latter, there will be a total of seven stages of *samâdhi* explicitly expressed by Patañjali in his system.

As we have seen, the four states of *samprajñâta* all involved the *citta* in various ways. *Asamprajñâta* is beyond the mind. It is therefore beyond thought and word. To underscore this, perhaps, Patañjali has used the simple pronoun *anya,* "the other," rather than a descriptive term, thereby pointing to *asamprajñâta* as a state which transcends all descriptive categories and nomenclatures. The commentators present *asamprajñâta samâdhi, samâdhi* "without support," as being the state where the awareness of *Purusa* is no longer aware of any external entity at all, including the *citta,* since the latter has dissolved itself. This state corresponds with *nirbîja,* "without seed" (I.51). In this final and ultimate state, the supreme goal of Yoga, the mind is not supported by any active thought. The *vrttis* of the mind exist simply as potential, and the *Samskâras,* the subconscious imprints that trigger thoughts, memories and *karma,* are also latent. Since the mind is now empty of all thoughts, the awareness of *Purusa* now no longer has any object whatsoever to be aware of, and thus, for the first time, can only become self-aware (loosely speaking). The final goal of Yoga has been attained.

Another way of considering this is that awareness is eternal, it cannot ever cease being aware. That being the case, the self's only options are of what it is aware of: it can be object aware, or (again, loosely speaking) subject aware – that is, aware of entities or objects other than itself, or exclusively aware of itself as awareness with no reference to any other entity. After myriad births being aware of the unlimited varieties of *Prakrtic* objects, *Purusa* has now come to the point of self-realization – realizing itself as distinct from not just objects of thought, but the very faculty and process of thought itself, the *citta* and its *vrttis*. When there are no objects to detain its awareness other than its own self, the *svarupa* of YS I.3, this is *asamprajñâta samâdhi*.

5. EPISTEMOLOGY

The Yoga school accepts three sources of receiving knowledge, *pramâna*, as valid (YS I.7), in accordance with the Sâmkhya tradition. The first is sense perception, *pratyâkca*, placed first on the list of *pramânas* because the other *pramânas* are dependent on it. Vyâsa defines sense perception as being the state or condition of the mind, *vrtti*, which apprehends both the specific (*visesa*) and generic (*sâmânya*) nature of an external object discussed further below. This apprehension is accomplished by the *citta* encountering a sense object through the senses and forming an impression of this object, a *vrtti*. More specifically, the *tâmasic* nature of sense objects imprint themselves upon the mind, and are then illuminated in the mind by the mind's *sâttvic* nature. Due to pervading the mind, the *Purusa*, or self, then becomes conscious of this mental impression, as if it were taking place within itself, indistinguishable from itself. In actual fact, the impression is imprinted on the *citta*, mind, which is pervaded by consciousness but external to it.

The second *pramâna*, source of receiving valid knowledge, is *anumâna*, inference (logic), defined as the assumption that an object of a particular category shares the same qualities as other objects in the same category – qualities which are not shared by objects in different categories. Yoga accepts Nyâya principles here.

Finally, *agama*, "verbal testimony," the third source of valid knowledge accepted by Patañjali, is the relaying of accurate information through the medium of words by a "trustworthy" person who has perceived or inferred the existence of an object, to someone who has not. "Trustworthy" is someone whose statements cannot be contradicted, has sense organs appropriately working in a suitable external environment, and is trustworthy and compassionate and free from defects such as illusion, laziness, deceit, dull-wittedness and so forth. The words of such a reliable authority enter the ear and produce an image, *vrtti,* in the mind of the hearer that corresponds to the *vrtti* experienced by the trustworthy person. The person receiving the information in this manner has neither personally experienced nor inferred the existence of the object of knowledge, but valid knowledge of the object is nonetheless achieved, which distinguishes this source of knowledge from the two discussed previously.

Returning to the most important episteme, perception, one must note that there are different types of *pratyakca*: the commentary on the *Sâmkhya Kârikâ*, the *Yuktidîpikâ,* speaks of *yogic* perception as well as sensual perception (38.2). Indeed, several schools make a distinction between *aparapratyakca*, conventional perception, and *parapratyakca,* supernormal perception, or, as the *Sâmkhya Sûtras* put it, external perception, *bahya-pratyakca,* and internal perception *abahya pratyakca* (I.90). The perception of interest to Yoga is the latter, that of a supernormal nature. But even the startling claims of omniscience that one encounters in the text are relevant only as signposts of *experiences* that the *yogî* will encounter on the path of Yoga, not as articles of faith.

Returning to the term *visesa,* "particularity" or "specificity," the term is best understood in contrast to "*sâmânya*," which refers to the general category of an object. Let us consider a "cow," or the standard item used to exemplify a generic object in philosophical commentarial discourse, a "pot." The word "cow" refers to a generic category of bovine creature with udders and horns, who give milk and go "moo"; and "pot" to a roundish container usually made of clay (in India) that holds liquids or other substances. Although there are millions of cows in the world, and each and every one is distinct, individual and unique in some way, the term "cow" does not particularize or distinguish one cow from another. It is a general term that refers to an entire category of creatures. Likewise with the term "pot." The term *sâmânya,* then refers to the genus, species or general category of something; terms like "cow" and "pot," indeed all words in human speech, refer to objects only in terms of their generic characteristics. *Visesa,* by contrast is what particularizes ultimate entities from each other, and ultimately one atom from another (the delimiting feature an atom has that makes it a unique specific individual, distinct from any other atom).

According to Yoga, these three forms of knowledge as conventionally accepted are all limited because they cannot provide information about "particulars" or specifics. Verbal testimony is dependent on words, and words, like "cow," can only point to the cow as a member of a general class of things – so when we say something like "there is a cow in the field," we are only really giving information about the cow as a member of a species, and not about particulars: we are not conveying precise information about the specifics of the particular individual cow in question.

Along exactly the same lines, inference, also, only deals with generalities (and is, in fact, dependent on perception in the first place). As for empirical sense perception, it is true, say the commentators, that when we look at a particular cow or pot, we might be able to pick up on some characteristic that distinguishes the particular cow or pot in front of us from other cows and pots – perhaps this cow has odd skin colour or the pot an odd shape. But conventional sense perception, says Vyâsa, cannot provide us information about the precisely specific or subtle nature of an object – its atomic composition for example, nor about distant or hidden objects beyond the range of the senses.

Only through the clear, unobstructed insight of *samâdhi* can one fully grasp the *visesa,* particularity, of an object, its subtle substructure of distinct atoms and subtle essences. Patañjali claims that the *yogî* can tell the difference between two identical items, since, although they appear identical to normal perception, the atoms comprising them are different, and it is these that the *yogî* can perceive. We must keep in mind that the *yogic* tradition claims one can actually *perceive* these essences through the undeviatingly concentrated focus of mind in the higher stages of *samâdhi,* not merely theorize their existence. This perception, then, is actually a form of *pratyakca,* but not that of conventional sense perception. As noted earlier, the *Yuktidîpikâ* commentary on Sâmkhya points out that *yogic pratyakca* transcends normal sense-based perception. It is *parapratyakca,* "higher," supreme, supernormal, perception.

Additionally, since the *citta* is by nature luminous, once the influences of *rajas* and *tamas* have been removed, there is nothing to obstruct its natural luminosity, and it can pass beyond the limitations inherent in finite objects due to the *tamas* preponderant in physical things. The ingredients of the mind itself are the same as those underpinning the object in external reality, the three *gunas*; we must keep in mind here that the gross and subtle elements are nothing other than *tamas*-dominant evolutes from *sattva*-dominant *buddhi* and *ahamkâra*. Thus when fully *sâttvic*, the mind can transcend its own *klesa* limitations (II.2ff) and merge into the common substratum of all things. This corresponds to such states as *savicâra* described in the section on *samâdhi*, when the *yogî's* awareness perceives that the subtle nature of the object of meditation as well as the meditating mind itself actually pervades all objects and thus all reality. So, once the obstructing qualities of *rajas* and *tamas* have been removed, then the pure luminosity of consciousness passes beyond the limitations of all boundaries and finite objects. In other words, the commentators claim that in the higher stages of *samâdhi*, the *yogî* becomes essentially omniscient since awareness is no longer limited to the body or dimensionality but can radiate out infinitely and permeate the subtle substratum in the form of *buddhi*, *ahamkâra*, the *tanmâtra*, etc. (as well as the specific conglomeration of atoms that emerge from these *tanmâtras*), underpinning all objects. It can thus perceive the *visesa*, particularity, that is, the specific atomic composition, of any particular object. As an aside, this ability reflects the metaphysics of the supernormal mystic powers inherent in the Yoga tradition, a discussion of which occupies almost a quarter of the text (but which are beyond the scope of this entry).

6. ETHICS

Patañjali outlines a practice essential for enhancing *sattva* and lucidity, the prerequisite for attaining steadiness in the mind. We have established by now that the path and attainments of Yoga are nothing other than the maximization of the *guna* of *sattva*. Central to the Yoga tradition, then, are the ethical and other practices indispensable to this objective. Verse I.33 states that as a result of cultivating an attitude of "friendship" with those who find themselves in a "situation of happiness," one of "compassion" towards those in "distress," one of "joy" towards "pious" selves, and one of "equanimity" or indifference towards the "impious," *sattva* is generated. Consequently, the mind becomes lucid – clarity being the nature of *sattva*. Once clear, one-pointed concentration, or steadiness, which is the goal of meditational Yoga, can be achieved by the mind.

From an ethical point of view, by being a well-wisher towards those who are happy, as well as those who are virtuous, the contamination of envy is removed. By compassion towards those miserable, that is, by wishing to remove someone's miseries as if they were one's own, the contamination of the desire to inflict harm on others is removed. By equanimity towards the impious, the contamination of intolerance is removed. By thus removing these traits of envy, desire to inflict harm, and intolerance, which are characteristics of *rajas* and *tamas*, the *sattva* natural to the mind can manifest. In the ensuing state of lucidity, the inclination towards seeking higher truths by controlling the *vrttis*, in other words towards cultivating a focused state of mind by the practice of *yoga*, spontaneously arises, because the inclination for enlightenment is natural to the pure *sâttvic* mind.

A further set of ethical practices indispensable for increasing the *sattva* component of the mind are the five *yamas*, observances (literally "restraints") of chapter II: non-violence, truthfulness; refrainment from stealing; celibacy and renunciation of [unnecessary] possessions. From these, *ahimsâ*, non-violence, is the *yama* singled out by the commentators for special attention, and therefore leads the list and thus, the entire eight limbs of Yoga (it seems important to note that the *yamas* themselves lead the list of the eight limbs suggesting that one's *yogic* accomplishment remains limited until the *yamas* are internalized and put into practice) (YS II.30).

Vyâsa accordingly takes *ahimsâ* as the root of the other *yamas*. He defines it as not injuring any living creature anywhere at any time. Just as the footprints of an elephant covers the footprints of all other creatúres, so does *ahimsâ* cover all the other *yamas* - one continues to undertake more and more vows and austerities for the sole purpose of purifying *ahimsâ*.

Vyâsa defines "truth," the second *yama*, as one's words and thoughts being in exact correspondence to fact, that is, to whatever is known through the three processes of knowledge accepted by the Yoga school. Speech is for the transfer of one's knowledge to others, and should not be deceitful, misleading or devoid of value. It should be for the benefit of all creatures, and not for their harm. However, underscoring the centrality of *ahimsâ* – truth must never result in violence. In other words, if there is ever a conflict between the *yamas* – if observing one *yama* results in the compromise of another – then *ahimsâ* must always be respected first.

"Refrainment from stealing," the third *yama*, is described as not taking things belonging to others, and not even harbouring the desire to do so. Vyâsa defines "celibacy" as the control of the sexual organs, and this is further refined by Vâcaspati Misra as not seeing, speaking with, embracing, or otherwise interacting with members of the opposite sex as objects of desire. In short, self-realization cannot be attained if one is sexually absorbed because this indicates that one is still seeking fulfilment on the sensual level, and thus misidentifying with the non-self.

Vyâsa defines "renunciation of possessions" as the ability to see the problems caused by the acquisition, preservation and destruction of things, since these only provoke attachment and injury. These *yamas* are considered the great vow; they are not exempted by one's class, place, time or circumstance. They are universal in all aspects of life's affairs and social interactions. Without them *rajas* and *tamas* cannot be curtailed, and the *sattva* essential to the higher stages of Yoga is unattainable.

7. THEISM

Patañjali in YS I.23 states that the goal of Yoga can be attained by the grace of God, *Isvara-prânidhânâd vâ*. The theistic, or *Isvaravâda* element in Indic thought stretches back at least to the late Vedic period. Of the six "schools" of traditional thought that stem from this period, five – Nyâya, Vaisesika, Vedânta, Yoga and Sâmkhya – were, or became, theistic. Sâmkhya, although often represented as nontheistic, was, in point of fact, widely theistic in its early expressions, and continued to retain widespread theistic variants outside of the later classical philosophical school associated with IsvaraKrsna, as evidenced in the Purânas and Bhagavad Gîtâ. Reflecting Patañjali's undogmatic and nonsectarian sophistication, although *Isvara-pranidhâna,* "devotion to God" may not be the exclusive or mandatory way to attain realization of the self (given the particle *vâ* "or" in I.23) it is clearly favoured by him. The term "*Isvara*" occurs in three distinct contexts in the Yoga Sûtras. The first, beginning with I.23, is in the context of how to attain the ultimate goal of Yoga, namely, the cessation of all thought, *samprajñâta samâdhi* and realization of *Purusa*. Patañjali presents dedication to *Isvara* as one such option. But it is important to note the word *va,* "or," in this *sûtra,* indicating that Patañjali presents devotion to *Isvara,* the Lord, as an optional means of attaining *samâdhi,* rather than an obligatory one.

In the ensuing discussion, Patañjali states that:

the Lord is a special self because he is untouched by the deposits of *Samskâras, karma* and its fructification, and the obstacles to the practice of yoga, the *klesas* of nescience, ego, attachment, aversion and the will-to-live. He is omniscient, and also the teacher of the ancients, because he is not limited by Time.

Given the primary context of the Sûtras, namely fixing the mind on an object, two *sûtras,* I.27–28, specify how *Isvara* is to be meditated upon: "his designation is the mystical syllable "om," and its repetition, *japa,* and the contemplation of its meaning should be performed." This points to the ubiquitous and most prominent form of Hindu meditation from the classical period to the present day: *mantra* recitation(*japa*). As a result of this devotional type of meditation, "comes the realization of the inner consciousness and freedom from all obstacles."

The second context in which Patañjali refers to *Isvara* is in the first *sûtra* in chapter II, where *kriyâ yoga,* the path of action, is described as consisting of austerity, study and devotion to the Lord. By performing such *kriyâ yoga, samâdhi* is attained and the obstacles (the *klesas* of II.3), are weakened. Finally, *Isvara* surfaces again in a third context in the second chapter, II.32, where the *niyamas* are listed. The *niyamas,* which are the second limb of the eight-limbed path of Yoga, consist of cleanliness, contentment, austerity, study and, as in the other two contexts, *Isvarapranidhâna,* devotion to *Isvara* (thus, the three ingredients of *kriyâ yoga* are all *niyamas*). The various benefits associated with following the *yamas* and *niyamas,* ethics and morals, are noted in the ensuing *sûtras* of the chapter, and II.45 states that the benefit from the *niyama* of devotion to God is the attainment of *samâdhi.* This is the final reference to *Isvara* in the text, but it is significant, because all the boons mentioned as accruing from the other *yamas* and *niyamas* (there are ten in all) represent *Prakrtic,* or material, attainments – vitality, knowledge of past lives, detachment, etc., etc. It is only from *Isvarapranidhâna,* the last item on the list of *yamas* and *niyamas,* that the ultimate goal of Yoga, *samâdhi,* is achieved. These then are the gleanings that can be extracted from Patañjali's characteristically frugal *sûtras.*

From these we can conclude that Patañjali is definitely promoting a degree of theistic practice in the Yoga Sûtras. Although in the first context, *Isvarapranidhâna,* devotional surrender to God, is optional as a means of attaining *samâdhi,* Patañjali does direct six *sûtras* to *Isvara,* which is not insignificant given the frugality of his *sûtras.* This devotional surrender is not optional in the second context, *kriyâ yoga.* Since it is likewise not optional in the third context as a *niyama,* which is a prerequisite to meditational *yoga,* Patañjali seems to be requiring that all aspiring *yogîs* be devotionally oriented in the preparatory stages to the higher goals of Yoga and, while in the higher, more meditational stages of practice they may shift their meditational focus of concentration to other objects – even, ultimately, to any object of their pleasing (I.39) – they would best be advised to retain *Isvara* as object thereafter, since this "special *Purusa*" can bestow perfection of *samâdhi* which other objects cannot (II.45).

Patañjali also states that *Isvara* is represented by the mystical syllable "*om.*" *Om* has been understood as a sonal incarnation of *Brahman* (which is the most common term used for the Absolute Truth in the *Upanisads*), since the late Vedic period. A scholastic such as Patañjali would most certainly have been well schooled in the Upanisads (especially given his own mandate of the prerequisite of study for success in *yoga,* II.1 & 44), which, as an orthodox thinker, he would have accepted as *sruti,* divine revelation. Even though he never refers to *Brahman* in the *Sûtras,* here again we must wonder whether along with *all*t he *Isvara* theologies of his time he is quite consciously equating the Upanisadic *Brahman* with this personal *Isvara,* by means of this common denominator of *om.*

It is through the sound *om* that the *yogi* is to fix the mind on *Isvara.* After all, since *Isvara,* as a type of *Purusa,* is beyond *Prakrti,* and therefore beyond conceptualization or any type of *vrtti,* how is one to fix one's mind upon him – the *Prakrtic* mind cannot perceive that which is finer than itself? Patañjali here provides the means: through the recitation of the syllable in which *Isvara* manifests. Such recitation is called *japa* (an old Vedic term common in the old Brâhmana texts, where it referred to the soft recitation of Vedic *mantras* by the priest.) By constantly repeating *om* and contemplating its meaning, *artha,* namely *Isvara,* the mind of the *yogî* becomes one-pointed – the goal of all *yoga* practice. Repeating the sound *om* and "contemplating its meaning," namely, that it is the sound representation of *Isvara,* the object of the *yogî's* surrender, when coupled with Patañjali's usage of the word *pranidhâna,* surrender, in I.23, points to chanting the *mantra* in a devotional mood. This is quintessential Hindu theistic meditation, the most prominent form of Hindu Yoga evidenced from antiquity to the present day.

REFERENCES :

a. Primary Sources

1.Aranya, Swami Hariharananda. 1984. *Yoga Philosophy of Patanjali [with the commentary of Vyasa].* Albany: State University of New York Press.

2.Ballantyne, James Robert. 1852. *The Aphorisms of the Yoga Philosophy of Patañjali with Illustrative Extracts from the Commentary By Bhoja Raja.* Allahabad: Presbyterian Mission Press.

3.Hariharânanda, Mukerji. 1963. *Yoga Philosophy of Patañjali.* Calcutta: Calcutta University (reprint, New York: SUNY, 1977).

4.Kumar Shiv & Bhargava, D.N. 1980. *Yultidipika*. Delhi: Eastern Book Linkers.

5.Manikar, T.G.1972. *Samkhya Karika of Isvarakrsna with Gaudabhasya*. Poona: Oriental Book Agency.

6.Rukmani, T.S.1981. *Yogavârttika of Vijñânabhikßu*. 4 vols. Delhi: Munshiram Manoharlal.

7.Sharma, Har Dutt. 1933. *The Samkhya Karika [with the commentary of Gaudapada]*. Poona: Oriental Book Agency.

8.Sharma, Har Dutt. 1934 *The Tattva Kaumudi*. Poona: Oriental Book Agency.

9.Woods, James Haughton. 1912. *The Yoga System of Patañjali* [*with the commentary of Vacaspati*]. Delhi: Motilal Banarsidass, (reprint, 1998).

b. Secondary Sources

1.Alter, Joseph. 2004. *Yoga in Modern India: The Body between Science and Philosophy*. Princeton: Princeton University Press.

2.Bhattacharya, Ram Shankar. 1985. *An Introduction to the Yoga Sütra*. Delhi: Bharatiya Vidya Prakasansa.

3.Bronkhurst, Johannes. 1993. *The Two Traditions of Meditation in Ancient India*. Delhi: Motilal Banarsidass.

4.Brockington, John, "Epic Yoga" *Journal of Vaishnava Studies* 14.1. Fall (2005): 123-138.

5.Bryant, Edwin. 2009. *The Yoga Sutras: A New Edition, Translation, and Commentary*. New York: North Point Press.

6.Chapple, Christopher. 2003. *Reconciling Yogas*. Albany: State University of New York.

7.Dasgupta, S. 1922. A *History of Indian Philosophy Motilal Banarsidass*.

8.Dasgupta, S. *Hindu Mysticism*. 1927. Chicago: The Open Court Publishing Company.

9.De Michelis, Elizabeth. 2004. *History of Modern Yoga: Patanjali and Western Esotericism*. New York and London: Continuum.

10.Eliade, Mircea. 1958. *Yoga: Immortality and Freedom*. Translated by Willard R. Trask. London: Kegan Paul.

11.Feuerstein, Georg. 1989. *The Yoga-Sutra of Patañjali: A New Translation and Commentary*. Rochester, VT: Inner Traditions.

12.Feuerstein, Georg. 1996. *The Philosophy of Classical Yoga*. Rochester, VT: Inner Traditions.

13.Feuerstein, Georg. 2001. *The Yoga Tradition: Its History, Literature, Philosophy, and Practice*. Prescott, AZ: Hohm Press.

14.Feuerstein, Georg. 2003. *The Deeper Dimension of Yoga: Theory and Practice*. Boston: Shambhala.

15.Hopkins, E.W. 1901 "Yoga Technique in the Great Epic" *Journal of the American Oriental Society*. Vol 22: 333-379.

16.Larson, Gerald James *Classical Sâmkhya*. 1979. Delhi: Motilal Benarsidass.

17.Larson, Gerald James. 1999. "Classical Yoga as Neo- Sâmkhya: a Chapter in the History of Indian Philosophy" *Asiatische Studien Studes Asiatiques*. LII.3: 723-732.

18.Larson, Gerald James and Bhattacharya. 2008. *Yoga: India's philosophy of Meditation*. Encyclopedia of Indian Philosophies. Volume XII. Delhi: Motilal Banarsidass.

19.Singleton, Mark. 2010. *Yoga Body: The Origins of Modern Posture Practice*. Oxford and New York: Oxford University Press.

20.Yamashita Koichi. 1994. *Pâtañjala Yoga Philosophy with Reference to Buddhism*. Calcutta: Firma KLM.

21.Whicher, Ian. 1998. *The Integrity of the Yoga Darsana*. New York: SUNY.

7

Nyaya Philosophy

Nyâya (literally "Logic") is a leading school of philosophy within the "Hindu umbrella"—those communities which saw themselves as the inheritors of the ancient Vedic civilization and allied cultural traditions. Epistemologically, Nyâya develops of a sophisticated precursor to contemporary reliabilism (particularly process reliabilism), centered on the notion of "knowledge-sources" (*pramâna*), and a conception of epistemic responsibility which allows for default, unreflective justification accorded to putatively veridical cognition. It also extensively studies the nature of reasoning in the attempt to map pathways which lead to veridical inferential cognition. Nyâya's methods of analysis and argument resolution influenced much of classical Indian literary criticism, philosophical debate, and jurisprudence. Metaphysically, Nyâya defends a robust realism, including universals, selves, and substances, largely in debate with Buddhist anti-realists and flux-theorists. Nyâya thinkers were also India's most sophisticated natural theologians. For at least a millennium, Nyâya honed a variety of arguments in support of a baseline theism in constant engagement with sophisticated philosophical atheists, most notably Buddhists and Mîmâmsakas (Hindu Ritualists).

Nyâya's prehistory is tied to ancient traditions of debate and rules of reasoning (*vâda-sâstra*). The oldest extant Nyâya text is the Nyâya-sûtra attributed to Gautama (c. 200 C.E.). Throughout much of Nyâya's formative period the philosophical development of the school took place through commentaries on the sûtras (with important exceptions including works of Jayanta, c. 875, Udayana,

c. 975, and the somewhat heterodox Bhâsarvajña, c. 875). Leading commentators include Vâtsyâyana (c. 450), Uddyotakara (c. 600) Vâcaspati Misra (c. 900) and Udayana. The school would enter its "new" phase (*navya-nyâya*) in the work of the eminent epistemologist Gangesa Upâdhyâya (c. 1325). This article focuses on the older tradition of Nyâya, beginning with the sûtras, with occasional gestures toward developments within the new school. Given the breadth of Nyâya thought, this discussion has to exclude some important topics for the sake of economy, such as aesthetics, philosophy of language, and theory of value. The article's primary focus is on epistemology and metaphysics. There is a brief consideration of Nyâya's philosophy of religion.

1. EPISTEMOLOGY

The Nyâya-sûtra opens with a list of its primary topics, sixteen items which may be grouped into the following four categories: epistemology, metaphysics, procedures and elements of inquiry, and debate theory. That Nyâya's initial topic is epistemology (*pramânas*, "knowledge-sources") is noteworthy. Both the sûtras and the commentarial tradition argue that epistemic success is central in the search for happiness, since we must understand the world properly should we desire to achieve the goods it offers. Vâtsyâyana claims that while Nyâya's metaphysical concerns overlap with other, more scripturally-based Hindu schools, what distinguishes Nyâya is a reflective concern with evidence, doubt and the objects of knowledge.

He further defines Nyâya's philosophical method as the "investigation of a subject by means of knowledge-sources" (NB 1.1.1). Importantly, the *pramânas* are not simply the means by which individuals attain veridical cognition. They are also the final court of appeals in philosophical dispute. Uddyotakara thus claims the best kind of demonstrative reasoning occurs when the *pramânas are* deployed in concert in order to establish a fact.

The four *pramânas* are perception, inference, analogical reasoning, and testimony. We will discuss them in order. Then, we will consider Nyâya's theory of knowledge in general.

a. Perception (*pratyakca*)

i. The Characteristics of Perception

Nyâya-sûtra 1.1.4 defines perceptual cognition as follows.

A perceptual cognition arises by means of the connection between sense faculty and object, is not dependent on words, is non-deviating, and is determinate.

This sûtra provides four conditions which must be met for cognition to be perceptual. The first, that cognition arises from the connection between sense faculty and object, evinces Nyâya's direct realism. It is such connection, the central feature of the causal chain which terminates in perceptual cognition, which fixes the intentionality of a token percept. Uddyotakara enumerates six kinds of connection (*sannikarca*) to account for the fact that that we perceive not only substances, but properties, absences, and so on: (i) conjunction (*samyoga*), the connection between a sense faculty and an object; (ii) inherence in what is conjoined (*samyukta-samavâya*), the connection between a sense faculty and a property-trope which inheres in an object; (iii) inherence in what inheres in what is conjoined (*samyukta-samaveta-samavâya*), the connection between a sense faculty and the universal which is instantiated in a property-trope; (iv) inherence (*samavâya*), the kind of connection which makes auditory perception possible; (v) inherence in what inheres (*samaveta-samavâya*), the connection between the auditory faculty and universals which inhere within sounds; (vi) qualifier-qualified relation (*visesya-visesana-bhâva*), the connection which allows for the perception of inherence and absence in objects. In all cases, the perceptual cognition is born of connection between a sense faculty and an occurrent fact or object.

The second condition, that the cognition produced is not dependent on words, has a somewhat complicated interpretive history. Generally, Nyâya holds that ordinary perception involves concept deployment. Therefore, this restriction does not endorse a view held by the Buddhist Dignâga and his followers, that genuine perception is non-conceptual (*kalpanâ-apodha*). Still, the meaning of *avyapadesya* is disputed amongst Naiyâyikas. On one reading, this qualification serves the purpose of distinguishing between perceptually and testimonially generated cognitions. The latter also require information provided by the senses but further require the deployment of semantic and syntactic knowledge. An allied reading suggests that while involving the application of concepts, perception of an object is often causally prior to speech acts involving it.

The third, "non-deviating" condition blocks false cognitions, like the misperception that an oyster shell is a piece of silver, from the ranks of *pramâna*-born. This is tied to the Nyâya notion that *pramânas* are by definition inerrant, and that false cognitive presentations are not truly *pramânas* but pseudo-pramânas (pramâna-âbhâsa). Though we may mistakenly take a pseudo-*pramâna*, like the illusion of a person in the distance, to be the real thing, it is not. "Perception" and similar *pramâna*-terms have success grammar for Nyâya.

The fourth, "determinate" condition blocks cognitions which are merely doubtful from the ranks of the pramâna-born. Dubious cognitions, like that of a distant person at dusk, do not convey misleadingly false information, but being unclear, they do not properly apprehend the object in question. It could be a person or a post. As such, one neither correctly grasps its character nor falsely takes it to represent accurately a certain object. Later Naiyâyikas, most notably Vâcaspati Misra, read the qualifiers "notdependent on words" and "determinate" disjunctively, in order to say that perception may be non-propositional or propositional. However anachronistic this may be as an interpretation of the Nyâya-sûtra, this division is accepted by later Nyâya.

ii. Extraordinary Perceptual States

Nyâya admits of certain kinds of extraordinary perception in order to account for cognitive states that are perceptual in character, but distinct from those commonly experienced. They involve modes of sense-object connection other than the six kinds noted above. Later Nyâya (beginning at least with Jayanta) recognizes three kinds of extraordinary perception: (i) yogic perception, (ii) perception of a universal through an individual which instantiates and (iii) perception of an object's properties as mediated by emory.

Yogic perception includes experiential states reported by ntemplatives in deep mediation. Their cognitive objects (usually e deep self or God) are taken to be experienced in a direct and ımediated way, but generally without the operation of the external nses. Given their experiential character and their putative reement with other sources of knowledge like scripture and ference, yogic experiences are *prima facie* taken to be veridical, oduced by non-normal perception.

Perception of a universal through an individual which stantiates it is Nyâya's response to the problem of induction. yâya holds that universals are perceptually experienced as stantiated in individuals (see the third of Uddyotakara's six ıds of connection above). But the notion that we may have prehension of all of the individuals which instantiate a universal, a their being instantiations of the universal, is further accepted Nyâya in order to explain how we attain to knowledge of *âpti*, or invariable relation between universals, which undergirds ısal regularities of various sorts. Unless one's experience of ne particular smoke instance as conjoined with a fire instance ows him to experience all instances of smoke *qua* smoke as ing conjoined with all instances of fire *qua* fire, through the tural tie between the universals *smokiness* and *fieriness*, inductive trapolation would be impossible. Nyâya thus solves the problem induction by appeal to extraordinary perception. This does not ply that we are always able to recognize such relations. It may e repeated experience for us to notice the ever-present nnection. But when such recognition arises, it is due to perceptual perience, not an extrapolative projection of past experience.

Perception of the properties of an object mediated by memory volves the visual experience of unpresented properties of an ject which is currently seen. Standard examples include seeing iece of sandalwood as fragrant or seeing a piece of ice as cold. re, there is a standard kind of sense object connection, but some the phenomenal features of the experience, while veridical, are generated by the ordinary connection. They are rather mediated by a special connection grounded in memory. What distinguish this kind of perception from straightforward inference is that th property in question is experienced with a phenomenal characte lacking in inference. This suggests that what may be considere inference for some may take the form of perception for other depending on their familiarity with the conceptual connectio between the properties in question.

iii. Introspection

Nyâya holds that while cognitions reveal or present the intentional objects, they rarely present themselves directly. Whe they are directly cognized, cognitions are grasped by othe apperceptive cognitions. As apperceptive awareness reveals cognition along with its predication content or "objecthood" (tha is, my cognition of a red truck is apperceptively cognized a having the predication content "red" and "truck-hood"), it i practically indefeasible. But, as Gangesa notes, this indefeasibilit does transfer to the content of the original cognition (which i itself object of the apperceptive awareness). I may have mistake a purple truck for a red truck, forgetting that my eyewear distort certain colours. Apperception is subsumed by Nyâya into the category of perception. In this case, the operative sense faculty is the "inner organ" (*manas*) and the object is a cognition conceived of as a property of a self. Gangesa argues at length with a Prâbhâkara Mîmâmsaka (a representative of another leading Hindu school), defending Nyâya's version of apperception against the Mîmâmsâ view that each cognition itself has a component of reflectively self-awareness.

A few words on *manas* (the inner organ): NS 1.1.16 argues that the absence of simultaneous cognition from all of the senses indicates the presence of a faculty which governs selective attention. The *manas* is identified as this faculty, an insentient psychological apparatus which processes the information of the senses. A formulation of perception by the Vaisesika school (Vaisesika-sûtra 3.1.18), accepted by Nyâya, is that it normally consists in a chain of connection between four things: a self and its *manas*, the *manas* and a sense organ, and the sense organ and an object. *Manas* also is the faculty which governs mnemonic retrieval and, as noted above, apperceptive awareness of mental states. Selves, in the Nyâya view, are fundamentally loci of awareness, cognition, and mnemonic dispositions (*samskâra*). But just as they rely on the five senses to experience the world, they rely on *manas* for the functioning of memory and apperception.

To conclude, we may note that perception is commonly called the *jyecmapramâna* (the "eldest" knowledge source) by Nyâya, since other *pramânas* depend on perceptual input, while perception operates directly on the objects of knowledge. Indeed, Gangesa suggests the following definition of a perceptual cognition: "a cognition that does not have another cognition as its proximate instrumental cause." Inference, analogy, and testimony, on the other hand, depend on immediately prior cognitions to trigger their functioning. The normative status accorded to veridical perceptual cognition is primarily a matter of causation and intentionality (*vicayatâ*). If a cognition is caused by the appropriate causal chain, starting with the contact of a sense faculty and an external object (or, in the case of apperception, the internal organ and an immediately prior cognition), and the cognition produced has an "objecthood" or intentionality which accurately targets the object in question, the cognition is veridical and has the status *prâmânya* (*pramânâ*-derived).

b. Inference (*anumâna*)

i. The Characteristics of Inference

Nyâya-sûtra 1.1.5 defines inference as follows.

[An inferential cognition] is preceded by that [perception], and is threefold: from cause to effect, from effect to cause or from that which is commonly seen.

This definition is somewhat elliptical. But it focuses on the fundamental character of inference: it is a cognition which follows from another cognition owing to their being conceptually connected in some way. Etymologically, *anumâna* means "after-cognizing". Inference follows from an earlier cognition, "that" in the *sûtra* above. Vâtsyâyana interprets "that" (*tat*) to refer to a perceptual cognition, and suggests that perceptual cognition precedes inference in two ways: (i) to engage in inference requires having perceptually established a fixed relationship between an inferential sign and the property to be inferred, and (ii) perceptual input triggers inference in that one must cognize the inferential sign as qualifying the locus of an inference. He provides a more explicit definition of inference as "a 'later cognition' of an object by means of cognition of its inferential sign" (NB 1.1.3).

Uddyotakara reasonably broadens the scope of "that" in NS 1.1.5 to refer to *pramâna*-produced cognitions of any kind which may trigger inference (NV 1.1.5). The meaning of reasoning from cause to effect and from effect to cause should be clear. Uddyotakara interprets reasoning from what is "commonly seen" as that which is grounded in non-causal correlations that have proven invariable. Vâtsyâyana offers another reading: when the relationship between an inferential sign and the inferential target is not perceptible, the target may be inferred owing to the similarity of the unseen prover with something known. The classic example of this kind of inference is as follows: Desire, aversion, and knowledge are properties. Properties require substances which instantiate them. Therefore there is anunseen substance which instantiates desire, aversion, and knowledge: the inner self (NB 1.1.5). Though the connection between mental states like desire and the self which supports them is unseen, the similarity between mental states and other, commonly seen properties (like the colour green) is enough to allow for the inference to a property-bearer.

The history of Nyâya's logical theory is extensive. Here, we will note a few salient points and focus on inference as understood in the period most important to this study (the final great creative period of what is normally known as "Old Nyâya"). First, in Nyâya, logic is subsumed within epistemology, and therefore tends to have a strong informal and cognitive flavor, mapping paths of reasoning that generate veridical cognitions and noting the common ways that reasoning goes wrong. Fundamentally, one makes inferences for oneself. Formal proofs are meant to mirror the kind of reasoning that takes place internally, for didactic or polemical purposes. The first explicit recognition of this dual nature of inference is commonly attributed to the Buddhist Dignâga, who coined the terms *svârthânumâna* (inference for oneself) and *parârthânumâna* (inference for another). Such a division is implicit, however, in the Nyâya-sûtra's distinction between inference as an individual's source of knowledge (NS 1.1.5) and as a systematic method of proof meant to convince another (NS 1.1.32-39).

Second, inference is triggered by the recognition of a sign or mark, whose relationship with some other object (property or fact) has been firmly established. The primary cause of an inferential cognition is an immediately prior "subsumptive judgment" (*parâmarsa*) which grasps an inferential sign as qualifying an inferential subject (the locus of the inference), while recollecting the sign's invariable concomitance with some other fact or object. The two fundamental requirements for inference are, therefore, awareness of *paksadharmatâ,* the inferential mark's qualifying the locus of the inference, and *vyâpti,* the sign's invariable concomitance with the target property or probandum. A paradigmatic act of inference to oneself is: "There is fire on that mountain, since there is smoke on it," which is supported by the awareness that fire is invariably concomitant with smoke. Naiyâyikas examine and standardize the conditions under which invariable concomitance (*vyâpti*) between a probans and a target fact is established.

Third, as logic's function is to generate veridical cognition, Nyâya does not stress the distinction between soundness and validity in respect to the quality of an argument. Both formal fallacies and the inclusion of false premises lead to *hetv-âbhâsa* ("pseudo provers" or logical defeaters), since they engender false cognition.

ii. The Structure of Inference

Concerning inference for polemical or didactic purposes, Nyâya employs a formal five-step argument illustrated by the following stock example.

1. There is fire on the hill (the *pratijñâ,* thesis).
2. Because there is smoke on the hill (the *hetu,* reason or probans).
3. Wherever there is smoke, there is fire; like a kitchen hearth and unlike a lake (the *udâharana,* illustration of concomitance).

4. This hill is likewise smoky (the *upanaya*, application of the rule).
5. Thus, there is fire on the hill (the *nigamana*, conclusion).

In practice, the five-membered "syllogism" is often truncated into three steps as follows.

A is qualified by S, because it is qualified by T.(Whatever is qualified by T is qualified by S) like (Tb & Sb)

Again the stock example:

The hill is qualified by fieriness because it is qualified by smokiness (Whatever is qualified by smokiness is qualified by fieriness) like a kitchen hearth and unlike a lake.

The basic components of the argument are:

The inferential subject (*paksa*), the locus of the inferential sign; *the hill* in our example. The general conditions for something to be taken up as a subject for inference, are that it be under dispute or currently unknown, with no reports from other knowledge sources available to definitively settle the issue.

The "prover" or inferential sign (*hetu*); *smoke* (more precisely, *smokiness*)

The probandum (*sâdhya*), the property to be proved by the inference; *fire* (more precisely, *fieriness*)

The "pervasion" or concomitance (*vyâpti*) that grounds the inference, which is implicit in the step: *"wherever there is smoke, there is fire"*

A corroborative instance (*sapaksa*); a locus known to be qualified by both the prover (*hetu*) and the probandum (*sâdhya*); this is a token of inductive support for the *vyâpti*; *a kitchen hearth*. There are also known negative examples, (*vipaksa*) of something that lacks both the prover property and the probandum; *where there is no fire, there is no smoke, like a lake*. Obviously, an instantiation of the prover property in the *vipaksa* class vitiates the argument.

This stock inference asserts that there is fire on the mountain (the mountain is qualified by the property of fieriness, Fm). Why? Because the mountain is qualified by the property of smokiness, Sm. There is an implied concomitance which grounds the inference: "Whatever is qualified by smokiness is qualified by fieriness," "x(Sx–>Fx). In the language of Nyâya, fire "pervades" smoke. This is an epistemic pervasion: we never find smoke instances without fire instances. As such, smoke is a *prover* property that allows us to infer the presence of fire. Finally, an example must be included in the syllogism to illustrate the inductive grounding which undergirds the invariable concomitance. In kitchen hearth k, fire is known to be concomitant with smoke, (Sk&Fk). In some instances, negative examples are used to indicate the *vyâpti* through contraposition. Wherever there is no fire there is no smoke, as illustrated in a lake, (~Fl& ~Sl).

Nyâya-sûtra 1.1.25 defines an example (*drstânta)* as "something about which experts and laypersons have the same opinion (*buddhi-sâmyam*)." Vâtsyâyana (NB Intro.; translation in Gangopadhyaya 1982: 5) elaborates:

Corroborative instance is an object of perception—an object about which the notions (*buddhi*) of the layman as well as the expert are not in conflict... It is also the basis of the application of *nyâya* (reasoning). By (showing) the contradiction of the *drstânta* the position of the opponent can be declared as refuted. By the substantiation of the *drstânta,* one's own position is well-established. If the skeptic (*nâstika*) admits a corroborative instance, he has to surrender his skepticism. If he does not admit any, how can he silence his opponent?

Regarding agreement between laypersons and experts, the basic idea, of course, is that supporting examples should be non-controversial. A good illustration of this is found in Uddyotakara's *Nyâya-vârttika* (2.1.16). Debating with a Buddhist interlocutor over the existence of property-bearing substances, he claims "there is no example whatever (*na hi kasciddrstântah*)... about which both parties agree (*ubhaya-paksa-sampratipannah*)."

In another interpretation of the three kinds of inference in the *sûtra,* Uddyotakara introduces three kinds of argument: wholly-positive, wholly-negative, and positive-negative. Wholly-positive inference occurs when there are attested cases of *sapaksa* but no *vipaksa* known. From a Buddhist perspective, the inference "whatever exists is momentary, like a cloud" would require this kind of inference, since there would be no available *vipaksa* to illustrate the non-presence of the prover. In cases where the property to be proven is entirely subsumed within the *paksa*, a wholly-negative form is employed. The *vyâpti* is contraposed, as in the following inference: "A living body has a self because it breathes. Whatever does not have a self does not breathe, like a pot." Most inferences are in principle amenable to the positive-negative form, like "There is fire on that hill, since there is billowing smoke over it. Wherever there is smoke, there is fire, like a kitchen hearth, and unlike a lake."

iii. Inferential Defeaters or Fallacies

Naiyâyikas provide various typologies of inferential fallacies and defeaters (*hetv-âbâsa*, "pseudo provers"). We may note five common kinds: (i) fallacies of *deviation* occur when the prover or inferential sign is not reliably correlated with the inferential target. To argue that "my mother must be visiting, since there is a Mazda parked outside" would involve the fallacy of deviation, since "Owning a Mazda" is a property that tracks not only my mother but many other drivers. It cannot, therefore, reliably indicate her presence. (ii) fallacies of *contradiction* occur when the prover in fact establishes a conclusion opposed to the thesis that someone defends. This would occur should someone argue that "Jones was not a kind man, since he gave his life for others," as giving one's life for others is an indicator of kindness or compassion. (iii) fallacies of *unestablishment* occur when a supposed prover is not actually the property of the inferential subject. Should someone argue "I know that your mother is in town, since I saw a Prius parked outside your home," the prover is *unestablished*, since my mother does not in fact own a Prius. (iv) argumentsare *rebutted*, when their conclusions are undermined by information gleaned by more secure knowledge sources. Someone may argue that my friend must be out of town, since he hasn't answered his phone all week. But if I just saw the friend in question at the local coffee shop, my perceptual knowledge *rebuts* his prover, invalidating it. Similarly, (v) arguments are *counterbalanced* when counterarguments of equal or greater force are put forth in support of an opposing conclusion. Disputant *a* argues that the inherent teleology of biological processes proves the existence of God. Disputant *b* argues that the existence of gratuitous evil proves that there is no God. Pending further philosophical work, argument *b*neutralizes the conclusion of argument *a*.

iv. Suppositional Reasoning

Tarka, suppositional or dialectical reasoning, is crucial to Nyâya's philosophical program. Still, according to Vâtsyâyana, it is not a full-fledged independent *pramâna*. Rather it is an "assistant to the *pramânas*" (*pramâna-anugrahaka*) (NB Introduction). *Tarka* is commonly employed as a form of *reductio* argument for the sake of judging competing claims or arguments, a *reductio* which depends not only on logical inconsistency, but on incoherence with deeply-held beliefs or norms. In the face of competing claims *x*and *y* about subject *s*, *tarka*is employed to show that *x* violates such norms, thereby shifting the presumptive weight to alternative *y*. Vâtsyâyana (NB1.1.40) offers the example of competing claims about the nature of the self. Some say that the self is a product which comes to exist within time while others claim that it is unproduced and eternal. The Naiyâyika deploys *tarka*by arguing that a consequence of the former view is that one's initial life circumstances would not be determined by his karmic inheritance from previous lives, a severe violation of fundamental metaphysical positions held by almost every Indian school. As such, strong presumptive weight should be given to the latter view. This example illustrates the way in which considerations of negative coherence govern *tarka's* deployment.

Vâtsyâyana notes that the reason *tarka*is not an independent *pramâna* is that it does not independently establish the nature of the thing in question (*anavadhâranât*). It provides consent (*anujânâti*) for one of two alternatives independently supported by apparent *pramânas*, by illustrating problems with the competing view. Uddyotakara (NV 1.1.1) adds that it is excluded from the ranks of *pramâna* because it does not provide definitive cognition (*pramânàmparicchedakamnatarkah*).

Later Naiyâyikas extol *tarka* as a means to test dubious inferential concomitances (*vyâpti*) by testing them against more fundamental holdings of various sorts. *Tarka* also has a crucial role in the management of philosophical doubt. Against the skeptic, Nyâya argues that doubt is not always reasonable. *Tarka* helps to distinguish legitimate doubt from mere contentiousness by illustrating which claims are better motivated and hence deserving of presumptive weight.

c. Analogical Reasoning (*upamâna*)

Nyâya-sûtra1.1.6 defines analogyas follows.

Analogy makes an object known by similarity with something already known.

Naiyâyikas commonly frame analogy as a means of vocabulary acquisition, and it has a severely restricted scope compared with the other *pramânas*. The standard example involves a person who is told that a water buffalo looks something like a cow and that such buffalo are present in a certain place in the countryside. Later, when out in the countryside, he recognizes that the thing he is seeing is similar to a cow, and therefore is a water buffalo. The cognition "That thing is a water buffalo," born of the recollection of testimony regarding its similarity with a cow and the perception of such common features, is paradigmatically analogical. Though most of the other schools either reduce analogy to a more fundamental *pramâna* or conceive of it in very different terms (Mîmâmsâ conceives of it as the capacity by which we apprehend similarity itself), Nyâya contends that the cognition in question is *sui generis* analogical, though it incorporates information from other *pramânas*.

d. Testimony (*sabda*)

NS1.1.5 defines testimony as follows.

Testimony is the assertion of a qualified speaker.

The semantic range of *âpta* ("authority," "credible person") includes expertise, trustworthiness, and reliability. Vâtsyâyana claims that an *âpta* possesses direct knowledge of something, and a willingness to convey such knowledge without distortion (NB 1.1.7). It is clear, though, that Nyâya does not require any kind of special expertise from such a speaker in normal situations. Nor does a hearer need positive evidence of trustworthiness. Mere absence of doubt in the asserter's ability to speak authoritatively about the issue at hand is enough. Testimony is thus thought of as a transmission of information or content. A person attains an accurate cognition through some *pramâna* token. In a properly functioning testimonial exchange, she bestows the information apprehended by the initial cognition to an epistemically responsible hearer. On such grounds, Uddyotakara notes that testimonial utterances may be divided into those whose contents are originally generated by perception or by inference. Jayanta likewise claims that the veridicality or non-veridicality of a testimonial cognition is dependent on the speaker's knowledge of the content of her statement and her honesty in relating it. Vâtsyâyana (NB 2.1.69) illustrates a levelheaded frankness about testimony's importance, noting that "in accord with knowledge gained by testimony, people undertake their common affairs." Uddyotakarasimilarly recognizes that testimony has the widest range of any source of knowledge, far outstripping what one may know from personal perception, inference or analogy.

e. Non-pramâna Epistemic Capacities

From the sûtra period, Nyâya recognizes a number of epistemic capacities which are nevertheless considered non-*pramâna* (NS 2.2.1-12). They are not considered independent *pramânas* for one of two reasons: (i) they are reducible to subspecies of other *pramânas*, or (ii) they do not produce the specific kind of cognitions which a *pramâna* must deliver. A core locus of debate amongst classical Indian thinkers is the nature and number of *pramânas*. Nyâya contends that the above four are the only irreducible sources of knowledge, which subsume all other kinds.

f. General Theory of Knowledge

i. A Causal Theory of Knowledge

Naiyâyikas speak of cognitive success in causal terms. "*pramâna*" normally refers to a means or process by which veridical awareness-episodes (*pramâ*) are generated, as seen above. Vâtsyâyana glosses the meaning of *pramânaas* "that by which something is properly cognized (*pramîtyateanena*)" (NB1.1.3).

Uddyotakara concurs: "what is spoken of as a *pramâna*? A *pramâna* is the cause of a [veridical] cognition" (*upalabdhi-hetupramânam*) (NV1.1.1). Moreover, despite its focus on reflective consideration of belief and valid cognition, Nyâya argues that the simple, unreflective functioning of a *pramâna* like perception or testimony is enough to generate knowledge in the absence of countervailing evidence.

ii. Internalist Constraints

Nyâya does maintain an internalist constraint: Once doubt arises—by adversarial challenge, peer disagreement, inconsistency between different cognitions, and so forth —a cognition must be validated in order to maintain the status of being "*pramâna*-produced." Doubt triggers a second-order concern with reflective inquiry and certification. The sûtras state that "Where there is doubt, there must be ongoing examination" (NS 2.1.7). Uddyotakara therefore claims that doubt is an essential component of investigation (*vicâra-anga*) (NV 1.1.23). Validation involves consciously reflecting on the etiology of a cognition to ensure that it is the product of a properly-functioning *pramâna*. It may also involve the deployment of other *pramânas* in the hopes for a convergence of knowledge-sources (*pramâna-samplava*) in support of the doubted cognition. In his opening comments on the Nyâya-sûtra, Vâtsyâyana famously provides a pragmatic test (but not definition) of truth: cognitions which guide us to successful action are likely veridical.

iii. A Relational Theory of Cognition

Nyâya epistemologists speak of cognition (*jñâna, buddhi, upalabdhi, pratyaya*): generally immediate awareness states of what Nyâya understands to be a mind-independent external reality. In the case of apperception, one cognizesher own mental states. Ontologically, cognitions are considered properties (*gunas*) of individual selves (*âtmans*). Memory dispositions, when triggered, generate cognition about the past. With a few exceptions, cognitions target things other than themselves.

For Nyâya, cognitions target their objects by means of a relation called "objecthood" (*vicayatâ*). Nyâya's theory is thus not exactly representational, but relational. "Objecthood" minimally has a threefold structure (with the possibility of iteration) corresponding to three features of the external object in question: a portion of the cognition targets an object itself, a portion of the cognition targets a property of the object, and finally, a portion of the cognition targets the relationship between the object and its property. In cases of veridical cognition (*pramâ*), the portion of cognition which targets a substantive and the portion which targets its property match up. Gangesa famously defines veridical cognition as "a cognitive state with predication content *x* about something in fact qualified by *x*" (*Tattvacintâmani, pramâ-laksana-vâda*). Seeing a male human being as qualified by "man" would be a paradigm case of veridical cognition. Error is generally classified as a misfire of the property-scoping portion of cognition. In error, a substantive is indeed cognized, but the property which is targeted does not actually qualify the substantive in question. The cognition's intentionality is bifurcated, so to speak, simultaneously scoping a substantive and a property which is in fact alien to it.

iv. Response to Skepticism

Nyâya is a staunchly anti-skeptical tradition of epistemology. While it does give an important role to doubt, which, as seen above, triggers reflection and philosophical review, it rejects the notion that doubt should be the starting place in philosophical reflection. Doubt itself should be motivated, as trust is a better default starting place in both ordinary life and philosophy. Pragmatically, Nyâya argues that the role of epistemology is to better hone our cognitive abilities in order to succeed in our life aims. But unrestricted doubt would undermine our ability to function on a basic level, and it therefore militates against the very point of epistemological inquiry. Theoretically, Nyâya argues that error and indeed doubt itself are conceptually parasitical on true cognition. Error and doubt only make sense against a background of true belief, and therefore reflection must start by taking putatively veridical cognition at face value. Allied to this is a strain of criticism that even the simple act of giving voice to skeptical arguments belays a philosopher's dependence on knowledge sources, including the inductively-supported tie between words and their meanings, which a skeptic relies on to speak his case. Given that everyone, the skeptic included, relies on *pramânas,* they are to be given the lion's share of default entitlement.

2. METAPHYSICS

Nyâya defends a realist and pluralist metaphysics of categories (*padârthas,* lit. "things denoted by words"), largely adapted, with some modifications, from its sister school Vaisesika. The categories are substance, quality, action, universal, individuator, inherence and absence. They will be discussed individually below.

a. Substance (*dravya*), Including Self (*âtman*)

Substances are the bedrock of Nyâya/Vaisesika metaphysics (hereafter, simply "Nyâya Metaphysics"), as other categories generally inhere within substances or are nested within properties that inhere within substances. Paradigmatic substances include the indestructible atoms of earth, water, air and fire; composite substances like pots and trees; inner "selves" (*âtman*) which are the eternal, reincarnating souls; and God, a unique *âtman.*

Naiyâyikas provide a number of arguments in support of a non-material self. A standard argument runs as follows: Things like desire, cognition, experiences of pleasure and pain and volition are qualities. All qualities inhere in substances. Therefore, there is a substance to which desire and the rest belong. This conclusion is then followed by an argument from elimination. None of the material elements like earth or water are the bearers of desire and the rest. Therefore, there must be a special, non-material substance, namely a self (see various commentaries on NS 1.1.10). This argument is bolstered by others meant to illustrate that the physical body, as a product of material elements cannot be the fundamental locus of conscious states.

Some of the richest debates in classical India take place between Nyâya and Buddhists over the reality of substances. The central concern of such debates is often the status of individual selves—an important substance, to say the least. Famously, the Buddha declared that reality is "lacking a self" (*anâtman*), and his followers develop a number of arguments which purport to illustrate this in two ways. (i) Diachronically: moment by moment, things are destroyed and new things arise, such that no substance (including selves) endures for longer than a moment. (ii) Synchronically: in a single moment, what we take to be wholes (including selves) are nothing more than heaps of micro-properties (illustrated by the famous chariot metaphor in *The Questions of King Milinda.*) The Buddhist position is that although there is no such thing as an enduring self, the need for moral continuity and other desiderata may be satisfied merely by the causal connections between events in a single causal stream which we refer to as a "person."

Nyâya's response is to defend the existence of substances generally and selves in particular. In defence of substances, it argues that composite substances have capacities beyond the mere collection of their parts (NS 2.1.35). Moreover, Nyâya argues that the Buddhist reduction, if carried out consistently, would lead to an absurdity. We can see composite substances, but we cannot seeentities like atoms, which exist below our perceptual threshold. But if substances are nothing but heaps of micro objects/properties, which themselves can be reduced, and so on, then we should not be able to perceive substances at all. Thus, there must be a unified identity for individual substances which undergirds their availability for perceptual experience (NS 2.1.36).

In defence of the diachronic existence of individual selves, Nyâya argues that our experience of recollection ("that is the very man I saw a week ago") requires a locus of memory which spans the time between the initial experience and the re-experience of an object (NS 1.1.10 and allied commentaries). In this spirit, Uddyotakara, following Vâtsyâyana, argues that if I am now a different self than the "me" of yesterday, I should not be able to recollect things which that "me" experienced, since one self is unable to recollect the content of another's experience. In defence of the synchronic identity of selves, Nyâya argues that cross-modal recognition ("that thing I see is the same thing I am touching") requires a single experiencer with the ability to synthesize data from various senses (NS 3.1.1-3). Early Nyâya's arguments for the self find their apex in Udayana's monograph *Determining the Truth of the Self.*

b. Quality

Qualities (*guna*), are property tropes which qualify substances. Unlike universals they are not repeatable. The red colour of some particular fire hydrant is a quality. Like other instances of the colour *red* it is inhered by the universal *redness*, but it is as particular as the hydrant which it qualifies. Qualities include colour, number (which is thought to inhere in objects), spatial location, contact, disjunction, and so forth, along with qualities which are unique to selves, like desire, cognition, and karmic merit.

c. Action

Like qualities, actions (*karma*) inhere in substances and are non-repeatable tropes. But they have causal capacities which qualities lack, particularly the ability to engender conjunction and disjunction between substances.

d. Universal

Universals (*sâmânya* or *jâti*) inhere in substances (for example*pot-hood*), qualities (*redness*) or motions (*contraction-hood*). Naiyâyikas argue that universals are required to account for common experiences of a recurring character, for the functioning of language, and to undergird causal regularities in nature (which are held to be relations between universals). As its theory of universals is developed, Nyâya recognizes entities which are like universals, but which are, for theoretical reasons, excluded from their ranks (*upâdhi*). Udayana would famously chart the reasons for such exclusion. These are: (i) A true universal must be capable of more than one instance. *Spacehood* would not be a true universal, as it can only have one instance. (ii) Two universals which have the same exact instances are in fact the same universal, simply under two designations. (iii) Should two apparent universals share an instance, while one is not entirely subsumed within the other, both are mere *upâdhis*. This criterion, which is the most controversial of the "universal-blockers," suggests that the operative notion of universal here is something akin to natural kinds. (iv) Any supposed universal that would, if accepted, lead to an infinite regress (for example*universal-hood*), is not accepted. (v) There is no universal for individuators (see below), as their ontic function is to introduce primitive differentiation. (vi) There is no universal for inherence (see below), as this would engender a vicious infinite regress: inherence would require further inherence between it and its universal "inherencehood", and so on.

e. Inherence

Inherence is a relation which is central to Nyâya's ontology, by which qualities, actions, universals, and individuators relate to substances, by which universals relate to qualities and actions, and by which wholes relate to their parts. In the first instance, the brown colour of a cow inheres in the cow. In the second, the universal brownness inheres in the quality trope brown. In the third, my car, a substance, is a single entity, which inheres in its various parts. Thus, your touching just one part of my car is enough to justify the claim "you touched my car" *simpliciter*. Nyâya contends that inherence is a self-linking property. It does not rely on other instances of inherence in order to "glue" it to the two elements which it relates. Thus it seeks to rebut regress arguments of the type advanced by recently by F. H. Bradley and by the classical Vedântin Sankarâcârya (c. 9th century C.E.) in classical India.

f. Individuator

Individuators are the finest-grained causes of ontological distinction. They are the means by which individual atoms within the basic kinds "earth", "water", and so forth, and by which individual selves are ultimately particularized. Individuators for Nyâya's ontology may be conceived as roughly analogous to haecceities within Western philosophical discourse.

g. Absence

The ontological reality of absence, however attenuated, isaccepted by Nyâya in order to account for both linguistic practice involving negation and cognitive states which correctly ascertain non-existence of some kind. Vâtsyâyana argues that the positive knowledge produced by a knowledge sourcegives immediate rise to knowledge of an absence insofar as one can reflect that if something was not made manifest at the time of the initial cognition (and provided that the thing in question is ordinarily cognizable), it was absent. Uddyotakara famously argues that negation is often perceptible: looking at my desk, I see the absence of a coffee mug, and such absence is "located" on the surface my desk. In this spirit, absence is generally thought of as a qualifier (*visesana*) of some object or property, which is the qualificand (*viœecya*). The four basic kinds of absences accepted by Nyâya in its mature period are prior absence (of something before it is created), absence-by-destruction (of an object after it is destroyed), absolute absence (of something for some locus where it could never exist), and mutual absence (between two separately existing objects).

h. Causation

Naiyâyikas speak of a cause or causal condition as something which is necessarily antecedent to aspecific kind of effect without being "causally irrelevant". Such causes are threefold. The (i) inherence cause, akin to a material cause, is the substratum out of which (or within which) an effect is made (the threads which together make up a cloth). The (ii) non-inherence cause includes properties of the inherence cause which influence the properties of the effect (the property of contact which inheres within the threads which make up a cloth). Finally, (iii), the instrumental/agential cause(s). This third category is a kind of catch-all which includes everything aside from the substratum and its properties. Central in this category are agents, their activities, and instruments used by then to produce effects. Out of the nexuṣ of causal conditions which come together in the production of an effect, Naiyâyikas tend to speak of a most important factor as the trigger cause (for example the striking of a match against a rough surface which produces a lit match).

In order to weed out unnecessary or unimportant factors from the causal nexus which produces an effect, Nyâya includes the caveat that a proper cause must not be "causally irrelevant". Causal irrelevance occurs in various ways. For example, something *x* which universally precedes a certain effect *y*, but whose relationship with the effect is mediated by some other factor *z* upon which it subsists is causally irrelevant. For example, a certain artist may create a unique kind of sculpture, and she is thus identified as a causal factor in its production. She may have certain properties (hair colour, eye colour, height) which also, by means of their subsisting in her, invariably precede the production of her sculptures. But since their participation in the causal event is derivative, they are deemed causally irrelevant and unworthy of being specified as causes.

3. PHILOSOPHY OF RELIGION

Nyâya expressly conceives of itself as a rational defender of classical Hindu religious and theistic culture. *Nyâya-sûtra* begins by claiming that ascertainment of the ultimate good (*nihsreya*) requires correct apprehension of reality, which gives rise to a sustained epistemological/metaphysical investigation of the kind the sûtras provide. Vâtsyâyanaargues that as a discipline of inquiry, Nyâya is the support of all practices of legitimate *dharma*. Jayanta claims that amongst the various research programs in the umbrella of classical Vedic culture, Nyâya is of chief importance, since it aims to defend Vedic tradition and its manifold subdivisions of study from the attacks of rival, anti-Vedic philosophers. Though the Nyâya-sûtra overwhelmingly focuses on theoretical issues and not praxis, it nonetheless recommends that students of Nyâya engage in yogic practice (4.2.42) and defends the possibility of enlightenment (4.2.44-5).

From fairly early in its history, Nyâya specifically takes it upon itself to defend the existence of God (*Îsvara*). Nyâya primarily employs versions of the design inference. Paradigmatic arguments include:

Primordial matter, atoms and *karma* function when guided by a conscious agent because they are insentient (*acetanatvât*) like an axe. As axes, due to insentience, operate only when directed by a sentient agent, so too do things like primordial nature, atoms and *karma*. Therefore, they too are directed by a cause possessed of intelligence. (Uddyotakara, NV 4.1.21)

Things like the earth have a maker as their cause, because they are products (*kâryatvât*). (Udayana *Nyâyakusumâñjali*, Fifth Chapter)

With various formulations like the above, and extensive supporting arguments, Nyâya defends a version of the argument from design. Buddhist, Mîmâmsâ (and later, Jain) philosophers respond by charging Nyâya with violations of inferential boundaries: only by extrapolating far beyond the correlation between ordinary products and makers is Nyâya able to argue for a unique God-like maker of the world.

A standard response, as seen in Vâcaspati (NVT 4.1.21) is that even in straightforward general-to-particular inductive reasoning, we employ some degree of inference to the best explanation. This allows enough flexibility to infer new kinds of entities while appealing to correlations generated from ordinary experience.

REFERENCES :

a. Sanskrit Source Materials

1.JayantaBhamma. *Nyâya-mañjarî.* Critically Edited by Vidvan, K. S. Varadacarya.Vol 1. Mysore: Oriental Research Institute 1969.

2.JayantaBhamma. *Nyâya-mañjarî.* Critically Edited by Vidvan, K. S. Varadacarya.Vol 2. Mysore: Oriental Research Institute 1983.

3.Nyâya-Tarkatirtha, Taranatha and Amarendramohan Tarkatirtha, eds. *Nyâyadarúanam: with Vâtsyâyana'sBhâsya* [cited as NB above], *Uddyotakara's Vârttika*[cited as NV], *Vâcaspati Misra's Tâtparyamîkâ* [cited as NVT] & *Viúvanâtha's Vrtti.* Calcutta: Munshiram Manoharlal 2003.

4.Udayana. *Nyâyavârttikatâtpâryaúuddhi of Udayanâcârya.* Edited by Anantalal Thakur. New Delhi: Indian Council of Philosophical Research.

b. Primary Texts in English Translation

1.Gangopadhyaya, Mrinalkanti, trans. *Nyâya: Gautama's Nyâya-sûtra with Vâtsyâyana's Commentary.*Calcutta: Indian Studies 1982.

2.Iyer, S. R., Editor and Translator, *Tarkabhâcâ* of Keœava Miœra. Varanasi: Chaukhambha Orientalia, 1979.

3.JayantaBhamma. *Nyâya-mañjarî.* Translated by Janaki Vallabha Bhattacaryya. Vol. 1. Delhi: Motilal Banarsidass 1978.

4.Jha, Sir Ganganatha, trans. *The Nyâya-sûtras of Gautama.*Vols 1-4. Delhi: Motilal Banarsidass 1999.

5.Phillips, Stephen and N. S. Ramanuja Tatacharya. *Epistemology of Perception: GaEgeœa's*TattvacintâmaGi *Jewel of Reflection on the Truth (About Epistemology), The Perception Chapter*(pratyakca-khaGa). New York: American Institute of Buddhist Studies 2004. [This also contains the Sanskrit text.]

6.Potter, Karl H., ed. *Encyclopedia of Indian Philosophies.*Vol. 2. *Nyâya-Vaisesika.* Delhi: Motilal Banarsidass 1977. [This volume contains summary translations and helpful historical and conceptual introductions to early Nyâya and its individual philosophers.]

7.Udayana. *Âtmatattvaviveka.* Translation and commentary by N. S. Dravid. Shimla: Indian Institute of Advanced Study 1995. [This also contains the Sanskrit text.]

8.Udayana. *Nyâyakusumâñjali.* Translation and commentary by N. S. Dravid. New Delhi: Indian Council of Philosophical Research 1996. [This also contains the Sanskrit text.]

C. Studies of Nyâya Epistemology, Metaphysics, and Philosophy of Religion in English

1.Bhattacaryya, Gopikamohan. *Studies in Nyâya-Vaisesika Theism.* Calcutta: Sanskrit College 1961.

2.Chakrabarti, Kisor Kumar. *Classical Indian Philosophy of Mind: The Nyâya Dualist Tradition.* Albany: State University of New York Press 1999.

3.Chemparathy, George. *An Indian Rational Theology: Introduction to Udayana's Nyâyakusumâñjali.*Publications of the De Nobili Research Library, Vol. 1. Vienna: Gerold& Co.; Delhi: Motilal Banarsidass 1972.

4.Ghokale, Pradeep P. *Inference and Fallacies Discussed in Ancient Indian Logic (with special reference to Nyâya and Buddhism).* Bibliotheca Indo-Buddhica Series, Sunil Gupta, ed.Delhi: Sri Satguru Publications 1992.

5.Halbfass, Wilhelm. *On Being and What There Is: Classical Vaisesika and the History of Indian Ontology.* Albany: State University of New York Press 1992. [*Though this text focuses on Vaisesika, it is relevant given the great overlap between Nyâya and Vaisesika in metaphysical theory.*]

6.Matilal, B. K. *Perception.* Oxford: Clarendon Press: Oxford 1986.

7.Matilal, B. K. *The Character of Logic in India.* Albany: SUNY Press 1998.

d. General Studies

1. Ganeri, Jonardon. *Philosophy in Classical India: The Proper Work of Reason.* London and New York: Routledge 2001.

2. Matilal, B. K. *Nyâya-Vaisesika.* A History of Indian Literature, Vol. 6, Fasc. 2. Edited by Jan Gonda. Weisbaden: Otto Harrassowitz 1977.

3. Mohanty, J.N. *Classical Indian Philosophy.* Lanham: Rowman & Littlefield Publishers, Inc., 2000.

4. Phillips, Stephen. *Classical Indian Metaphysics: Refutations of Realism and the Emergence of "New Logic."* Chicago: Open Court 1995.

8

Vaisheshika Philosophy

Kanada, a learned sage, founded this system. This system is believed to be as old as Jainism and Buddhism. Kanada presented his detailed atomic theory in Vaisheshika-Sutra. Basically, Vaisheshika is a pluralistic realism. It explains the nature of the world with seven categories:

Dravya (substance), guna (quality), karma (action), samanya (universal), vishesha (particular), amavaya (inherence) and abhava (non-existence).

Vaisheshika contends that every effect is a fresh creation or a new beginning. Thus this system refutes the theory of pre-existence of the effect in the cause. Kanada does not discuss much on God. But the later commentators refer to God as the Supreme Soul, perfect and eternal. This system accepts that God (Ishvara) is the efficient cause of the world. The eternal atoms are the material cause of the world.

Vaisheshika recognizes nine ultimate substances : Five material and four non-material substances.

The five material substances are: Earth, water, fire, air and akasha.

The four non-material substances are: space, time, soul and mind.

Earth, water, fire and air are atomic but akasha is non-atomic and infinite.

Space and time are infinite and eternal. The concept of soul is comparable to that of the self or atman. This system considers consciousnessas an accidental property. In other words, when the soul associates itself to the body, only then it 'acquires' consciousness. Thus, consciousness is not considered an essential quality of the soul.

The mind (manas) is accepted as atomic but indivisible and eternal substance. The mind helps to establish the contact of the self to the external world objects.

The soul develops attachment to the body owing to ignorance. The soul identifies itself with the body and mind. The soul is trapped in the bondage of karma, as a consequence of actions resulted from countless desires and passions. It can be free from the bondage only if it becomes free from actions. Liberation follows the cessation of the actions.

9

Purva Mimamsa

The first major orthodox philosophical system to develop was Purva Mimamsa. The other one to follow was the Uttar Mimamsa. The orthodox systems accept the authority of the Vedas.

The Sanskrit word '*mimamsa* means a 'revered thought'. The word is originated from the root 'man' which refers to 'thinking' or 'investigating'. The word '*mimamsa*' suggests "probing and acquiring knowledge" or "critical review and investigation of the Vedas".

Each of the Vedas is considered to be composed of four parts: The *Samhitas,* the *Brahmanas,* the *Aranyakas* and the Upanishads. The first two parts are generally focused on the rituals and they form the *Karma-kanda* portion of the Vedas. The later two parts form the *Jnana-kanda*(concerned with knowledge) portion of the Vedas.

Purva-Mimamsa is based on the earlier (*Purva* = earlier) parts of the Vedas.

Uttar-Mimamsa is based on the later (*Uttar* = later) parts of the Vedas.

Purva-Mimamsa is also known as *Karma Mimamsa* since it deals with the *Karmic* actions of rituals and sacrifices. Uttar-Mimamsa is also known as *Brahman Mimamsa* since it is concerned with the knowledge of Reality. In popular terms, Purva-Mimamsa is known simply as Mimamsa and Uttar-Mimamsa as Vedanta.

Jaimini is credited as the chief proponent of the Mimamsa system. His glorious work is Mimamsa-Sutra written around the end of the 2nd century A.D. Mimamsa-Sutra is the largest of all the philosophical *Sutras*. Divided into 12 chapters, it is a collection of nearly 2500 aphorisms which are extremely difficult to comprehend.

Earlier scholars wrote commentaries on Mimamsa-Sutra. Unfortunately they are lost with the passage of time. The earliest available commentary is Sabarasvamin's Sabara-bhasya, which is still the authoritative basis of all subsequent works on Mimamsa. Renowned scholars Kumarila Bhatta and Prabhakara independently wrote their commentaries on Sabara-bhasya. Prabhakara was a student of Kumarila Bhatta. However, they differed, to some degree, on the interpretation of Sabara-bhasya and wrote separate commentaries. (Mandan Mishra, the erudite scholar, was a follower of Kumarila Bhatta. He also wrote a commentary, but at a later stage he changed his thinking and became a disciple of Shamkaracharya.)

This system out rightly accept the Vedas as the eternal source of 'revealed truth.' Thus though it differs from the earlier four philosophical systems (Vaisheshika, Nyaya, Samkhya, Yoga which neither accept nor reject the authority of the Vedas), a great chunk ofMimamsa philosophy is derived from the Vaisheshika-Nyaya duo.

Mimamsa system attaches a lot of importance to the Verbal testimony which is essentially the Vedic testimony. Jaimini accepts the 'Word" or the '*Shabda*' as the only means of knowledge. The 'word' or the '*Shabda*' is necessarily the Vedic word, according to Jaimini. This system strongly contends that the Vedas are not authored by an individual. Since they are 'self-revealed' or '*apaurusheya*', they manifest their own validity.

The system is a pluralistic realist. It endorses the reality of the world as well as that of the individual souls. The soul is accepted as an eternal and infinite substance. Consciousness is an accidental attribute of the soul. The soul is distinct from the body, the senses and the mind. Though Kumarila Bhatta and Prabhakara differ on issues like the self, the soul and it attribute. The earlier *mimamsakas* do not give much importance to the deities. Hence they do not endorse God as the creator of the universe. But later *mimamsakas* show a bent towards theism.

This system has a profound faith in the Vedas. The system supports the law of *karma*. It believes in the Unseen Power or '*apurva*'. Apart from accepting the heaven and the hell, the system supports the theory of liberation.

10

Uttar Mimamsa

Uttar Mimamsa is the Vedanta, one of the most significant of all Indian philosophies. As compared to other systems, its advent and growth is recent. Still it is the most influential orthodox philosophical systems of India.

The Vedas are the most valuable scriptures of the mankind. They present the most exalted form of superhuman knowledge and wisdom. The Vedas are eternal. They are timeless since they might have taken ages to acquire the written form.

The four Vedasare: Rig Veda, Yajur Veda, Sama Veda and Atharva Veda. Each of the Vedas is divided into four parts : The *Samhitas*, the*Brahmanas*, the *Aranyakas* and the Upanishads. The Upanishads are the concluding parts of the Vedas. They expound the supreme philosophical knowledge. The word 'Vedanta' usually refers to the Upanishads. The word is a compound of '*Veda*' and '*Anta*'. It means the ending portion of the Vedas. However, the word 'Vedanta', in a broad sense, covers not only the Upanishads but all the commentaries and interpretations associated with the Upanishads. All these works constitute the Vedanta philosophy.

The great scholar Badarayana (?500-200 B.C) initiated the efforts to simplify the Upanishadic philosophy. Badarayana is also known as Ved Vyasa. He was the first scholar to take up the challenging task of systemizing the immensely vast philosophical doctrines of the Upanishads. The result of his efforts was one of the most illustrious works on Vedanta. Badarayana's work is known as Brahma-Sutra or Vedanta-Sutra. It is also referred to as Uttar-Mimamsa-Sutra. The Brahma-Sutra has 555 sutras. Most of them are aphoristic and almost unintelligible at first sight. Hence, a number of commentaries were written to interpret them. Among these the commentaries of Shamkaracharya, Ramnujacharya and Madhavacharya are regarded authentic and are held in very high view.

They are regarded as the greatest scholars of Indian philosophy. They are not only the principal commentators of Brahma-Sutra (Vedanta-Sutra) but are also its leading interpreters. Thus, we have three major schools of Vedanta based on the philosophy of the distinguished trio: *Advaita*(non-dualism) of Shamkaracharya, *Vishishtadvaita* (qualified non-dualism) of Ramnujacharya and *Dvaita*(dualism) of Madhvacharya.

All three schools are founded on the Vedanta philosophy. However, there have been differences among them. Even the followers of a particular system, within their own fold, differ to some degree on certain issues.

The Vedanta philosophy is focused on the *Jagat* (the universe), the *Jiva* (individual soul) and the Brahman (the Supreme Being). Brahman is the repository of all knowledge and power. *Jivas* are trapped in the Jagat. Attached to the physical world and driven by passions and desires, they remain chained to ceaseless actions (*karma*). As a result, they subject themselves to countless births in various forms. Their transmigration from this birth (life) to the next depends on the *karma* (the quality of action). *Moksha* or *mukti* (liberation) is the goal of life. This philosophy, in general, is accepted by all the three schools. Now let us understand the basic difference among the three schools.

Dvaita refers to 'two'. *Dvaita* school is based on the concept of dualism. Madhavacharya emphasizes the distinction between God and individual soul (*Jiva*). In addition, the school differentiates God from matter as well as the soul from matter. The school maintains that the God, *Jiva* and the *Jagat* are three separate and everlasting entities. God governs the world and has control over the souls. The souls in its ignorance remains shackled in the world. By devotion and God's mercy, the soul can migrate to the Heaven above. It can obtain *Mukti* from the cycle of life and death and live with God forever in the Heaven.

Vishishtadvaita literally means "qualified non-dualism". Ramanujacharya stresses that God alone exists. He says that Brahman is God. He is not formless. The Cosmos and the *Jivas* form his body. When the *Jiva* (soul) realises that he is a part of *Paramatman* (God), the soul is liberated. On liberation, his soul enjoys infinite consciousness and infinite bliss of God. The soul is in communion with God, but it does not share the power of the creation or destruction.

Advaita means "non-dualism". Brahman is the sole Supreme Reality. Brahman, *Jagat* and *Jiva* are not different, separate entities.

11

Advaita Vedanta Philosophy

Advaita Vedânta is one version of Vedânta. Vedânta is nominally a school of Indian philosophy, although in reality it is a label for any hermeneutics that attempts to provide a consistent interpretation of the philosophy of the Upanisads or, more formally, the canonical summary of the Upanisads, Bâdarâyana's Brahma Sûtra. Advaita is often translated as "non-dualism" though it literally means "non-secondness." Although Sankara is regarded as the promoter of Advaita Vedânta as a distinct school of Indian philosophy, the origins of this school predate Sankara. The existence of an Advaita tradition is acknowledged by Sankara in his commentaries. The names of Upancadic teachers such as Yajñavalkya, Uddalaka, and Bâdarâyana, the author of the Brahma Sûtra, could be considered as representing the thoughts of early Advaita. The essential philosophy of Advaita is an idealist monism, and is considered to be presented first in the Upanisads and consolidated in the Brahma Sûtra by this tradition. According to Advaita metaphysics, Brahman—the ultimate, transcendent and immanent God of the latter Vedas—appears as the world because of its creative energy (mâyâ). The world has no separate existence apart from Brahman. The experiencing self (jîva) and the transcendental self of the Universe (âtman) are in reality identical (both are Brahman), though the individual self seems different as space within a container seems different from space as such. These cardinal doctrines are represented in the anonymous verse "brahma satyam jagan mithya; jîvo brahmaiva na aparah" (Brahman is alone True, and this world of plurality is an error; the individual self is not different from Brahman). Plurality is experienced because of error in judgments (mithya) and ignorance (avidya). Knowledge of Brahman removes these errors and causes liberation from the cycle of transmigration and worldly bondage.

1. HISTORY OF ADVAITA VEDÂNTA

It is possible that an Advaita tradition existed in the early part of the first millennium C.E., as indicated by Sankara himself with his reference to tradition (*sampradâya*). But the only two names that could have some historical certainty are Gaudapâda and Govinda Bhagavadpâda, mentioned as Sankara's teacher's teacher and the latter Sankara's teacher. The first complete Advaitic work is considered to be the *Mandukya Kârikâ,* a commentary on the *Mandukya Upancad,* authored by Gaudapâda. Sankara, as many scholars believe, lived in the eight century. His life, travel, and works, as we understand from the*digvijaya* texts are almost of a superhuman quality. Though he lived only for 32 years, Sankara's accomplishments included travelling from the south to the north of India, writing commentaries for the ten *Upanisads,* the cryptic *Brahma Sûtra,* the *Bhagavad Gîtâ,* and authoring many other texts (though his authorship of only some is established), and founding four *pîtas,* or centers of (Advaitic) excellence, with his pupils in charge. Sankara is supposed to have had four (prominent) pupils: Padmapâda, Sureúvara, Hastamalaka and Tomaka. Padmapâda is said to be his earliest student. *Panchapadika,* by Padmapâda, is a lucid commentary on Sankara's commentary on the first verses of the *Brahma Sûtra*. Sureœvara is supposed to have written *Naickarmya Siddhi,* an independent treatise on *Advaita*. Mandana Misra (eight century), an earlier adherent of the rival school of Bhatta mîmâmsâ, is responsible for a version of Advaita which focuses on the doctrine of *sphota,* a semantic theory held by the Indian philosopher of language Bhartrhari. He also accepts to a greater extent the joint importance of knowledge and works as a means to liberation, when for Sankara knowledge is the one and only means. Mandana Miœra's *Brahmasiddhi* is a significant work, which also marks a distinct form of Advaita. Two major sub-schools of Advaita Vedânta arose after Sankara: *Bhamati* and *Vivarana*. The *Bhamati* School owes its name to Vacaspati Micera's (ninth century) commentary on Sankara's *Brahma Sûtra Bhâsya*, while the *Vivarana* School is named after Prakashatman's (tenth century) commentary on Padmapâda's *Pancapadika*, which itself is a commentary on Sankara's commentary on the *Brahma Sûtra*. The prominent names in the later Advaita tradition are Prakâsâtman (tenth century), Vimuktâtman (tenth century), Sarvajñâtman (tenth century), Srî Harca (twelfth century), Citsukha (twelfth century), ânandagiri (thirteenth century), Amalânandâ (thirteenth century), Vidyâranya (fourteenth century), Sankarânandâ (fourteenth century), Sadânandâ (fifteenth century), Prakâsânanda (sixteenth century), Nrsimhâsrama (sixteenth century), Madhusûdhana Sarasvati (seventeenth century), Dharmarâja Adṿarindra (seventeenth century), Appaya Dîksita (seventeenth century), Sadasiva Brahmendra (eighteenth century), Candrasekhara Bhârati (twentieth century), and Sacchidânandendra Saraswati (twentieth century). *Vivarana*, which is a commentary on Padmapâda's *Panchapadika*, written by Vacaspati Mshra is a landmark work in the tradition. The *Khandanakhandakhadya* of Srî Harca, *Tattvapradipika* of Citsukha, *Pañcadasi* of Vidyâranya, *Vedântasâra* of Sadânandâ, *Advaitasiddhi* of Madhusadana Sarasvati, and *Vedântaparibhasa*of Dharmarâja Advarindra are some of the landmark works representing later Advaita tradition..Throughout the eigteenth century and until the twenty-first century, there are many saints and philosophers whose tradition is rooted primarily or largely in Advaita philosophy. Prominent among the saints are Bhagavan Ramana Maharsi, Swami Vivekananda, Swami Tapovanam, Swami Chinmayânandâ, and Swami Bodhânandâ. Among the philosophers, KC Bhattacharya and TMP Mahadevan have contributed a great deal to the tradition.

2. METAPHYSICS AND PHILOSOPHY

The classical Advaita philosophy of Sankara recognizes a unity in multiplicity, identity between individual and pure consciousness, and the experienced world as having no existence apart from Brahman. The major metaphysical concepts in Advaita Vedânta tradition, such as *mâyâ*, *mithya* (error in judgment), vivarta (illusion/

whirlpool), have been subjected to a variety of interpretations. On some interpretations, Advaita Vedânta appears as a nihilistic philosophy that denounces the matters of the lived-world.

a. Brahman, *Jîva, îsvara,* and *Mâyâ*

For classical Advaita Vedânta, Brahman is the fundamental reality underlying all objects and experiences. Brahman is explained as pure existence, pure consciousness and pure bliss. All forms of existence presuppose a knowing self. Brahman or pure consciousness underlies the knowing self. Consciousness according to the Advaita School, unlike the positions held by other Vedânta schools, is not a property of Brahman but its very nature. Brahman is also one without a second, all-pervading and the immediate awareness. This absolute Brahman is known as *nirguna* Brahman, or Brahman "without qualities," but is usually simply called "Brahman." This Brahman is ever known to Itself and constitutes the reality in all individuals selves, while the appearance of our empirical individuality is credited to *avidya* (ignorance) and *mâyâ* (illusion). Brahman thus cannot be known as an individual object distinct from the individual self. However, it can be experienced indirectly in the natural world of experience as a personal God, known as *saguna* Brahman, or Brahman with qualities. It is usually referred to as *Îsvara* (the Lord). The appearance of plurality arises from a natural state of confusion or ignorance (*avidya*), inherent in most biological entities. Given this natural state of ignorance, Advaita provisionally accepts the empirical reality of individual selves, mental ideas and physical objects as a cognitive construction of this natural state of ignorance. But from the absolute standpoint, none of these have independent existence but are founded on Brahman. From the standpoint of this fundamental reality, individual minds as well as physical objects are appearances and do not have abiding reality. Brahman appears as the manifold objects of experience because of its creative power, *mâyâ*. *Mâyâ* is that which appears to be real at the time of experience but which does not have ultimate existence. It is dependent on pure consciousness. Brahman appears as the manifold world without undergoing an intrinsic change or modification. At no point of time does Brahman change into the world. The world is but a*vivarta,* a superimposition on Brahman. The world is neither totally real nor totally unreal. It is not totally unreal since it is experienced. It is not totally real since it is sublated by knowledge of Brahman. There are many examples given to illustrate the relation between the existence of the world and Brahman.

The two famous examples are that of the space in a pot versus the space in the whole cosmos (undifferentiated in reality, though arbitrarily separated by the contingencies of the pot just as the world is in relation to Brahman), and the self versus the reflection of the self (the reflection having no substantial existence apart from the self just as the objects of the world rely upon Brahman for substantiality). The existence of an individuated *jîva* and the world are without a beginning. We cannot say when they began, or what the first cause is. But both are with an end, which is knowledge of Brahman. According to classical Advaita Vedânta, the existence of the empirical world cannot be conceived without a creator who is all-knowing and all-powerful. The creation, sustenance, and dissolution of the world are overseen by *Îsvara*. *Îsvara* is the purest manifestation of Brahman. Brahman with the creative power of *mâyâ* is *îsvara*. *Mâyâ* has both individual (*vyaœti*) and cosmic (*samasti*) aspects.

The cosmic aspect belongs to one *Îsvara*, and the individual aspect, *avidya*, belongs to many *jîvas*. But the difference is that *îsvara* is not controlled by *mâyâ*, whereas the *jîva* is overpowered by *avidya*. *Mâyâ* is responsible for the creation of the world. *Avidya* is responsible for confounding the distinct existence between self and the not-self. With this confounding, *avidya* conceals Brahman and constructs the world. As a result the *jîva* functions as a doer (*karta*) and enjoyer (*bhokta*) of a limited world. The classical picture may be contrasted with two sub-schools of Advaita Vedânta that arose after Sankara: *Bhamati*and *Vivarana*. The primary difference between these two sub-schools is based on the different interpretations for *avidya* and *mâyâ*. Sankara described *avidya* as beginningless. He considered that to search the origin of *avidya* itself is a process founded on *avidya* and hence will be fruitless. But Sankara's disciples gave greater attention to this concept, and thus originated the two sub-schools. The *Bhamati* School owes its name to Vacaspati Miœra's (ninth century) commentary on

Sankara's *Brahma Sûtra Bhâsya,* while the *Vivarana* School is named after Prakâcâtman's (tenth century) commentary on Padmapâda's *Pañcapadika,* which itself is a commentary on Sankara's *Brahma Sûtra Bhâsya.* The major issue that distinguishes *Bhamati* and *Vivarana* schools is their position on the nature and locus of *avidya.* According to the *Bhamati* School, the *jîva* is the locus and object of *avidya.* According to the *Vivarana*School, Brahman is the locus of *avidya.* The *Bhamati* School holds that Brahman can never be the locus of *avidya* but is the controller of it as *Îsvara.* Belonging to *jîva, tula-avidya,* or individual ignorance performs two functions – veils Brahman, and projects (*vikcepa*) a separate world. *Mula-avidya* ("root ignorance") is the universal ignorance that is equivalent to *Mâyâ,* and is controlled by *Îsvara.* The *Vivarana* School holds that since Brahman alone exists, Brahman is the locus and object of *avidya.* With the help of epistemological discussions, the non-reality of the duality between Brahman and world is established. The *Vivarana* School responds to the question regarding Brahman's existence as both "pure consciousness" and "universal ignorance" by claiming that valid cognition (*prama*) presumes *avidya,* in the everyday world, whereas pure consciousness is the essential nature of Brahman.

b. Three Planes of Existence

There are three planes of existence according to classical Advaita Vedânta: the plane of absolute existence (*paramarthika satta*), the plane of worldly existence (*vyavaharika satta*) which includes this world and the heavenly world, and the plane of illusory existence (*pratibhâsika* existence). The two latter planes of existence are a function of *mâyâ* and are thus illusory to some extent. A *pratibhâsika*existence, such as objects presented in a mirage, is less real than a worldly existence. Its corresponding unreality is, however, different from that which characterizes the absolutely nonexistent or the impossible, such as a sky-lotus (a lotus that grows in the sky) or the son of a barren woman. The independent existence of a mirage and the world, both of which are due to a certain causal condition, ceases once the causal condition change. The causal condition is *avidya,* or ignorance. The independent existence and experience of the world ceases to be with the gain of knowledge of Brahman. The nature of knowledge of Brahman is that "I am pure consciousness." The self-ignorance of the *jîva* (individuated self) that "I am limited" is replaced by the Brahman-knowledge that "I am everything," accompanied by a re-identification of the self with the transcendental Brahman. The knower of Brahman sees the one non-plural reality in everything. He or she no longer gives an absolute reality to independent and limited existence of the world, but experiences the world as a creative expression of pure consciousness. The states of waking (*jâgrat*), dreaming (*svapna*) and deep sleep (*susupti*) all point to the fourth nameless state *turiya,* pure consciousness, which is to be realized as the true self. Pure consciousness is not only pure existence but also the ultimate bliss which is experienced partially during deep sleep. Hence we wake up refreshed.

3. EPISTEMOLOGY

The Advaita tradition puts forward three lesser tests of truth: correspondence, coherence, and practical efficacy. These are followed by a fourth test of truth: epistemic-nonsublatability (*abâdhyatvam* or *bâdharâhityam*). According to the *Vedânta Paribhâca* (a classical text of Advaita Vedânta) "that knowledge is valid which has for its object something that is nonsublated." Nonsublatablity is considered as the ultimate criterion for valid knowledge. The master test of epistemic-nonsublatability inspires a further constraint: foundationality (*anadhigatatvam,* lit. "of not known earlier"). This last criterion of truth is the highest standard that virtually all knowledge claims fail, and thus it is the standard for absolute, or unqualified, knowledge, while the former criteria are amenable to mundane, worldly knowledge claims. According to Advaita Vedânta, a judgment is true if it remains unsublated. The commonly used example that illustrates epistemic-nonsublatabilty is the rope that appears as a snake from a distance (a stock example in Indian philosophy). The belief that one sees a snake in this circumstance is erroneous according to Advaita Vedânta because the snake belief (and the visual presentation of a snake) is sublated into the judgment that what one is really seeing is a rope. Only wrong cognitions can be sublated. The condition of foundationality disqualifies memory as a means of knowledge. Memory is the recollection of something already known and is thus derivable and not foundational. Only genuine knowledge of the Self, according to Advaita Vedânta, passes the test of foundationality: it is born of immediate knowledge (*aparokca jñâna*) and not memory (*smrti*). Six natural ways of knowing are accepted as valid means of knowledge (*pramâna*) by Advaita Vedânta: perception (*pratyakca*), inference (*anumâna*), verbal testimony (*sabda*), comparison (*upamana*), postulation (*arthapatti*) and non-apprehension (*anupalabdhi*). The *pramânas* do not contradict each other and each of them presents a distinct kind of knowledge. Nonfoundational knowledge of Brahman cannot be had by any means but through *Sruti*, which is the supernaturally revealed text in the form of the Vedas (of which the Upanisads form the most philosophical portion).

Inference and the other means of knowledge cannot determinately reveal the truth of Brahman on their own. However, Advaitins recognize that in addition to *Sruti*, one requires *yukti* (reason) and *anubhava* (personal experience) to actualize knowledge of Brahman. *Moksa* (liberation), which consists in the cessation of the cycle of life and death, governed by the karma of the individual self, is the result of knowledge of Brahman. As Brahman is identical with the universal Self, and this Self is always self-conscious, it would seem that knowledge of Brahman is Self-knowledge, and that this Self-knowledge is ever present. If so, it seems that ignorance is impossible. Moreover, in the *adhyâsa Bhâsya* (his preamble to the commentary on the *Brahma Sûtra*) Sankara says that the pure subjectivity—the Self or Brahman—can never become the object of knowledge, just as the object can never be the subject. This would suggest that Self-knowledge that one gains in order to achieve liberation is impossible. Sankara's response to this problem is to regard knowledge of Brahman that is necessary for liberation, derived from scripture, to be distinct from the Self-consciousness of Brahman, and rather a practical knowledge that removes ignorance, which is an obstacle to the luminance of the ever-present self-consciousness of Brahman that does pass the test of foundationality. Ignorance, in turn, is not a feature of the ultimate

Self on his account, but a feature of the individual self that is ultimately unreal. Four factors are involved in an external perception: the physical object, the sense organ, the mind (*antahkarana*) and the cognizing self (*pramata*). The cognizing self alone is self-luminous and the rest of the three factors are not self-luminous being devoid of consciousness. It is the mind and the sense organ which relates the cognizing self to the object. The self alone is the knower and the rest are knowable as objects of knowledge. At the same time the existence of mind is indubitable. It is the mind that helps to distinguish between various perceptions. It is because of the self-luminous (*svata-prakâca*) nature of pure consciousness that the subject knows and the object is known. In his commentary to *Taittirîya Upanisad*, Sankara says that "consciousness is the very nature of the Self and inseparable from It." The cognizing self, the known object, the object-knowledge, and the valid means of knowledge (*pramâna*) are essentially the manifestations of one pure consciousness.

a. Error, True Knowledge and Practical Teachings

Sankara uses *adhyâsa* to indicate illusion – illusory objects of perception as well as illusory perception. Two other words which are used to denote the same are *adhyâropa* (superimposition) and *avabhâsa* (appearance). According to Sankara the case of illusion involves both superimposition and appearance. *Adhyâsa,* as he says in his preamble to the *Brahma Sûtra,* is the apprehension of something as something else with two kinds of confounding such as the object and its properties. The concept of illusion, in Advaita Vedânta, is significant because it leads to the theory of a "real substratum." The illusory object, like the real object, has a definite locus. According to Sankara, *adhyâsa*is not possible without a substratum. Padmapâda says in *Pañcapadika* that *adhyâsa* without a substratum has never been experienced and is inconceivable. Vacaspati affirms that there cannot be a case of illusion where the substratum is fully apprehended or not apprehended at all. The Advaita theory of error (known as *anirvacanîya khyâti,* or the apprehension of the indefinable) holds that the perception of the illusory object is a product of the ignorance about the substratum. Sankara characterizes illusion in two ways in his commentary on the *Brahma Sûtra*. The first is an appearance of something previously experienced—like memory—in something else (*smrtirupah paratra pûrva drstah avabhâsah*). The second is a minimalist characterization—the appearance of one thing with the properties of another (*anyasya anyadharma avabhâsatam*. Sankara devotes his introduction to his commentary on the *Brahma Sûtra,* to the idea of *adhyâsa* to account for illusory perception relating to both everyday experience and also transcendent entities. This introduction, called the *adhyâsa Bhâsya* (commentary on illusion) presents a realistic position and a seemingly dualistic metaphysics: "Since it is an established fact that the object and subject which are presented as *yusmad*—'you' /the other, and *asmad*—'me' are by very nature contradictory, and their qualities also contradictory, as light and darkness they cannot be identical."

Plurality and illusion, on this account, are constructed out of the cognitive superimposition of the category of objects on pure subjectivity. While two conceptual categories are superimposed to create objects of illusion, the Adavita Vedânta view is that the only possible way of metaphysically describing the object of illusion is with the help of a characteristic, other than those of non-existence and existence, which is termed as the "indeterminate" (*anirvacaniya*) which also somehow connects the two usual possibilities of existence and non-existence. The object of illusion cannot be logically defined as real or unreal. Error is the apprehension of the indefinable. It is due to the "illegitimate transference" of the qualities of one order to another. Perceptual illusion forms the bridge between Advaita's soteriology, on the one hand, and its theory of experience, on the other. The relationship between the experience of liberation in this life (*mukti*) and everyday experience is viewed as analogous to the relation between veridical and delusive sense perception. Sankara formulates a theory of knowledge in accordance with his soteriological views. Sankara's interest is thus not to build a theory of error and leave it by itself but to connect it to his theory of the ultimate reality of Self-Consciousness which is the only state which can be true according to his twin criteria for truth (non-sublatability and foundationality). The characteristic of indeterminacy that qualifies objects of illusion is that which is truly neither real nor unreal but appears as a real locus. It serves as a stark contrast to the soteriological goal of the Self, which is truly real and determinate. On the basis of his theory of knowledge, Sankara elucidates the fourfold (mental and physical) practices or qualifications—*sâdana catucmaya*—to aid in the achievement of liberation: (i) the discrimination (*viveka*) between the permanent (*nitya*) and the impermanent (*anitya*) objects of experience; (ii) dispassion towards the enjoyment of fruits of action here and in heaven; (iii) accomplishment of means of discipline such as calmness, mental control etc.; (iv) a longing for liberation. In his commentary to the *Brahma Sûtra,* Sankara says that the inquiry into Brahman could start only after acquiring these fourfold qualifications. The concept of liberation (*moksa*) in Advaita is cashed out in terms of Brahman. The pathways to liberations are defined by the removal of self-ignorance that is brought about by the removal of *mithyajñâna* (erroneous knowledge claims). This is captured in the formula of one Advaitin: "[He] is never born again who knows that he is the only one in all beings like the ether and that all beings are in him" (*Upadesa Sahasri* XVII.69). Many thinkers in the history of Indian philosophy have held that there is an important connection between action and liberation. In contrast, Sankara rejects the theory of *jñâna-karma-samuccaya,* the combination of karma (Vedic duties) with knowledge of Brahman leading to liberation. Knowledge of Brahman alone is the route to liberation for Sankara. The role of action (karma) is to purify the mind (*antahkaranasuddhi*) and make it free from likes and dislikes (*raga dvesa vimuktah*). Such a mind will be instrumental to knowledge of Brahman.

REFERENCES:

a. Primary Sources

1.Alladi Mahadeva Sastri (Trans.). *The Bhagavad Gita with the commentary of Srî Sankara*. Madras: Samata Books, 1981.

2.Madhusudana, Saraswati. *Gudartha Dipika*. Trans. Sisirkumar Gupta. Delhi: Motilal Banarsidass Pubs., 1977.

3.*Brahma Sûtra Sankara Bhâsya: 3.3.54.* Found in, V.H. Date, *Vedânta Explained: Sankara's Commentary on the Brahma-Sûtra,* vols. 1 and 2 (Bombay: Book Seller's Publishing Com., 1954).

4.Date, V. H. *Vedânta Explained: Sankara's commentary on the Brahma Sûtra*. Vol. I. Bombay: Book Seller's Publishing Company, 1954.

5.*Taittiriya Upanisad Sankara Bhâsya*: 2.10. Found in Karl H. Potter, Gen. Ed. *Encyclopedia of Indian Philosophies*, Vol. III. 1st Ind. ed. Delhi: Motilal Banarsidass Publishers, 1981.

6.*Upadesa Sahasri of Sankaracharya*, Trans. Swami Jagadananda. Mylapore: Srî Ramkrishna Math, 1941.

7.*D[g-d[cya Viveka of Sankara*. Trans. Swami Nikhilananda. 6th ed. Mysore: Srî Ramakrishna Ashrama, 1976.

b. Secondary Sources

1.Potter, Karl H. *Advaita Vedânta up to Sankara and his Pupils*. Vol. III of *Encyclopedia of Indian Philosophies*. Delhi: Motilal Banarsidass, 1981.

2.Mahadevan, T M P. *Sankara*. New Delhi: National Book Trust, 1968.

3.Mahadevan, T M P. *Superimposition in Advaita Vedânta*. New Delhi: Sterling Publishers Pvt. Ltd., 1985.

4.Satprakashananda, Swami. *Methods of Knowledge According to Advaita Vedânta*. Calcutta: Advaita Ashrama, 1974.

5.Dasgupta, Surendranath. *A History of Indian Philosophy*. Vol. I. Delhi: Motilal Banarsidass, 1975.

6.Radhakrishnan, S. *Indian Philosophy*. Vol. II. Delhi: Oxford University Press, 1940.

7.Rangacarya, M. (Trans.). *The Sarva Siddhânta-Sangraha of Sankara*. New Delhi: Ajay Book Service, 1983.

12

Gaudapada (555 CE)

Gauapâda is one of the early and most reputed philosophers of the Vedânta school in the Indian system of thought, who is believed to have lived roughly during 500 C.E. In the spiritual lineage, Gauapâda is regarded as the grand preceptor of Sankaracarya [8th c. C.E.], the systematizer of Advaita Vedânta. Gauapâda is best known for his analytical exposition on the tenets of Advaita Vedânta that provided a firm ontological grounding to Vedânta philosophy. Gauapâda's expository interpretation of the Upanisadic literature in the light of logical reasoning is a critical apparatus of epistemological exposition in the Advaita tradition.

According to Gauapâda's thesis, the ultimate ontological reality is the pure consciousness, which is bereft of attributes and intentionality. The world of duality is nothing but a vibration of the mind (*manodrsya* or *manaspandita*). The pluralistic world is imagined by the mind (*sankalpa*) and this false projection is sponsored by the illusory factor called *mâyâ*. The origination of the individual soul, which experiences the world of duality, is figurative. The finitude of the individuality of the soul is caused due to nescience (*avidyâ*), while in reality its nature is identical with the ultimate soul – pure consciousness. The knowledge of non-difference between the individual and the supreme soul alone leads to liberation.

Gauapâda's influence has probably been most far-reaching in the development of Advaita Vedânta through the ages. He is well-known for his conception of 'contact-less contemplation' (*asparsa yoga*) a key soteriological notion of Advaita Vedânta. More famous is his doctrine of non-origination (*ajâti-vâda*), with which he establishes the eternality and non-duality of consciousness. The philosophy of Gauapâda may be characterized as absolute non-dualism and establishes this doctrine both by the method of affirmation and negation (*adhyâropa* and *apavâda*). He explains the doctrine of *advaita-vâda* using illustrations such as "quenching of fire-brand" (*alâtaúânti*) and the phantasmagoric city (*gandharva-nagara*) to systematically expound the falsity of the world.

1. LIFE AND WORKS OF GAUAPÂDA

Within the Advaita tradition, Gauapâda is regarded as the disciple of the legendary sage sukha and is the teacher of Govinda bhagavadpâda, who is Sankarâcârya's direct preceptor. Sankara, in his works, exhibits extreme reverence to Gauapâda. Gauapâda is referred to by the terms *sampradâyavit* – knower of the tradition, *paramaguru* – grand preceptor, *'vrddha âcârya'* – ancient preceptor, and so on. All that is known about Gauapâda is mostly derived from his name. The term *'Gaua'*, according to some scholars, indicates his geographical origin, which is the region of Bengal. Alternatively, we find some references to Gauapâda by the term *'Gauâcârya'* – a compound word which means the 'teacher of the *Gaua*'. Here again the term *'Gaua'* clearly denotes a place and is not a proper name. Also, Suresvarâcârya (a direct disciple of Sankara), in his work *Naickarmya Siddhi* IV.44, refers him as *'Gauah'*. From a 13th century prolific glossator, ânandagiri, we gather that Gauapâda spent some time in Badrikâsrama absorbed in deep meditation. Another legend about Gauapâda, narrated by a 17th c. advaitin, informs us that there was a place near a river Hîraravati in Kurukshetra (the northern region of today's Bengal), a place where some *Gaua* people lived. According to this note, the term *'Gaua'* connotes a specific ethnic group belonging to a particular geographical origin. It was in this place the *âcârya* was absorbed in meditation and hence the name Gauapâdâcârya. Apart from these abstract conjectures on the life of Gauapâda, his dates are also not clearly established. From the references from the Buddhist writers who cite Gauapâda as the source of substantial evidence, some scholars attempt to give a rough idea on Gauapâda's date. Vidhushekhara Bhattacarya and T. M. P. Mahadevan bring to our notice that three Buddhist writers, namely, Bhavaviveka, Santaraksita and Kamalasila have cited Gauapada's *kârikâ*-s in their works. Karl Potter suggests that Bhavaviveka is the younger contemporary of Dharmapala, who according to early Chinese travel accounts seems to have flourished during 5th c. C.E From this information we may fix Gauapada's date not later than 5th c. C.E. A few other scholars fix Gauapâda's date in accordance to Sankara's date, which then would push his date further to 6th c. C.E. Some other scholars bring to our notice that Gauapâda himself cites some Buddhist views of Nâgârjuna and Asanga, with which we could fix the upper limit to 4th c. C.E.

All the scholars agree that Gauapâda's most prominent work, is his metrical commentary on the *Mândûkya Upanisad* called the *Mândûkya kârikâ.* It is otherwise called *Gauapâdîya* or *Gauapâda kârika.* Thanga Swamy and Tandalam Narayana Swamy Iyer indicate that there is a commentary on the *Nrsimha Uttara Tâpini Upanisad* authored by Gauapâda. A commentary (*Bhâsya*) on the *Sâmkhya kârikâ* of Îsvara Krsna is attributed to Gauapâda. There is yet another commentary – a *vrtti* on the *Uttara gîta* is also attributed to Gauapâda. In the tantric tradition, works like the *Durgâsaptasati, Subhagodaya stuti* and *œri Vidyâratna Sûtra*'s authorship is ascribed to Gauapâda. These works are supposedly on the Srî *Vidyâ* tradition. Some scholars maintain that there are multiple Gauapâda-s who belong to different times and places while the *Mândûkya kârikâ* is the only work of Gauapâda who is Sankara's grand preceptor.

2. AN OVERVIEW OF GAUAPÂDA'S MÂNDÛKYA KÂRIKÂ

A *kârikâ* is usually a crisp condensation of a subject matter or an explication of a specific doctrinal position. The *Mândûkya kârikâ* is a metrical commentary on the *Mândûkya Upanisad*, which belongs to the Atharva Veda. The Gauapâda *kârikâ* seems to be a collection of terse aphorisms consolidated under different topics of Advaita Vedânta. The *kârikâ* is pedagogically instructive in its tone. Traditionally, the *Mândûkya kârikâ* is regarded as an exhaustive manual for the fundamentals of Advaita Vedânta and hence called *Upadesa grantha.* Gauapâda's *kârikâ* has 215 verses distributed in four chapters. The relation between the *Mândûkya Upanisad* and the *kârikâ*-s remains abstract. The four chapters are namely, a. *âgama prakarana* – the chapter regarding the scriptures consisting of 29 verses b. *Vaitathya prakarana* – the chapter regarding illusion consisting of 38 verses c. *advaita prakaraṇa* – the chapter on non-duality constituting 48 verses and d. *alâtasanti prakarana* – the chapter on the fire-brand comprising of 100 verses. There are some traditional views, which consider the 29 verses in the first chapter of the *kârikâ* as the Upanisad itself. The main purport of these four chapters of the *kârikâ* is to delineate the quintessence of Vedântic content as commenced in the Upanisad. The first chapter is an exposition of the Upanisadic content mainly to describe the nature of the absolute ontological being. Expounding upon the states of psycho-physical experiences (waking, dream and profound sleep) as primary constituents of metempsychic existence, the *kârikâ* discusses various positions on the theories of creation. Based on the Upanisadic cohort, the *kârikâ,* in this chapter, attempts to initiate the Advaitic position that the template of creation is temporally apparent and ultimately unreal. The second chapter of the *kârikâ* proposes to logically establish the theory of illusion. The rationality of the third chapter of the *kârikâ* is to firmly establish the position of non-duality (*advaita*) by the method of methodical assertion and negation (*adhyâropa* and *apavâda*). Finally, the objective of the fourth chapter mainly seeks to explicate the notion of the 'contactless yoga' (*asparsa*) to assert the theory of non-origination (*ajâti*) of the eternal soul as expounded in the third chapter. The refutation of the creation theories remains to be the prime focus of all the four chapters.

There is an intense controversy in modern scholarship over the correct interpretation of the philosophy and the structure of *Mândûkya kârikâ.* Vidhushekhara Bhattacarya advocates that the four chapters do not constitute a unitary text of the *Mândûkya kârikâ.* According to Bhattacarya, the four chapters of the*Mândûkya kârikâ* are four independent treatises and were later consolidated into one title called *âgamasâstra.* He also observes that the first chapter of the *Mândûkya kârikâ* does not systematically expound the prose content of the *Mândûkya Upanisad* and this led Bhattacarya to conclude that the first chapter of the *kârikâ* predates the *Upanisadic* content. Owing to copious references to *'Buddha'* in the fourth chapter (IV.19, 42,80, 88, 98, 99) and for the claim that the term *'alâtasânti'* is a peculiar to Buddhists, Bhattacarya advocates that *Mândûkya kârikâ* is more inclined to Buddhist philosophy than to Vedânta. However, Richard King in his detailed analysis on the date and authorship of the text rejects the Bhattacarya's hypothesis, while he arrives at a conclusion that the final or the fourth chapter (the *alâtasânti prakaraṇa*) is a later text composed perhaps for a different audience by some other author who is heavily influenced by Gauapâda. According to King, the fourth chapter profuṣely adopts Buddhist terminologies especially from the Mâdhyamaka and the Yogâcâra philosophical traditions. Richard King also shows that the prominent Advaitins (beginning from 8th to 17th C.E) completely omit any reference to the fourth chapter in their respective works. King also contends that the first three chapters of the Mândûkya *kârikâ* were linked by the Sankarite tradition by the 8th century of the Common Era and was eventually attributed to the author who bore the title *'Gaua'*.

3. GAUAPÂDA'S ONTO-THEOLOGY

The sacred syllable *OM*, also known as *pranava* is regarded as the absolute being. Gauapâda suggests that the structure of the sacred syllable has linguistic connections to, and homologically implies, onto-theological connotations. The *kârikâ* of the *âgama prakarana* begins with the appraisal of the method of contemplation of the *pranava*. Gauapâda regards *OM* as the sound from which the entire creation springs forth. *OM* is the root for all speech. Gauapâda suggests that the sonic *pranava* is discerned with its four fold linguistic measures (*mâtra*-s) representing the gradational states of consciousness. The four *mâtra*-s are *a, u, m & the OM*. According to the phonetic rules of Sanksrit, the first two *mâtra*-s, *'a' & 'u'* combine to render a diphthong *'o'* resulting in the sonic *OM*. Each of these phonetic elements is homologous to the states of experience of the individual soul. The sound *'a'* of the *pranava* represents the waking state (*jâgrat*), which Gauapâda calls the all pervasive, external, universal consciousness known by the term *'âpti'*. In this state, the individual soul bears the name *viœva* – who is the enjoyer of the gross objects (*sthûla bhuk*). Secondly, the phonetic element *'u'* represents the dream state in which the individual soul becomes the enjoyer of the internal objects (*antahprajña*) and is called the *sûksma bhuk.* In this state the soul bears the name *'taijasa'*. Gauapâda refers to the nature state of the internal consciousness by the term *'utkarsa'* meaning ecstasy. The third state is of profound sleep (*sucupti*) and is represented by the sound *'m'*. The individual soul in profound sleep is the enjoyer of bliss (*ânanda bhuk*). The profound sleep, as Gauapâda describes, is a state of intense consciousness in its causal state in which the gross and subtle state of objective experiences get dissolved (*laya*). Finally, the fourth state is known as the *turîya* and is absolutely transcendental to all the phenomenal states of apparent realities. The fourth state is measureless (*amâtra*) and is devoid of all attributes whatsoever. This *turîya,* as Gauapâda conveys, is non-dual (*advaita*), the reality of Lord-hood (*isâna*), the seer of everything (*sarva drk*). It is in this state, as Gauapâda in *kârikâ* I.17 points out, all the phenomenal realities of the world would cease (*prapañcopasamam*) to have any existence. All the dualities are merely sponsored by the indiscernible factor of *mâyâ* and in reality they do not exist at all.

Gauapâda identifies this fourth state of the absolute attributeless Being – the *pranava* and the phonetic components of *pranava* with the state of individual experience relegated in different gradations of consciousness. The realization of *turîya* as the attributeless consciousness is the real awakening from the state of profound sleep. The awakening is accomplished by contemplating on the *pranava and* this is called the *pranava yoga.* Apophatically, the *pranava yoga* is the final salvific process and Gauapâda considers it to be an onto-soteriological guarantee for the emancipation of the individual soul.

4. METAPHYSICS

a. Theory of Non-origination (ajâti vâda)

The fulcrum of Gauapâda's philosophy of non-duality is the theory of non-origination known as the *ajâti vâda* in Sanskrit. The theory of non-origination is constructed on the fundamental premise that 'nothing is ever born, nothing is created whatsoever and there is no transactional reality at any rate'. The phenomenal reality is figurative and is imagined upon the Self by its own magical power called *mâyâ.* In the second and the third chapter of the *kârikâ,* Gauapâda discusses this theory in detail. Gauapâda primarily adopts the logical method of superimposition and subsequent negation (*adyâropa-apavâda*) to establish the concept of non-origination of the Self. The Self is the only non-dual reality and whatever exists apart from that reality is logically reduced as unreal and is subsequently negated to absolute non-existence.

The doctrine of *ajâti vâda* – the theory of non-origination aims at dismantling all the theories of creation in order to suggest that there is no creation that has ever occurred. Gauapâda's logical postulation is that when the Self is the only reality that remains eternal, whatever it is that seems to exist apart from the non-dual self must be unreal and hence non-existent. Gauapâda in the *kârikâ* I.17 maintains the premise that 'if the world ever existed then it would at some point cease to exist. But since the Self alone is the eternal existence, the phenomenal world is known to be absolute non-existence only'. Gauapâda also points out that the creation has no purpose in any metaphysical sense. Creation cannot serve the purpose of any experience to the divine Being since the Upanisadic import insists that the ultimate being is ever-accomplished and it transcends all phenomenal relations. Secondly, purpose of creation cannot be taken as the God's sport or the divine play (*lîla*) since it is an unwelcome position to suppose that the cosmogenically omnipotent God has some desire to be accomplished.

Gauapâda introduces the concept of non-origination in the *vaitathya prakarana* where he aims to prove the falsity of the phenomenal world. He maintains that the existence of conventional mundane reality of the material world is an apparatus or the means (*upâya*) to apprehend the absolute non-dual being. In *kârikâ* II.31, Gauapâda points out that the existence of the world is false; just as a city that exists in the sky (*gandharva nagara*), so does the whole universe upon the Self. Likewise, the modifications of material reality in terms of creation, subsistence and dissolution are merely imagined upon the Self. Gauapâda also uses the illustration of dream to posit that just as the dream vanishes to non-existence once the individual returns to the waking state; so does the world cease to exist once the reality of the absolute is known. Gauapâda insists on the point that there exists neither the dream nor the waking and hence the universe never existed at all upon the unborn Self. Gauapâda also uses the analogy of rope-snake in this context. The *kârikâ* II.17 states that 'as a rope whose nature has not been well known is imagined in the dark like a snake, so also is the pattern of duality imagined being manifested from the unborn Self'. The final illustration that Gauapâda employs can be noted from the *kârikâ* III.8 that says 'Just as the sky is seen by the ignorant young boys as being covered by the dust etc., so does the Self in being associated with the impurities of mundane transformations' (*yathâ bâlânam gaganam malinammalaih*). Origination (*jâti*) is a magical projection (*vivarta*) of the Self and is operative only through *mâyâ* (*sato hi mâyayâ janma* – GK.III.27.) The Self that is bereft of any transformation in terms of origination and so forth, by its own innate nature is self-established (*svastha*), tranquil (*úânta*), self-effulgent (*sakrd vibhâta*), nameless and formless (*anâmaka, arûpaka*).

b. Contact-less Contemplation (asparsa yoga)

The third chapter of *Mândûkya kârikâ,* introduces the notion of 'contact-less contemplation' (*asparsayoga*). According to Gauapâda, *asparsa yoga* is a transcendental mental state in which the mind is stripped from all desires and afflictions. *Sparsa* in Sanskrit means contact. In this context, it is the contact with the sense organs that results in the identification of Self with the non-Self causing bondage. *Asparsa*is the counter state in which there no contact with the sense organs (*sarva abhilâpa vigatah; sarva cintâ samutthitah* III.37) and the function of the mind in material sense is nullified. The ephemeral realities in multitude names and forms, those that are movable and immovable and so on, are perceived only by the mind (*manodrsya)* causing desires, disappointments, pleasure, pain and so on. Once the mind is nullified, the duality does not exist. When mind is pure, the Self dwells in the supra-sensible state of tranquillity. Gaupâda, in the *kârikâ* IV.2, offers salutations to the transcendental state of *asparsa* stating that this *yogic* state is free from all mundane relations in the nature of highest bliss, free from any dispute or doubt and that which is well established in the Vedic scriptures. 'Those who perceive the contact of the consciousness with the external objects, may as well see footmarks in the open space' (*kârikâ* IV.28). Control of mind, according to Gauapâda, is the key to accomplish this state of *asparsa*. The mind when under complete control (*manonigraha*) through the ability to discriminate between the eternal Self and the ephemeral non-Self, in Gauapâda's opinion, is equated with the nature of mind in the state of profound sleep. Gauapâda calls this state of non-mind *'amanîbhâva'*.

5. PHENOMENOLOGY OF CONSCIOUSNESS – QUENCHING OF FIRE-BRAND ALÂTA SÂNTI

The Advaita philosophy holds the position that the consciousness is attributed with the functionality of perception only with regard to the waking state wherein the objectivity is merely projected and thus appears in various names and forms. This figurative intentionality of consciousness is merely a mental simulation caused by the apparent conjugation of Self and the non-self. The objectivity provided by the mind attributes the intentionality to the consciousness. Thus consciousness acquires varied degrees of functionality in terms of intentional acts such as perception, memory, imagination and the like. In reality, however, suspending the objective world constituting the universals and particulars, the phenomenological residuum is the pure supra-Consciousness that does not stand in any causal relation with the objective entities; nor does it have any intentionality and hence is apodictically transcendental. Though the consciousness is the substratum for all cognitive experiences that precipitate out of subject-object interactions, it in 'actuality' remains untouched by any of these transactions.

Gauapâda uses the simile called 'fire-circle' (*alâta cakra*) in order to explain the onto-phenomenology of consciousness. When a stick with a fire tip is waved (*alâta spandita*) during the night, it forms different appearances in accordance to the movement of the fire-brand and so does the vibration of the consciousness that appears to exist in terms of known, knower and the like, (*grahana-grâhaka*) in accordance to the nature of limiting adjuncts (*kârikâ* IV.47). Just as the same fire-brand when not in motion is free from all appearances, the consciousness too when not vibrated remains in its true intrinsic nature is free from all names and forms. Gauapâda insists that, even when the fire-brand is in motion the appearances that seem to exist do not come from anywhere and they do not go anywhere. Appearances do not originate from the fire-brand and they do not dissolve into it. There is no causal relation between the resultant products of appearances with the seeming cause. Similarly, the entire universe that exist in pairs of dualities are not products of consciousness and nor is the consciousness a product of the physical universe. The existence of cause-effect result, according to Gauapâda , is a mental pre-occupation (*phala-âvesah*) which is a mere projection (*phala-udbhavah*). In the domain of ignorance these mental pre-suppositions manifest as multi-fold appearances, which is purely due to concealment (*samvrtya – samvarana*) of the nature of absolute self as pure consciousness.

REFERENCES:

a. Primary References

1.Gauapâda, '*sagau*apâda mânûkya kârikâ atharvavedîya mânûkyopanicad: *with Sankarâcârya's Bhâsya & ânandagiri's tîka*', Ed. by Vinaya Ganesa Apte, Anandasrama Press, 1936.

2.Gauapâda, '*Sânkhya kârikâ: commentary of Gauapâda – Îsvara Krsna*', Mainkar Tryambak Govind, Poona Oriental Book Agency, 1964.

3.Gauapâda, '*mânûkya kârikâ*', Swami Gambhirananda Trans., Ramakrishna Mutt, Trichur, 1987.

4.Samkarâcârya, '*Prasthâna traya Bhâsya: mânskya kârikâ Bhâsya*', Vol.II, V.Panoli Trans., Mathrubhumi Grandhavedi Publication, Calicut, 2006.

b. Secondary Sources

1.Mahadevan T.M.P, '*Gauapâda: A study in early Vedânta*', University of Madras, Madras, 1960.

2.Vidhushekhara Bhattacarya, *'âgamasâstra of Gauapâda'*, University of Calcutta, Calcutta, 1943.

3.Douglas Fox, *'Dispelling Illusion: Gauapâda's Alâtasânti with an introduction'*, SUNY, New York, 1993.

4.Colin A. Cole, *'A Study of Gau*apâda's mânskya *kârikâ'*, Motilal Banarsidass, Delhi, 2004.

5.Natalia Isayeva, *'From Early Vedânta to Kashmir Shaivism: Gauapâda, Bhatrhari & Abhinavagupta'*, SUNY, New York, 1995.

6.Richard King, *'Early Advaita Vedânta and Buddhism'*, SUNY, New York, 1995.

13

Bhedabheda Vedanta

Bhedâbheda Vedânta is one of the several traditions of Vedânta philosophy in India. "Bhedâbheda" is a Sanskrit word meaning "Difference and Non-Difference." The characteristic position of all the different Bhedâbheda Vedânta schools is that the individual self (*jîvâtman*) is both different and not different from the ultimate reality known as Brahman. Bhedâbheda reconciles the positions of two other major schools of Vedânta. The Advaita (Monist) Vedânta that claims the individual self is completely identical to Brahman, and the Dvaita (Dualist) Vedânta that teaches complete difference between the individual self and Brahman. However, each thinker within the Bhedâbheda Vedânta tradition has his own particular understanding of the precise meanings of the philosophical terms "difference" and "non-difference." Bhedâbheda Vedântic ideas can traced to some of the very oldest Vedântic texts, including quite possibly Bâdarâyana's *Brahma Sûtra* (app. 4th c. CE). Bhedâbheda ideas also had an enormous influence on the devotional *(bhakti)* schools of India's medieval period. Among medieval Bhedâbheda thinkers are Vallabha (1479-1531 CE), founder of the Pucmimârga devotional sect now centered in Nathdwara, Rajasthan, and Caitanya (1485-1533 CE) the founder of the Gaudîya Vaisnava sect based in the northeastern Indian state of West Bengal.

1. HISTORICAL OVERVIEW

Bhedâbheda is often presented as a school of Vedânta. Vedânta, in turn, is sometimes spoken about as a single philosophy, when in reality "Vedânta" has different uses. Its most inclusive use is as a label for a philosophy that purports to be expressed at length in the latter part of the Vedas, that is, the Upanisads. It is centrally concerned with the inquiry into the nature of an ultimate entity called "Brahman." There are many different accounts of this synoptic philosophy, and the various accounts are often considered schools of philosophy themselves. Unlike the well-known schools of Advaita (Non-Dualist) Vedânta, Visistâdvaita (Non-Dualism of the Qualified) Vedânta, and Dvaita (Dualist) Vedânta, it makes more sense to refer to Bhedâbheda Vedânta as a "tradition" or "family" of philosophies rather than as a single "school." This is because, unlike the three aforementioned schools, Bhedâbheda has no single founder who created an institutionalized network of monasteries dedicated to the study, development, and propagation of the founder's teachings. The history of Bhedâbheda in India stretches back at least until the 7th century CE and likely quite earlier, and continues into the present day. Although there are substantial philosophical disagreements among the many Bhedâbheda thinkers, their philosophies also show certain characteristic similarities. After a short historical introduction to several major Bhedâbhedavâdins, I will discuss a few viewpoints that almost all Bhedâbheda schools share. These include the understanding of the relation between individual self (*jîvâtman*) and Brahman as one of part and whole; the doctrine that the phenomenal world is a real transformation of Brahman (*Parinâmavâda*); and the doctrine that liberation can only be attained by means of a combination of knowledge and ritual action (*Jñânakarmasamuccayavâda*), not by knowledge alone.

a. Bâdarâyana and Bhartrprapañca

Numerous scholars have concluded that Bâdarâyana's *Brahma Sûtra* (circa 4th c. CE), one of the foundational texts common to all Vedânta schools, was written from a Bhedâbheda Vedântic viewpoint (Dasgupta 1922: vol. 2, p. 42; Nakamura 1989: p. 500). While that claim is disputed by other schools, there is little doubt that Bhedâbheda predates Sankara's Advaita Vedânta. In his commentary on the *Brhadâranyaka Upanisad,* Sankara (8th c.) repeatedly criticizes interpretations by an earlier Vedântin named Bhartrprapañca, who characterized the relation between Brahman and individual souls as one of difference and non-difference. One of the central disagreements between the two is that Sankara claims that Brahman's entire creation is a mere appearance (*vivarta*), while Bhartrprapañca maintains that it is real (Hiriyanna 1957: vol. 2, pp. 6-16).

b. Bhâskara

The first Bhedâbhedavâdin widely recognized as such by the later tradition is Bhâskara (8th-9th c.). He was either a younger contemporary of Sankara or perhaps lived slightly after Sankara. His only extant work is a commentary on the *Brahma Sûtra*. That work is expressly written in order to defend the earlier claims of Bhedâbhedavâdins against Sankara's interpretation of the *Brahma Sûtra*. Although he never mentions Sankara by name, he makes it clear from the beginning that his primary intention in commenting on the *Brahma Sûtra* is to oppose some predecessor: "I am writing a commentary on this *sûtra* in order to obstruct those commentators who have concealed its ideas and replaced them with their own" (Bhâskara 1903: p. 1). Bhâskara is the earliest in a long line of Vedântic authors concerned to refute Advaita (including Râmânuja and Madhva, not to mention numerous Bhedâbhedavâdins). Many of the stock arguments used against the Advaita originated with Bhâskara, if indeed he did not borrow them from an even earlier source. He also seems to have been remembered by the collective Advaita tradition as a thorn in its side. So, for instance, in the 14th century hagiography of Sankara, the *Sankaradigvijaya,* Mâdhava depicts one "Bhamma Bhâskara" as a haughty and famous Bhedâbhedavâdin whom Sankara defeats in a lengthy debate.

c. Yâdavaprakâúa and Nimbârka

While the Visistâdvaita philosopher Râmânuja (11th-12th c.) is widely acknowledged as the most influential Vedântin after Sankara, Râmânuja's complicated relationship with Bhedâbhedavâda is rarely discussed. Râmânuja's teacher Yâdavaprakâsa was a Bhedâbhedavâdin. Yâdavaprakâsa's works have been lost, and therefore almost all of what we know of his ideas comes from Râmânuja and one of Râmânuja's commentators, Sudarsanasári. However, it is possible from these numerous hints to draw a sketch of Yâdavaprakâsa's basic views. Râmânuja depicts Yâdavaprakâsa as an exponent of Svâbhâvika Bhedâbhedavâda, the view that Brahman is both different and not different than the world in its very nature, and that difference is not simply due to difference of artificial limiting conditions (see Oberhammer 1997: p. 10). Yâdavaprakâsa shares this basic viewpoint with Nimbârka (13th c.?), and disagrees with the Aupâdhika Bhedâbhedavâda of Bhâskara, who maintains that the difference of the world and Brahman is due to limiting conditions. Another characteristic of Yâdavaprakâsa's thought is his repeated insistence that Brahman has the substance of pure existence (*sanmâtradravya*). The relationship between Brahman and the world is not merely one of class and individual, but rather both are existent entities, standing in the relationship of cause and effect (see Oberhammer 1997: p. 14).

d. Vallabha

In the late medieval period, the doctrine of Bhedâbheda became increasingly associated with devotional (*bhakti*) movements in North India. It is largely on the basis of their reputations as the founders of religious sects, and not as philosophers *per se*, that thinkers such as Vallabha (1479-1531) and Caitanya (1485-1533) became widely known. Among the former's most influential works are a commentary on the *Brahma Sûtra*entitled the *AnuBhâsya*, and his commentary on the *Bhâgavata Purâna*, entitled the *Subodhinî*. Vallabha founded the Vaisnava sect of the *Pucmimârga* ("path of nourishment") now based in Nathdwara, Rajasthan.

His philosophical system, called Suddhâdvaita (Pure Non-Dualism), takes its name from his view that there is no dualism whatsoever between a real Brahman and an unreal world. Since both are completely real, he denies that there can be any sort of ontological dualism of real and unreal between the two—therefore it is a "pure" non-dualism. Obviously, this refers to the Advaita school's view that the phenomenal world is not real in an ultimate sense, and is a clever attempt to re-appropriate the valued label "Advaita" for his own school. Yet in this regard all Bhedâbhedavâdins might claim the name Suddhâdvaita, since they all assert the reality of the phenomenal world.

e. Caitanya

Caitanya was another medieval Vaisnava philosopher/ theologian, famous for a school of thought known as Acintya

Bhedâbhedavâda (Inconceivable Difference and Non-difference). Although Caitanya never wrote down his teachings, numerous followers authored works based on his philosophy, such as Jîva Gosvâmin, author of a well-known commentary on the *Bhâgavata Purâna*. This system's notion of "inconceivability" (*acintyatva*) is a central concept used to reconcile apparently contradictory notions, such as the simultaneous oneness and multiplicity of Brahman, or the difference and non-difference of God and his powers. The tradition of Acintya-Bhedâbheda, also commonly known as Gaudîya Vaisnavism, thrives to this day in the Indian state of West Bengal. Perhaps the most famous offshoot of this devotional tradition is the International Society for Krishna Consciousness (ISKON), more popularly known in the West by the name the "Hari Krishnas."

f. Vijñânabhiksu

The last major Bhedâbheda thinker in pre-modern India, Vijñânabhiksu (16th c.), did not follow the path of *bhakti*. Vijñânabhiksu sought to show the ultimate unity of the schools of Vedânta, Sânkhya, Yoga, and Nyâya, and is most well known today for commentaries on Sânkhya and Yoga texts. In his innovative sub-commentary on Patanjali's *Yoga Sûtra,* Vijñânabhiksu argues that yoga is the most effective means to liberation, although he never repudiates the Bhedâbheda metaphysical framework of his earliest writings (Nicholson 2005). Vijñânabhiksu was a theist who considered Visnu the supreme God. In his commentary on the *Sânkhya Sûtra,* he argues that the Sânkhya school requires an omnipotent God in order to cause the union of its two fundamental principles, primordial nature (*Prakrti*) and pure consciousness (*Purusa*). Vijñânabhiksu grounds his reinterpretations of fundamental concepts in Sânkhya-Yoga in Bhedâbheda metaphysics. In his earliest works, such as his Bhedâbheda Vedântic commentary on the *Brahma Sûtras,* he understands the concepts of difference and non-difference in terms of separation and non-separation (Ram 1995). Although for him the fundamental relation of the individual self and Brahman is one of non-separation, the Sânkhya-Yoga analysis of the individual selves as multiple and separate from one another is correct, as long as it is understood that this state of separation is temporary and adventitious. While

Vijñânabhiksu's acceptance of Sânkhya-Yoga philosophical truths puts him at odds with some earlier Bhedâbhedavâdins, he continues in the tradition of Bhâskara in his trenchant criticism of the Advaita Vedântins, whom he decries as "crypto-Buddhists" (*pracchannabauddha*) and "Vedântins in name alone" (*vedântibruva*).

2. ONTOLOGY

One of the most notable differences between Bhedâbheda Vedânta and Advaita (Monistic) Vedânta is their views on the existence of the phenomenal world. While Advaita holds that the phenomenal world is ultimately unreal (*mithyâ*) and that only Brahman truly exists, Bhedâbheda thinkers insist that the phenomenal world is real, and not at all illusory. In this basic assertion they are in line with the majority of Indian philosophical schools, including the schools of Qualified Non-Dualist (Visistâdvaita) Vedânta, Dualist (Dvaita) Vedânta, Nyâya, Sânkhya, and Mîmâmsâ. Although Advaitins cite certain passages from the Upanisads as supporting the notion that the world is akin to a mirage or a magical trick, Bhedâbhedavâdins accuse Advaitins of borrowing this idea from the Mind-only (Cittamâtra) school of Buddhism, and frequently employ the epithet of "crypto-Buddhist" (*pracchannabauddha*) to refer to Advaitins.

a. Part and Whole

Bhedâbhedavâdins understand the relation between Brahman and the individual souls to be a relation between a whole and its parts. They frequently employ stock examples to illustrate this relation. Some of the most common are a fire and its sparks, the sun and its rays, a father and his son, and the ocean and its waves. Each of these is an example of a part-whole relation, which is also a variety of difference and non-difference (Bhedâbheda). So, to take one example, the sparks that come off of a fire are both the same as that fire and different from it. They are the same insofar as they came from the fire, and are constituted by the same substance as fire. But they are also distinguishable from the original fire, as occupying a separate point in space. Although these four examples each seem to illustrate a different relation (and it may seem to make no sense at all to understand a son as a "part" of his father),

Bhedâbhedavâdins cite these familiar examples from the physical world in order to shed light on the true metaphysical relation between Brahman and the individual selves. While each might capture some aspect of that relation, inevitably they are mere approximations, requiring further commentary and philosophical analysis.

Advaita Vedântins object to the characterization of the individual self as a part, and characterize Brahman as partless. All schools of Vedânta understand the Veda as the ultimate epistemic authority, and arguments from scripture play a large part in intra-Vedântic disputes. Advaitins point out that both the Upanisads and the *Brahma Sûtras* say that Brahman is partless (*niravayava, nickala*). Furthermore, the assertion that Brahman has parts seems to defy logic. It is inconceivable that Brahman could be made up of parts, for things that are made up of parts are dependent on those parts, and impermanent. Advaitins offer their own stock examples to show that Brahman cannot be divided up, and that any such division is purely an artificial limitation on an indivisible entity. For example, Advaitins commonly liken Brahman to the element called "space" (*âkâsa*). According to traditional science in India, space is an element that is omnipresent in the world, just as all Vedântins agree that Brahman is omnipresent. Although we can talk about space as being delimited (the space inside a room, the space inside a pot), such limitations of space are purely accidental, not essential to the element itself. It may appear to an observer that the space inside a pot and the space outside the pot are two different entities, but this is a misunderstanding of the fundamental nature of space.

The Bhedâbhedavâdins can themselves appeal to textual authority for the idea that the relation between Brahman and the individual self is a relation between a whole and its parts. In *Brahma Sûtra* 2.3.43, The individual self is referred to as a "part" (*amsa*), and Bhedâbhedavâdins cite this passage whenever they require a textual support for their views. However, Advaitins take this description of the relation as a figurative, and not literal description of the status of the individual self. Otherwise, this passage will conflict with *Brahma Sûtra* 2.1.26, which says that Brahman is "partless" (*niravayava*). For Advaita, the world appears *as if* to be made of parts. But when it is understood correctly, all of the many entities in the world are seen to be false, and only one entity, a single, partless Brahman remains. Bhedâbhedavâdins, in their assertion of the world's phenomenal reality, insist that multiplicity is real. Brahman is simultaneously one and many, depending on the perspective from which it is viewed, just as the ocean can be described as one or many, depending on the perspective from which it is described. Bhedâbhedavâdins maintain that Brahman's being made up of parts in no way diminishes the perfection of Brahman, just as the existence of waves in the ocean in no way diminishes the amount of water therein.

b. Aupâdhika and Svâbhâvika Bhedâbheda

All Bhedâbhedavâdins maintain the reality of the phenomenal world and the multiplicity of individual selves. However, some Bhedâbheda thinkers edge closer to the Advaita position by arguing that although multiplicity is real, it is in some way *less real* than the absolute unity of Brahman. The early Bhedâbheda thinker Bhâskara (8th-9th c. CE) exemplifies this tendency to reduce the ontological status of the phenomenal world, while still maintaining its reality. Bhâskara's philosophy is an example of Aupâdhika Bhedâbhedavâda ("Difference and Non-difference Based on Limiting Conditions"). According to Bhâskara, the one, absolute Brahman becomes finite and multiple by means of limiting conditions (*upâdhis*). Just as a pure diamond appears to be red when it is placed next to a red flower, so too the absolute Brahman appears finite when it is transformed through limiting conditions. This transformation is a real one; the individual self really is finite, subject to ignorance, suffering, and bondage, so long as it is filtered through limiting conditions. Although the individual self is real as differentiated from Brahman, for Bhâskara difference is merely a temporary state. In its natural state, Brahman is one and not many. Although it undergoes limitations to become finite, the ultimate goal of the individual is to realize his or her absolute state. Liberation is precisely the removal of such limiting conditions. At the other end of the spectrum from Bhâskara's Aupadhika Bhedâbhedavâda is Nimbârka's philosophy of Svâbhâvika Bhedâbheda (Natural Difference and Non-Difference). For Nimbârka (13th c.), Brahman is different and non-different not because of artificial limiting conditions, but contains both non-difference and non-difference as its essential nature. Along with Yâdavaprakâsa (11th c.), Nimbârka comes closest to upholding both difference and non-difference as equally real states of Brahman. The tendency among most Bhedâbhedavâdins, however, is to subordinate difference to non-difference. Although difference is a real state that Brahman undergoes as it transforms into multiple individual selves, Bhâskara in essence makes the state of non-difference "more real" than the state of difference. In this way, school of Bhedâbheda Vedânta is often closer to the school of Advaita (Monist) Vedânta than it is to the school of Dvaita (Dualist) Vedânta.

3. CAUSALITY

a. Parinâmavâda (Theory of real transformation)

Closely related to Bhedâbheda Vedânta's ontology is its theory of causality. Bhedâbheda Vedântins subscribe to the theory of *Parinâmavâda,* which states that the phenomenal world is a real transformation (*parinâma*) of the material cause of the world. They share this theory with the Sânkhya school of philosophy, as well as with most other schools of Vedânta. The major difference between the Vedântic theory of *Parinâmavâda* and the Sânkhya's *Parinâmavâda* is the understanding of what constitutes the material cause of the world. For Sânkhya, primordial nature (*Prakrti*) transforms itself into the phenomenal world. The principle of primordial nature is completely insentient, and the process of transformation that creates the world is a blind, automatic process. For Bhedâbheda Vedântins, Brahman is both the material and efficient cause of the universe. Brahman, unlike the Sânkhya's *Prakrti,* is sentient. Yet both the sentient (individual souls) and insentient (physical things) have their origin in Brahman, according to Bhedâbhedavâdins. In spite of their apparent proximity to the Sânkhya school on the issue of causality, early Bhedâbheda thinkers such as Bhâskara took pains to critique the Sânkhya notion of *Prakrti,* accusing it of being both contrary to scripture and contrary to logic. A few later Bhedâbheda thinkers took a softer line on Sânkhya. The most notable of these was Vijñânabhiksu (16th c.), who argued for the ultimate unity of Sânkhya and Bhedâbheda Vedânta doctrines.

b. Vivartavâda (Theory of unreal manifestation)

Once again, it is useful to contrast the doctrines of the Bhedâbheda school with Advaita Vedânta. Advaita Vedânta maintains the doctrine of *Vivartavâda,* which states that the world is an unreal manifestation (*vivarta*) of Brahman. Advaita, like other schools of Vedânta, identifies Brahman as both material and efficient cause. But for the Advaitins, Brahman is the cause of an unreal effect. Although the world can be described as conventionally real (*paramârthasat*), the Advaitins claim that all of Brahman's effects must ultimately be acknowledged as unreal before the individual self can be liberated. Although the theory of *Vivartavâda* is traditionally accepted as a theory shared by the entire Advaita school, some recent historians have questioned this, noting passages in the work of Sankara, the founder of the Advaita, that appear to be closer to the theory of *parinâma* (Hacker 1953: pp. 24ff.; Rao 1996: pp. 265ff.). It is likely that the theory of *Vivartavâda* is a theory that emerged gradually out of the earlier Vedântic theory of *Parinâmavâda,* rather than one that sprang fully formed out of the head of Sankara. It also bears repeating that some Bhedâbheda Vedântins come perilously close to the Advaita view of the phenomenal world as only conventionally real, as they often emphasize that multiplicity is an unnatural, temporary state.

c. Satkâryavâda (Theory of pre-existent effect)

Proponents of both Vedântic theories of causality, *Parinâmavâda* and *Vivartavâda,* justify each by citing a central passage at *Chândogya Upanisad* 6.1.4-5. There, the sage Aruni describes the nature of causality to his son, Svetaketu, using the example of the relation of clay to a pot: It is like this, son. By means of just one lump of clay one would perceive everything made of clay—the transformation is a verbal handle, a name—while the reality is just this: 'It's clay.' It is like this, son. By means of just one copper trinket one would perceive everything made of copper—the transformation is a verbal handle, a name—while the reality is just this: 'It's copper.' (Olivelle 1996: 148)

This passage uses the examples of an everyday material cause, clay or copper, to shed light on the nature of cause and effect. It expresses the doctrine of *Satkaryavâda*, which says that the effect preexists in its cause. All Vedântins subscribe to this theory—the doctrines of real tranformation (*parinâma*) and unreal manifestation (*Vivartavâda*) can be understood as two different versions of the theory of *Satkâryavâda*. According to *Satkâryavâda*, the lump of clay does not go out of existence when it is transformed into a pot, a cup, a saucer, or the like, only to be replaced by something entirely new. Although the form of the clay has changed, its essence, its clay-ness, remains. The same logic applies to everything caused by Brahman. The entire world, in all of its many forms, nonetheless shares the same essence, as being Brahman. This view, something like an early Indian theory of the conservation of matter, suggests that nothing ever arrives in the universe completely new, but only as a transformation of some earlier material cause. Nothing can be created *ex nihilo*. In this belief, the Vedântins are at odds with the Buddhist and Nyâya schools, who for separate reasons argue that the effect does not preexist in the cause.

Although Bhedâbheda Vedântins and Advaita Vedântins have the theory of *Satkâryavâda*in common, they part ways when asked to characterize the status of the effect. Is the effect a real transformation (*parinâma*) of the cause, or merely an unreal manifestation (*vivarta*)? The passage at *Chândogya Upanisad* 6.1.4-5 has been interpreted in both ways. Advaitins emphasize the apparent nominalism expressed by Aruni in this passage: "the transformation is a verbal handle, a name—while the reality is just this: 'It's copper.'" This might suggest that the effect is unreal, and only the cause is truly real. But Bhedâbhedavâdins see this passage as simply another instantiation of the principle of difference and non-difference, just as it is illustrated by the examples of a fire and its sparks or the sun and its rays. From one perspective, focusing on substance, we can say that all of the various cups, saucers, and plates are one—they are all clay. Yet at the same time, they have been transformed by the pot-maker into different forms, multiple in number, occupying different points in space. From this perspective, the effects are real. Just as the many pots, plates, and saucers are simultaneously different and non-different from the original lump of clay, so too all of the individual selves are both different and non-different from Brahman, the original material cause.

4. THEOLOGY AND SOTERIOLOGY

a. God in Bhedâbhedavâda

In the medieval period, Bhedâbheda Vedânta became closely associated with theism in general, and the movement of *bhakti* devotionalism in particular. There is a reason that*bhaktas* such as Vallabha (1479-1531 CE) and Caitanya (1485-1533) built the foundations of their theological systems on centuries-old Bhedâbheda concepts. Like the schools of Râmânuja and Madhva, Bhedâbhedavâda is a realist school. Whereas in the Advaita school even God has to be understood as ultimately unreal, since He too is merely Brahman limited by the artificial condition of lordliness, certain types of Bhedâbheda philosophy can accommodate a God who is real in his qualified (*saguna*) form. Although on a certain level, an Advaitin can profess a belief in God, he or she knows that ultimately God is merely a crutch, a heuristic to enable human beings to go one step closer to that ultimate Brahman devoid of qualities (*nirguna*). Such a God is ultimately unsatisfying for those whose primary interest is devotion—in any system of Advaita, devotion must occupy a lower position than pure knowledge. On the other hand, many worshippers will also be unsatisfied with the Dvaita school's uncompromising notion that they themselves are completely separate from God, and that ultimate unification with the Godhead is impossible. Both Bhedâbhedavâda and Visistâdvaita offer the possibility to bridge these two alternatives, by offering the alternative of both a real God possessing qualities and the possibility of personal participation in that Godhead.

b. Knowledge combined with ritual acts leads to liberation

Besides insistence that the phenomenal world is a real transformation (*parinâma*) of Brahman, another view shared by Bhedâbhedavâdins is the necessity of ritual acts in combination with knowledge (*Jñânakarmasamuccayavâda*) in order to obtain liberation. Bhâskara devotes much of the beginning of his commentary on the *Brahma Sûtra* to a critique of Sankara's radical view that knowledge alone is sufficient for the attainment of Brahman, as long as one has fulfilled one's ritual requirements at an earlier stage. Although today polemics between Vedântins are usually depicted in solely philosophical or theological terms, this suggests that above all, Sankara's new teachings were seen by other Vedântins in the 8th century as a serious threat to the ritual-social order. Bhâskara's arguments in favour of Brahmanic ritualism are an important reminder of the continuities between early Vedânta and the Pûrva Mîmâmsâ (Prior Exegesis) school of ritual hermeneutics. The two schools are so close that Sanskrit authors in pre-modern India typically refer to Vedânta by the names "Brahma Mîmâmsâ" (Exegesis of Brahman) or "Uttara Mîmâmsâ" (Later Exegesis), emphasizing the central importance of Vedic interpretation for all Vedântic thinkers.

The notion of *bhakti* finds a home in Bhedâbhedavâda, since Bhedâbheda takes activity in the world (*karman*) seriously, believing that activities in the world are real, and produce real effects. But it should not be thought that all Bhedâbhedavâdins were proponents of *bhakti*. The early Bhedâbheda of Bhâskara was not concerned at all with *bhakti*. Instead, Bhâskara uses Bhedâbheda conceptual terminology as a conservative apologist, to defend the importance of Brahmanical ritual orthodoxy from Sankara, a radical who rejected the ultimate efficacy of Vedic ritual. It is only with Nimbârka, a Bhedâbheda thinker heavily influenced by the *bhakti* system of Râmânuja, that we first fully see the union of *bhakti*worship and Bhedâbhedavâda. Even in medieval northern India, where *bhakti* was influential and widespread, not all Bhedâbhedavâdins were *bhaktas*. Vijñânabhiksu, for example, was more interested in espousing a modified, Bhedâbheda Vedântic form of Patañjali's Yoga than he was to proselytize for the path of devotion. Such flexibility of the Bhedâbheda philosophical apparatus has allowed it to survive as a living tradition for over 1500 years in a number of very different historical contexts. Although in the modern period Bhedâbheda Vedânta has been eclipsed in popularity by neo-Vedântic interpretations of Advaita Vedânta philosophy, its lineage continues today among traditional scholars in Pucmimârga and Gaudîya Vaicnava religious communities. And, for the first time in its long history, in the early 21st century Bhedâbheda Vedânta is beginning to receive the attention it deserves among historians, philosophers, and theologians outside of India.

REFERENCES

1.Bhâskara (1903). *Brahmasûtra Bhâsyam*, ed. Pandit Vindhyeshvari Prasada Dvivedin. Benares: Chowkhamba Sanskrit Book Depot.

2.Dasgupta, Surendranath (1922). *A History of Indian Philosophy, vol III*. Delhi: Motilal Banarsidass.

3.Hacker, Paul (1953). *Vivarta: Studien zur Geschichte der illusionistischen Kosmologie und Erkenntnistheorie der Inder*. Wiesbaden: Franz Steiner Verlag.

4.Kapoor, O.B.L (1976). *The Philosophy and Religion of Sri Caitanya*. Delhi: Munshiram Manoharlal.

5.Marfatia, Mrdula I. (1967). *The Philosophy of Vallabhâcarya*. Delhi: Munshiram Manoharlal.

6.Nakamura, Hajime (1989). *A History of Early Vedânta Philosophy*, part 1. Delhi: Motilal Banarsidass.

7.Nicholson, Andrew (2005). "Vijñânabhiksu's Yoga," *Journal of Vaishnava Studies* vol.14, no. 1: pp. 43-53.

8.Oberhammer, Gerhard (1997). *Materialien zur Geschichte der* Râmânuja-*Schule III:*Yâdavaprakâúa, *der vergessene Lehrer Râmânujas*. Wien: Verlag der Osterreichische Akademie der Wissenschaften.

9.Olivelle, Patrick, translator (1996). *Upanisads*. New York: Oxford University Press.

10.Ram, Kanshi (1995). *Integral Non-Dualism: A Critical Exposition of* Vijñânabhiksu'*s System of Philosophy*. Delhi: Motilal Banarsidass.

11.Rao, Srinivasa (1996). "Two 'Myths' in Advaita," *Journal of Indian Philosophy* vol. 24: pp. 265-279.

12.Smith, Frederick M. (2005). "The Hierarchy of Philosophical Systems According to Vallabhâcârya," *Journal of Indian Philosophy* vol. 33: pp. 421-453.

13.Srinivasachari, P.N. (1972). *The Philosophy of Bhedâbheda*. Madras: Adyar Library.

14

Visistadvaita Philosophy

Ramanuja (c.1017-c113 CE): Râmânuja (*âcârya*), the eleventh century South Indian philosopher, is the chief proponent of Vishishtâdvaita, which is one of the three main forms of the Orthodox Hindu philosophical school, Vedânta. As the prime philosopher of the Vishishtâdvaita tradition, Râmânuja is one of the Indian philosophical tradition's most important and influential figures. He was the first Indian philosopher to provide a systematic theistic interpretation of the philosophy of the Vedas, and is famous for arguing for the epistemic and soteriological significance of *bhakti*, or devotion to a personal God. Unlike many of his contemporaries, Râmânuja defended the reality of a plurality of individual persons, qualities, values and objects while affirming the substantial unity of all. On some accounts, Râmânuja's influence on popular Hindu practice is so vast that his system forms the basis for popular Hindu philosophy. His two main philosophical writings (the *Shrî Bhâshya* and *Vedârthasangraha*) are amongst the best examples of rigorous and energetic argumentation in any philosophical tradition, and they are masterpieces of Indian scholastic philosophy.

1. RAMANUJA'S LIFE AND WORKS

On traditional accounts, Ramanuja lived the unusually long life of 120 years (twice the average lifespan at the time), from 1017 to 1137 AD, though recent scholarship places his life between 1077 to 1157 AD, with a life of 80 years (Carman p.27). He was born in the Southern, Tamil speaking region of India, in the small township of Shri Perumbudur on the outskirts of modern day Chennai (Madras) into a family that hailed from a subclass of Brahmins (the Hindu priestly caste) known for their scholarship and learning in the Vedas. His family was likely bilingual, fluent in both the local vernacular (Tamil) and the language of scholarship (Sanskrit). From a young age he is reputed to have displayed a prodigious intellect and liberal attitudes towards caste. At this time he became friendly with a local, saintly Sudra (member of the servile caste) by the name of Kancipurna, whose occupation it was to perform services for the local temple idol of the Hindu deity Vishnu. Ramanuja admired Kancipurna's piety and devotion to Vishnu and sought Kancipurna as his guru-much to the horror of Kancipurna who regarded Ramanuja's humility before him as an affront to caste propriety.

Shortly after being married in his teenage years, and after his father passed away, Ramanuja and his family moved to the neighboring city of Kancipuram. There Ramanuja found his first formal teacher, Yadavaprakasha, who was an accomplished professor of the form of the Vedanta philosophy that was in vogue at the time-a form of Vedanta that has strong affinities to Shankara's Absolute Idealistic Monism (Advaita Vedanta) but was also close to the Difference-and-non-difference view (Bhedabheda Vedanta). ("Vedanta" means the 'end of the Vedas' and refers to the philosophy expressed in the end portion of the Vedas, also known as the Upanishads, and encoded in the cryptic summary by Badharayana called the*Vedanta Sutra* or *Brahma Sutra*. The perennial questions of Vedanta are: what is the nature of *Brahman*, or the Ultimate, and what is the relationship between the multiplicity of individuals to this Ultimate. Vedanta comprises one of the six orthodox schools of Hindu philosophy.)

At first Yadavaprakasha was thrilled to receive a talented and intelligent student of the likes of Ramanuja. But disagreements between the two, on the proper interpretation of the Upanishads, soon broke out. Yadavaprakasha favoured an amoral, impersonal, non-theistic interpretation of the Upanishads. Ramanuja, in contrast, favoured a theistic interpretation of the Upanishads that placed a premium on the aesthetic and moral excellences of *Brahman*. Yadavaprakasha found Ramanuja's skill at offering alternative interpretations threatening both to his authority and the popularity of his philosophy. He thus hatched a plan, with some of his other students, to murder Ramanuja while on a pilgrimage. Ramanuja however got word of the plan from his classmate and cousin (Govinda) and escaped from the pilgrimage with his life. Ramanuja (surprisingly) did not make public his knowledge of the failed assassination attempt and resumed classes with Yadavaprakasha when he returned to Kancipuram. Yadavaprakasha for his part did not reveal his complicity in the plot to take Ramanuja's life, and feigned happiness at continuing to be his teacher. Not too long afterwards, however, Yadavaprakasha ordered Ramanuja to leave his school, after a final disagreement on the interpretation of scripture occurred.

Without a teacher, Ramanuja returned dejected to his childhood mentor, Kancipurna, who assured him that a teacher would come his way. For the time being, Kancipurna instructed Ramanuja to help him in his manual service to the temple idol of Vishnu.

At the same time Yamuna, the spiritual head of the fledgling Tamil Vaishnava (Vishnu worshiping) community, was near the end of his life and in search of a successor. This community, known as the Shri Vaishnava Sampradaya, was formed around the memory of the Four Thousand Tamil Verses (*Nalayira Divya Prabhandam*) of twelve Tamil Vaishnava saints (*Alvars*), renowned for their devotional poetry on Vishnu. While it had a modest popular base, it lacked a formal and legitimizing articulation in the Sanskrit academic community. Though a competent and accomplished philosopher in his own right who authored the impressive *Siddhi Trayam*, Yamuna came into the fold too late in his life to fully articulate the philosophy of Shri Vaishnavas to the pan-Indian academic community. He thus held out the hope that Ramanuja would, amongst other things, take up the task of articulating the philosophical ethos of the tradition that had been entrusted to him, in the form of a formal, Sanskrit commentary on the *Brahma Sutra* (the cryptic summary of the philosophical purport of the Upanishads). Upon finding out that Ramanuja had been freed from ties to Yadavaprakasha, and had returned to the company of Kancipurna (himself a member of Yamuna's Shri Vaishnava community) Yamuna was overjoyed and sent word to Ramanuja to come and take up the post as his successor. Yamuna however died just before Ramanuja could reach him, and once again Ramanuja found himself without the teacher he had been searching for.

After Ramanuja had gained his composure, he made his way over to the crowd centered on Yamuna's new corpse. He noted that three fingers of Yamuna's were curled. Yamuna's senior disciples explained to Ramanuja that they likely represented three wishes of Yamuna, one of which being that a commentary on the *Brahma Sutra* should be written. When Ramanuja pledged to try to fulfill those wishes, the fingers uncurled. The crowd took this as a sign that Ramanuja was the heir apparent of Yamuna. Ramanuja was however vexed at the local temple idol of Vishnu for not even allowing him a brief meeting with Yamuna, and would not formally join the community for nearly a year.

When Ramanuja did decide to formally join the Shri Vaishnava fold, Yamuna's senior disciple, Mahapurna, supervised his initiation. For a matter of six months, Ramanuja had found himself the teacher he was looking for in the form of Mahapurna. Under Mahapurna, Ramanuja learned the verses of the Tamil Vaishnava saints. However, his learning under Mahapurna came to an abrupt end when Ramanuja's wife picked a fight with Mahapurna's wife, on the premise that the latter was a member of a lower Brahminic subcaste. Upon hearing this, the hurt Mahapurna and his wife departed from Ramanuja's company without notice. Ramanuja, once again lost his teacher. But this was not the first time that Ramanuja's wife had interfered with his spiritual development.

At an earlier point, Ramanuja had invited his childhood mentor, Kancipurna, for a meal. Ramanuja had hoped to partake of Kancipurna's leavings as a sacrament. However, Kancipurna arrived early in absence of Ramanuja. Ramanuja's wife fed Kancipurna, sent him off, and ritually purified the dining area, by, amongst other things, discarding Kancipurna's leftovers.

Having lost the benefits of a teacher twice over as a result of his wife's caste-pretensions, Ramanuja was incensed. He thus sent his wife back to her natal home, and promptly became a renounciate (*sannyasin*). He earned the title "king of ascetics (*yatiraja*) from the temple deity of Vishnu speaking through Kancipurna at this point.

Ramanuja's separation from his wife and his initiation into the order of ascetics marks the beginning of his career as an independent and self-assured philosopher. He travelled around India and participated in public debates with exponents of rival philosophies. Many of the philosophers that Ramanuja defeated became prominent disciples in his fold. Ramanuja standardized and reformed temple worship in those Vaishnava temples that he gained control over (often through winning debates with the custodians of the temple). To this day his instructions are the norm of Shri Vaishnava temple and home worship in India and abroad.

The Shri Vaishnava tradition is unanimous in holding that Ramanuja authored nine, and only nine, works: all in Sanskrit. While Ramanuja is reported by the writings of his disciples to have lectured in Tamil on the verses of the Tamil Vaishnava saints, he left no writings on their work, and no explicit mention of them in his writings. At first glance, this seems remarkable, given that the *Divya Prabhandam* is regarded by the Shri Vaishnava tradition, as the Tamil equivalent of the Vedas. However, Ramanuja's silence on the*Alvars* in his Sanskrit writings may have been a result of his aim as philosopher to not preach to the converted, but to articulate his philosophy to the pan-Indian academic community.

Ramanuja's first work was likely the *Vedarthasangraha* ('Summary of the Meaning of the Vedas'). It sets out Ramanuja's philosophy, which is theistic (it affirms a morally perfect, omniscient and omnipotent God) and realistic (it affirms the existence and reality of a plurality of qualities, persons and objects). This work is referred to several times in Ramanuja's *magnum opus,* his commentary on the *Brahma Sutra,* the *Shri Bhashya* (also known as his *Brahma Sutra Bhashya*). This is the work that Ramanuja is best known by outside of the Shri Vaishnava tradition. In addition to this large commentary on the *Brahma Sutra,* Ramanuja apparently wrote two more shorter commentaries: *Vedantapida,* and *Vedantasara.* Aside from the *Vedarthasangraha* and *Shri Bhashya,* Ramanuja's most important philosophic work is a commentary on the *Bhagavad Gita* (*Bhagavad Gita Bhashya*). In addition to these philosophic works, Ramanuja is held by tradition to have written three prose hymns called collectively the *Gadya Traya*, which include the*Sharanagati Gadya, Shriranga Gadya* and the *Vaikuntha Gadya*). The *Sharanagati Gadya* is a dialogue between Ramanuja and the Hindu deities Shri (Lakshmi) and Narayana (Vishnu) (which jointly comprise God, or *Brahman*, for Ramanuja) in which Ramanuja surrenders himself before God and petitions Vishnu, through Lakshmi, for his Grace. Vishnu and Lakshmi, for their part, respond favorably to Ramanuja's act of surrender. The *Shriranga Gadya* is a prayer of surrender to the feet of Ranganatha. (This is Vishnu in his repose on the many headed serpent Adiœesa -'ancient servant,' 'ancient residue,' or 'primeval matter' - on the milk ocean.) The *Vaikuntha Gadya* describes in great detail the eternal realm of Vishnu, called Vaikuntha, on which one should meditate in order to gain liberation. Finally Ramanuja is held to have authored a manual of daily worship called the *Nityagrantha*.

The authenticity of all but the three large works attributed to Ramanuja – *Shri Bhashya, Vedarthasangraha* and the *Bhagavad Gita Bhashya* – have come into question in recent times. The argument against the authenticity of these texts appears to be a minority position amongst scholars. With respect to the two smaller commentaries on the *Brahma Sutra*, it has been argued that they must be inauthentic, because it seems unlikely that Ramanuja would himself have bothered to take the time to abridge his larger commentary, the *Shri Bhashya* (cf. Buitenen p.32). With respect to the short religious works attributed to Ramanuja, it has been argued that they present doctrines that go beyond those that are found in his major commentaries (cf. Lester p.279).

2. RAMANUJA'S COSMOLOGY AND METAPHYSICS

a. Background

Subsequent tradition has applied the label "Vishishtadvaita" to the philosophy of Ramanuja. It is meant to contrast his philosophy from leading competing views, such as Advaita (Non-Dualist), Bhedabheda (Difference-and-non-difference) and Dvaita

(Dualist) Vedanta. The term "Vishishtadvaita" is often translated as 'Qualified Non-Dualism.' An alternative, and more informative, translation is "Non-duality of the qualified whole," or perhaps 'Non-duality with qualifications." The label attempts to mark out Ramanuja's effort to affirm the unity of the many, without giving up on the reality of distinct persons, qualities, universals, or aesthetic and moral values.

Where all versions of Vedanta intersect is in their effort to provide a consistent and defendable interpretation of the *Brahma Sutra,* on philosophical and hermeneutic grounds. Given the common textual bases, there are certain doctrinal invariances amongst the various sub-schools of Vedanta.

In accordance with the Upanishads, the various schools of Vedanta hold that there is an ultimate entity, called *Brahman,* which also is referred to by scripture as "*Atma*" ("Self"). The Vedanta schools recognize, in accordance with the Upanishads, that *Brahman* plays a key role in the organization of the universe. Attainment of *Brahman* by an individual constitutes its highest good: soteriological liberation or *moksha.*

The chief areas of disagreement amongst the various schools of Vedanta are on the nature and ontological status of individual selves, objects of cognition and *Brahman,* as well as the relevance and importance of ethics or duty (*dharma*) to the good life.

Ramanuja's foils in the articulation of his philosophy are two forms of Vedanta that were not clearly distinguished during his day: these are the Bhedabheda view, and the Advaita philosophy. Both these views take a similar stance on the relationship of an individual's subjectivity and *Brahman*: on both accounts, the conscious principle of the individual is of a piece with *Brahman.* In the case of Advaita Vedanta, the consciousness of an individual is regarded as numerically identical with the consciousness of*Brahman*. On this view, the psychological ego or sense of individuality is something distinct from consciousness: it is its object. The Bhedabheda view similarly asserts the numerical identity of an individual's consciousness and *Brahman,* but it emphasizes that this identity is counteracted by a separating off, or differentiating effort, on the part of *Brahman* to compartmentalize itself and mysteriously constitute the world of plurality and difference. On this view, the individual ego is constituted by *Brahman*. According to the versions of Bhedabheda and Advaita that Ramanuja was acquainted with, mere knowledge of one's identity with *Brahman* is sufficient to bring about liberation; works, such as ritual and moral obligations, can at best play a preparatory role in bringing an individual to the state of being desirous for liberation, but they have no intrinsic value. Corollaries of these views are the position that consciousness, and not plurality, is metaphysically fundamental; that consciousness does not require objects for its existence; that belief in plurality consists in the uncritical acceptance of ordinary experience; and that dialectical reasoning can yield substantive knowledge with practical import. On many fronts (on the reality of universals, particulars, and moral values) both the Bhedabheda Advaita schools are classic forms of anti-realism.

Students of Ramanuja's thought may wish to know whom Ramanuja is arguing against. In all likely hood, it is his former teacher, Yadavaprakasha. However, Ramanuja does not attribute the Advaita or Bhedabheda views to any particular philosopher. Rather, these views are voiced by the opponent, or the ubiquitous *purvapaksin*, everywhere in Indian philosophy, expressing the views to be criticized.

Ramanuja's arguments that he presents against his opponent are of roughly three varieties. Some are negative, and focus on philosophical problems of the opponent's view. Some are positive, and concern arguing for theses that Ramanuja wishes to defend. And some arguments are hermeneutic. This last category of arguments combines criticism and positive philosophical argument, but it centers on the proper interpretation of the Vedas.

b. Negative Philosophical Criticisms of Bhedabheda and Advaita Vedanta

i. Logical Criticism

Ramanuja criticizes many of the arguments of the Bhedabheda and Advaita views on logical grounds. These schools employed dialectical arguments that conclude on the basis of logical puzzles that arise in accounting for distinctions and difference in perception that difference (which includes the idea of a distinct quality) is an unintelligible notion. From such considerations, these philosophers would typically conclude that only undifferentiated consciousness is the real (*Brahman*). Ramanuja at many points in the *Shri Bhashya* and the *Vedarthasangraha* attempts to argue against such views by an argument *ad absurdum*. Particularly, Ramanuja argues that the arguments presented by the Bhedabheda and Advaita Vedantins lead to intolerable contradictions and further conclusions that go against common sense. At one point he suggests that those who would make such arguments are "no better than a man who would claim that his own mother never had any children" (*Shri Bhashya*, I.i.1. *"Great Siddhanta"* p.44).

ii. Argument from Epistemology

Ramanuja argues that the epistemic considerations that his opponents adduce for their positions undercut their own views. The philosophers that Ramanuja takes aim at argue that all means of cognition involve error. Ramanuja argues that if this is so, it follows that we could never know that all cognition involves error, for such putative knowledge would itself involve an erroneous cognition, and hence not qualify as genuine knowledge. If Ramanuja's opponents view is correct, then it follows that some cognitions are not erroneous. But this is exactly what the disputed conclusion rules out (*Shri Bhashya*, I.i.1. *"Great Siddhanta"* pp.74-78).

c. Substantive Theses

i. Intentionality of Consciousness

While the previous two strategies that Ramanuja employs in his criticism of the Bhedabheda and Advaita views are largely negative, and involve criticizing these views on formal grounds, Ramanuja also defends philosophical theses that these two schools rule out. The most important of these theses is the view that consciousness is always consciousness of some object distinguished by a characteristic (cf. *Shri Bhashya*, I.i.1. *"Great Siddhanta"* p.53 and *"Great Purvapaksa"* p.32). This is the doctrine known as "*dharmabhutajnana*" in the Vishishtadvaita tradition (Shrinivasadisa VII.2). It implies the view that all epistemic states, be it consciousness or perception, are *intentional* or object oriented. If it is the case that even consciousness requires an object for its existence, it follows that there can be no such thing as pure consciousness apart from difference (such as qualities, properties and objects of consciousness). Thus, on this account, if consciousness exists, it follows that difference and plurality does as well. With this one thesis, and against the backdrop of Vedantic idealism, Ramanuja is able to generate one limb of his organismic cosmology.

ii. Consciousness is a Property of Something

Another important substantive philosophical thesis that Ramanuja defends is that consciousness is itself a property. To modern readers, this may seem to be a trivial point. However, it is central to the project of Ramanuja's opponents that *Brahman* is the only reality, and it is a reality devoid of distinctions or qualities. Ramanuja's opponents are happy to affirm that certain things can be said of *Brahman*, for instance, that it is (as affirmed in the *Taittitriya Upanishad* II.i.1.) truth (*satyam*) knowledge (*jnanam*) and infinite (*anantam*). However, they take the stand that these are not properties of *Brahman*, but the very being of *Brahman* (*Shri Bhashya*, I.i.1. "*Great Purvapaksa*" p.29). Ramanuja, in contrast, defends the view that such attributions bring attention to the reality of *Brahman*'s qualities (cf. *Shri Bhashya*, I.i.1. "*Great Purvapaksa*" p.28).

iii. Individuals are Real

A third and important substantive thesis that Ramanuja defends is the reality of the individual. According to Advaita Vedanta (and the Bhedabheda view to a lesser extent), the individual person, in contradistinction to other persons, is an illusion (*maya*) that comes about by nescience (*avidya*). Ramanuja argues that the very idea that something can be ignorant presumes that there is an individual capable of being ignorant. For all Vedantins affirm that *Brahman* is of the nature of consciousness and knowledge. Hence, to say that *Brahman* is ignorant is absurd. If anything is subject to ignorance, it must be an individual other than *Brahman*. However, if this is so, then ignorance cannot be brought into explain the existence of individuals, for it presumes the existence of an individual capable of being ignorant. Ramanuja's positive view is thus that there are, indeed, distinct individuals, many who are under the spell of ignorance. However, their individuality is ontologically and logically prior to their ignorance (*Shri Bhashya,* I.i.1. *"Great Siddhanta"* p.103)

d. Hermeneutic Criticism

All Vedanta philosophies must turn to the Vedas, and particularly the Upanishads, for scriptural grounding. Hence, in criticizing his fellow Vedantins, Ramanuja makes use of arguments that concern the proper interpretation of scripture.

i. Vedas as Doctrinally Unified Corpus

According to Ramanuja, his opponents have failed to arrive at an interpretation of the Vedas based on all Vedic texts. Rather, they emphasize some passages that support a monistic interpretation, and ignore those passages that either presume or emphasize plurality. Ramanuja notes that his opponents hold to the view that those Vedic texts that come later in the corpus are to be emphasized (the fact that they come later is presumed, on this account, to show that they contain the more advanced and esoteric teachings) (*Shri Bhashya,* I.i.1. *"Great Purvapaksa"* p.27). These, more than other portions of the Vedas, emphasize the oneness of reality with *Brahman.*

Ramanuja argues that even these portions of the Vedas presume and affirm plurality. Even if it were not the case that these portions of the Vedas mentioned plurality, we would have to take all the Vedas on par for Ramanuja. According to Ramanuja, one cannot attempt to give interpretations of isolated portions of the Vedas. Rather, one must take the Vedas as one unified corpus, aiming at the expression of a single doctrine (cf. *Shri Bhaṣhya* pp.92-3, I.i.1. *"Great Siddhanta"*). Hence, any tenable interpretation of the philosophy of the Vedas must not only affirm the reality of plurality, but also the importance of ritual and moral obligations (dharma), for these are spoken about at length in the earlier portions of the Vedas.

ii. "Tat tvam asi" and Co-ordinate Predication

Even if the Vedic corpus as a whole is taken to present a single doctrine, Ramanuja is still left with the task of accounting for how the seemingly monistic portions of the Upanishads are consistent with the reality of a plurality of distinct individuals. To overcome this hermeneutic hurdle, Ramanuja introduces the doctrine of *samanadhikaranya*, sometimes translated as "co-ordinate predication" or "the principle of grammatical coordination" but literally meaning 'several things in a common substrate.' The etymology of the word suggests an ontological doctrine. However, Ramanuja means to employ it as a semantic doctrine. According to Ramanuja, "The experts on such matters define it thus: `The signification of an identical entity by several terms [*shabda*] which are applied to that entity on different grounds is co-ordinate predication" (*Vedarthasangraha* §24).

In both the *Shri Bhashya* and the *Vedarthasangraha*, Ramanuja draws a distinction between the object*denoted* by a term, and the quality that it can be identified in connection with. The possibility of using various terms with the same denotation but with different qualitative content is what Ramanuja calls "ço-ordinate predication."

The doctrine that Ramanuja advances under the heading of co-ordinate predication strikingly anticipates the Fregean distinction between sense and reference. In the writings of Ramanuja, the doctrine is used to interpret monistic passages of the Vedas in a manner that affirms both the unity of the thing designated, via the coreferentiality of the various terms, while affirming that the various terms bring to the sentence an emphasis on distinct properties of the unitary thing so identified. With respect to the famous formula "that thou art" (*tat tvam asi*) from the *Chandyogai Upanishad* (which Advaitins quote as support for the absolute identity of the individual's self with *Brahman*), Ramanuja understands the indexicals "that" and "thou" as signifying an underlying unity, while containing distinct qualitative content. Hence, "that" in this context, brings to fore the quality of the underlying substantial unity of all individuals in *Brahman*, while "thou" emphasize that we, as individuals, are qualities or distinctions in this underlying unity (*Shri Bhashya,* I.i.1. *"Great Siddhanta"* pp.129-39).

iii. Brahman and Atman

Even if the doctrine of co-ordinate predication is granted, there is yet another hermeneutic hurdle for Ramanuja to contend with: this is the Upanishadic equation of *Brahman* (the Ultimate) with *Atma* (or Self). If the Ultimate and the Self are one, then it would seem that there is no room for the existence of a plurality of individual persons.

The problem might be solved by denying that *"Atma"* means self, but this would be to stipulate a meaning for the word *"Atma"* that it does not have in Sanskrit or Vedic. Ramanuja's solution to this problem is the cosmological doctrine of *sharira* and *shariri* (body and soul), or*shesha* and *sheshin* (dependant and dependant upon). According to Ramanuja, *Brahman* is the Self of all. However, this is not because our individual personhood is identical with the personhood of *Brahman,* but because we, along with all individuals, constitute modes or qualities of the *body* of *Brahman*. Thus, *Brahman* stands to all others as the soul or mind stands to its body. The metaphysical model that Ramanuja thus argues for is at once cosmological in nature, and organic. All individuals are *Brahman* by virtue of constituting its body, but all individuals retain an identity in contradistinction to other parts of *Brahman,* particularly the soul of *Brahman.*

In accordance with much of the monism of Upanishadic passages, Ramanuja maintains that there is a way in which the individual self (*jiva,* or *jivatma*) is identical with the Ultimate Self (*Atma* or *Paramatma*). This is in our natures. According to Ramanuja, each *jiva* shares with *Brahman* an essential nature of being a knower. However, due to beginningless past actions (karma) our true nature (as being knowers and dependants upon *Brahman*) are obscured from us. Moreover, our sharing this nature in no way implies that we have the same relationship to other things (*Shri Bhashya,* I.i.1. *"Great Siddhanta"* pp.99-102). In other words, our likeness in one respect with *Brahman* does not imply that we ourselves are either omnipotent, omniscient or all good.

3. RAMANUJA'S THEISM

In contrast to preceding commentators on the *Brahma Sutra*, Ramanuja's version of Vedanta is explicitly theistic. *Brahman* as *Atman* (the Highest Self of all) is the union of two deities: Vishnu, or Narayana, and His Consort Shri, or Lakshmi. (In Hinduism, Vishnu is the God who upholds and preserves all things, while Lakshmi is the Goddess of prosperity.) The unity of both the father (Vishnu) and mother (Lakshmi) element in *Brahman* is essential to Ramanuja. It is a consequence of the view that *Brahman* is*ubhayalingam*, or having both sexes: this accounts for *Brahman*'s creative potency. According to Ramanuja, *Brahman* (considered as the *Atman*) is antagonistic to all evil lacks all faults (*papam, heya,mala* or *dosha*), and is comprised of innumerable auspicious qualities (*kalyanaguna*): these auspicious qualities are both moral and aesthetic (*Vedarthasangraha* §§ 2, 6, 9, 19, 92, 112, 147, 161, 163, 198, 234, *Shri Bhashya*, I.i.1. pp.5, 80, 89, 92, 94, 125, 132, 133, 136, 144, I.i.2. p. 157, I.i.4. p.201,*Bhagavad Gita Bhashya* I. Intro, IX.34, to name just a few references-Ramanuja never tires or speaking of God's excellences.).

The highest Self (*Atma*) stands to all other persons as their parent, on Ramanuja's account. However, Ramanuja, like many Vedantins, does not subscribe to the Medieval Christian doctrine of creation *ex nihilo*: *Brahman* does not create individual persons, or basic, non-relational qualities for that matter, for these are eternal features of its Body. *Brahman* does engage in a form of creation, which consists in granting individual persons the fruits of their desires (whatever they are). The result of this dispensation is the organization of the elements comprising *Brahman*'s body into the cosmos (*Shri Bhashya*, I.i.1. "*Great Siddhanta*" p.124)

4. RAMANUJA'S SOTERIOLOGY

On Ramanuja's account, our greatest good consists of being ever aware of our true nature (as modes of*Brahman*) and of being aware of the nature of *Brahman*. When all impediments to this awareness are removed, the individual attains *moksha* (liberation). Knowledge of *Brahman* consists in liberation, for Ramanuja, mainly because of the character of *Brahman*. He writes:

Entities other than *Brahman* can be objects of such cognitions of the nature of joy only to a finite extent and for limited duration. But *Brahman* is such that cognizing of him is an infinite and abiding joy. It is for this reason that the *shruti* [scripture] says, '*Brahman* is bliss' (*Taittitriya Upanishad* II.6.) Since the form of cognition as joy is determined by its object, *Brahman* itself is joy. (*Vedarthasangraha*§241)

Ramanuja is explicit in holding that theoretical knowledge of *Brahman*'s nature will not suffice to procure liberation (*Shri Bhashya*, I.i.1. "*Small Siddhanta*" pp.13-14). Our embodied state places psychological constraints upon us that must be nullified. The remedy to be employed, for Ramanuja, is what he calls, after the *Bhagavad Gita*, *bhakti* yoga, or the discipline of devotion or worship. This type of yoga is comprised of two essential elements: (a) an attendance to one's duties with a deontological sense that they are the things that ought to be done for their own sake, and not for their consequences (also known as *karma* yoga), and (b) the constant worship of *Brahman*, particularly in the form of offering all of the fruits of one's labor to *Brahman*. These features of *bhakti* yoga serve two complimentary purposes. First, they counteract past undesirable actions (karmas) whose residual effects impede a full appreciation of reality. Secondly, they inculcate subservience before *Brahman*. This is valuable for Ramanuja, for service to God, on his account, is constitutive of an unbroken appreciation of *Brahman*'s nature.

5. RAMANUJA'S EPISTEMOLOGY

Epistemic concerns figure centrally in Ramanuja's arguments, and his diagnosis of the state of bondage (*samsara*), or non-liberation. Like many Indian philosophers, Ramanuja holds that liberation comes about by the cessation of nescience (*Shri Bhashya*, I.i.1. "*Small Siddhanta*" p.12). However, unlike many of his contemporaries, Ramanuja does not believe that reason is an independent means of knowledge, capable of dispelling ignorance.

a. Perception

Ramanuja holds a position that is similar to naïve empiricism. According to naïve empiricism, the only knowledge that one can have is knowledge that one has gained by one's own experience. Ramanuja's view is like naïve empiricism, in so far as his intentional account of the nature of all epistemic states (*dharmabhutajnana*) leads him to the view that all genuine or first-rate knowledge (*jnana*) consists in a perceptual relationship between a knower and an object of knowledge-knowledge *de re*-and not between a believer and a sentence or proposition-knowledge *de dicto*. Unlike some proponents of naïve empiricism, Ramanuja does not think that it suffices to intermittently have an acquaintance with objects of knowledge. Knowledge (*jnana*) only occurs when there is direct perception of an object. Unlike proper empiricists, Ramanuja does not restrict knowledge to that which can be gathered from the senses. The individual self (*jiva*) on Ramanuja's account is also capable of having a direct vision of transcendent entities, like *Brahman*. Yet, the character of the epistemic state in which one is acquainted with *Brahman*is a type of perception for Ramanuja.

b. Scripture

Because of Ramanuja's perceptual conception of knowledge, he does not regard acquaintance with scripture (*shruti*) as anything more than knowledge of the sentence meaning of scripture (cf. *Shri Bhashya*, I.i.1. "*Small Siddhanta*" pp.13-14). Yet, like many of his fellow Vedantins, Ramanuja regards scripture (*shruti*) as a *pramana*, or a *means* of knowledge. *Shruti*, or the revealed literature, consists of a very specific corpus of texts: the Vedas. (If Ramanuja believed that the *Divya Prabhandam* authored by the Tamil Vaishnava saints is the Tamil equivalent of the Vedas, then he would have held these to also be within the purview of *shruti*). Scripture is an important source of knowledge, for Ramanuja, for it is the only place that we can learn of our moral obligations (dharma) and what our liberation consists in (*moksha*). On the basis of the validity of scripture, several texts gain a derivative authority. These texts are *smriti* (remembered) texts, which include the law books (*dharmashastras*) of eminent figures, and seemingly sacred texts like the *Bhagavad Gita*. On the question of the justification of taking scripture seriously, Ramanuja holds that none can be given. Scripture is self-justifying. Scripture, for its part, can lead people to have cognitions of independent entities, such as *Brahman*, after providing them directions to perceive *Brahman*: without it one would never know what to look for. However, sensuous perception cannot vouch for the veracity of its contents, nor can reason independently provide a rational proof of its veracity. Having followed scripture's dictates, one will eventually have proof of its validity (*Shri Bhashya*I.i.4. p.175) (direct perceptual contact with objects such as *Brahman*). However, prior to embarking on the journey outlined in scripture, it must be taken on faith alone. Thus, on the position of the validity of scripture, Ramanuja is a fideist (see *Shri Bhashya* I.i.3. for Ramanuja's classic criticism of natural theology pp.162-74). (Some critics are apt to think that Ramanuja is correct on the ungroundability of the validity of scripture on either sensuous perception or reason, but that this impossibility makes Ramanuja's whole philosophy implausible.)

While according scripture great weight, Ramanuja shows his preference for common sense by tempering his interpretations of scripture in light of ordinary, sensuous experience. Contrary to the dialectically minded philosophers of his day, Ramanuja presumes in his defence of Vishishtadvaita in the *Shri Bhashya*(I.i.1.) that scriptural interpretation must accord with ordinary experience.

c. Bhakti

Ramanuja's unique contribution to Indian epistemology is the view that *bhakti*, or devotion, is itself an epistemic state. We have noted that, for Ramanuja, knowledge of *Brahman* consists in directly perceiving it. When *bhakti* takes firm root in an individual, it turns into *parabhakti,* which is the highest order of *bhakti*. In all cases, however, *bhakti* is a direct awareness of *Brahman*'s nature, and thus constitutes a type of knowledge (*jnana*) (*Vedarthasangraha* §238). The perceptual character of *bhakti* is sometimes obscured by Ramanuja's synonyms for this state. He sometimes calls it meditation or worship (*upasana*). However, he also insists that it is a kind of seeing, which has the character of direct perception (*pratyakshata* or *sakshatkara*) (cf. *Shri Bhashya,* I.i.1. *"Small Purvapaksha"* pp.15-7).

d. Error

Ramanuja's object oriented account of knowledge has the

problem of accounting for error. If knowledge corresponds to objects, what do false beliefs correspond to: mental objects? His response anticipates Bertrand Russell's account of error in *On Denoting*, which does away with ersatz objects in the explanation of error. According to Ramanuja, erroneous experiences, like dream states, are real, and they can be genuine objects of knowledge (as in the statement 'I dreamt last night' or 'I am dreaming'). However, the objects that the experience claims to be about are absent in false cognitions. This absence of the proper objects of knowledge explains the erroneousness of beliefs in them (*Shri Bhashya* I.i.1. "*Great Siddhanta*" p.78). Thus, on Ramanuja's account, mistaking mother of pearl for a piece of silver does not consist in mistakenly seeing something silver in colour, but in the mistaken cognition that the object perceived is a piece of silver.

6. RAMANUJA'S ETHICS

Ramanuja's ethics divides into his views on substantive matters, and metaethical issues.

a. Substantive Ethics

Ramanuja's substantive ethics in turn has two sources. Like other orthodox Hindu thinkers, Ramanuja holds that the primary source of moral knowledge is the Vedas. This is particularly true of the earlier portion of the Vedas, which sets forth prescribed and optional works (karmas) that constitute *dharma*. The importance of dharma, derived from the Vedas, is stressed in all three of Ramanuja's major works. Like other orthodox Hindu thinkers, Ramanuja also holds that the venerable tradition, or *smriti* literature, supplements the Vedic texts' account of dharma. The most important of the *smriti* texts, for Ramanuja, is the *Bhagavad Gita*.

The *Gita* emphasizes the importance of adopting a deontological attitude (concern for duty for duty's sake and not for its consequences) in order to perfect the execution of prescribed duties, particular to one's place in society. But the *Gita* also emphasizes the importance of certain virtues. The *Gita* praises being a friend (*mitra*) and showing compassion (*karuna*) to all creatures (*Bhagavad Gita* XII.13), and enumerates *ahimsa*, or non-injury, as one of the virtues essential to having *jnana,* or gnosis (*Bhagavad Gita* XIII.7-11).

On what is to be done when the requirements of virtues conflict with prescribed duties, Ramanuja is uncompromising. For Ramanuja, dharma, as set forth in the Vedas, is inviolable. This puts Ramanuja in the awkward position of having to defend the propriety of animal sacrifices, sanctioned and prescribed in the earlier portion of the Vedas.

Shri Vaishnava Brahmins, as a rule, are vegetarians. Ramanuja was, in all likelihood, himself a vegetarian. However, his general inclination to positively endorse the *Bhagavad Gita*'s disavowal of animal cruelty did not stop him from affirming the propriety of animal sacrifices.

In this respect, Ramanuja agrees with his Advaitin predecessor, Shankara, who held that while violence in general is evil, ritual slaughter is not any ordinary act of violence: because it is sanctioned by the Vedas, it cannot be evil (Shankara, *Brahma Sutra Bhashya,* III.i.25). Ramanuja however goes further and argues that ritual slaughter is not only not evil; it is also not really a form of violence. Rather, it is a healing act like a physician's procedure, which causes temporary pain but is ultimately to the benefit of the patient. The sacrificed animal, on Ramanuja's account, is more than compensated in the next life for being ritually slaughtered (*Shri Bhashya,* III.i.25. pp.599-600).

b. Foundations of Ethics

Ramanuja's metaethical comments concern the ground and validity of morality. Ramanuja seems to have always presumed that morality is intrinsically valuable. The intrinsic merit of God Himself, on Ramanuja's account, is tied to His moral excellences. Given that God has nothing to gain by being moral, the value of morality, at least in God's case, cannot be instrumental. However, for all other creatures, morality, or dharma, has an instrumental value: it helps counteract consequences of past karmas. Importantly, it is also the easy way to propitiate God. Ramanuja notes that, in theory, it is possible to achieve liberation through mental efforts alone. However, this is only a theoretical possibility, and is in reality impossible for creatures like us. *Jnana* yoga, or mental disciplines geared towards achieving liberation by solely meditating upon the Self (and not availing oneself of ancillary aids, like attendance to one's duties) is difficult and likely to lead to error. Karma yoga, or attendance to one's duties, on the other hand, is easy for our duties are those obligations suited to our capacities and nature (Ramanuja *Gita Bhashya,* XVIII.47 p.583). Morality, on Ramanuja's account, has both intrinsic and instrumental value. This account of the instrumental value of our obligations also contains, within it, the seeds of an account of the validity of our obligations: our obligations are those appropriate acts that are suited to us to perform. Thus, morality is not simply a law imposed from outside, on Ramanuja's account, but the best mode of action, given our personal natures. However, because of our context, we are unable to determine what is best for us, independently of scripture. Hence, our reliance on scripture to tell us our duties leads to the appearance that dharma is a law imposed on us from outside.

Dharma (duty or morality) is of the utmost importance for Ramanuja. It thus might seem ironic that the *Bhagavad Gita* itself advises us to give up our dharmas. At the very end of the work, after the importance and benefits of living the virtuous life are extolled, Krishna (the incarnation of Vishnu delivering a sermon in the *Bhagavad Gita*) advises us to 'give up all dharmas' and seek refuge in Him alone (*Bhagavad Gita*XVIII.66). Ramanuja offers two interpretations of this verse: (1) it can be taken as implying that we are to abandon the sense of agency that is incompatible with our cosmological dependence upon God, or (2), it can be taken as implying that we ought to give up recourse to expiatory rituals (sometime called "*dharmas*") to nullify the effects of past actions. Neither interpretation allows for abandoning our prescribed obligations (Ramanuja, *Bhagavad Gita Bhashya* XVIII.66, p.599). Ramanuja's views contrast sharply with the views of the Advaita Vedantin Shankara, who argues that morality (dharma) for the seeker of liberation (*moksha*) is an evil, for it ensnares a person in things of the world (Shankara, *Bhagavad Gita Bhashya,* IV:21 pp.202-203).

7. INTERPRETING RAMANUJA: THE NORTHERN AND SOUTHERN SCHOOLS AND THE AUTHENTICITY OF THE GADYAS

Within two centuries after Ramanuja, the Shri Vaishnava tradition split into two separate sub-traditions. Both schools claim to have the authority of Ramanuja in support of their views. These traditions are the Northern or Vadakalai school, and the Southern or Tenkalai school. The respective founding figures of these schools are Vedanta Deshika and Manavalamamuni, two of many eminent Shri Vaishnava scholars to follow Ramanuja. One manner in which the Northern and Southern schools differ is with respect to the importance that the Vedas are to play in the devotees life: the Northern school holds that Vedic observances are essential to proper Shri Vaishnava practices, while the Southern school emphasises the importance of emulating the examples of the twelve Alvars.

Most importantly, the two schools differ on the relationship between divine grace and individual effort. Both schools agree that Grace is necessary for liberation, but they disagree as to the conditions under which Grace is dispensed. According to the Northern school, Grace is conditional on the effort of the individual. Liberation, on this view, is a cooperative effort between God and the aspirant. According to the Southern school, Grace is dispensed freely. Liberation, on this view, is the sole responsibility of God. (On some accounts, the two schools can also be defined with respect to eighteen points of difference. See Govindacarya for one of the few but regrettably unbalanced accounts of this controversy).

Both schools agree that the intercession of Grace is tied to the devotee performing the spiritual act of*sharanagati* or *prapatti*-surrender before God. The act of *prapatti*, or the formal surrender to God, with the understanding that one has no other refuge, is central to Shri Vaishnava cultic life. However, Northern and Southern schools differ with respect to what is to follow. For the Southern school, a one-time act of *prapatti* is sufficient. Subsequent lapses in devotion or attitude do not alter God's disposition to save the individual. However, for the Northern school, lapses on the part of the devotee require a fresh commitment on the part of the individual to surrender before God, in addition to constant effort on the part of the individual to attend to their moral duties in the spirit of *bhakti* yoga.

The controversy between the two schools could be circumvented if it could be shown that the very doctrine of *sharanagati* or *prapatti* is foreign to the thought of Ṛamanuja. This is what some recent scholars have attempted to show. Robert C. Lester, following the arguments of the Vadakalai Shri Vaishnava scholar, Agnihothram Ramanuja Thatachariar of Kumbakonam, argues that the doctrine of *sharanagati* or *prapatti*, at the heart of latter day Shri Vaishnava controversy, is only found in the *Sharanagati Gadya* and the *Shriranga Gadya*, and are absent from Ramanuja's main philosophic works. On this basis, Lester argues that the *Gadyas* (specifically the *Sharanagati Gadya* and *Shriranga Gadya*) and the doctrine of *sharanagati* or *prapatti* are spurious.

According to this argument, the *Gadyas* present, for the first time, the view that *surrendering* to God constitutes a unique means of gaining liberation. And, moreover, Lester argues that this idea is foreign to the arguments that Ramanuja presents in the *Shri Bhashya*, the *Vedarthasangraha* and the *Gita Bhashya*. These works are unanimous in stressing the role of *bhakti* as both the beginning and end of liberation.

In defence of the authenticity of the *Gadyas*, one might argue that the very idea of *bhakti* contains with in it the notion of *sharanagati*-that to love or be devoted to God is to surrender oneself to God. However, Lester argues that the notion of *bhakti* promulgated in the three main works of Ramanuja is distinct from the notion of *prapatti* or *sharanagati* in the *Gadyas*. First, the *Sharanagati Gadya* makes it clear that the devotee is seeking God, not out of love, but out of desperation, with the request that God grant the devotee *bhakti*, and the favour of being eternally in His service. *Sharanagati* or *prapatti* thus constitutes an act that is logically distinct from what is involved in *bhakti*, which is the steady remembrance of God, and attendance to one's duties in a spirit of sacrifice. Secondly, the *Gadyas* have suggested to many that the act of surrendering to God is *sufficient* to procure liberation. The critic persuaded by Lester's view holds that such a view is nowhere to be found in Ramanuja's three main works.

In response to Lester's arguments, one might take a holistic stance: the import of the *Gadyas* and Ramanuja's larger works must be assessed together. This is the stand that has been traditionally adopted by Shri Vaishnavas of both schools. If this approach is adopted, one is likely to read Ramanuja's account of *bhakti* as implying an implicit understanding of our dependence and helplessness before God (a view shared by both the Northern and Southern schools), and one may also regard the *Gadyas* as not putting forth the radical notion that the act of surrender is sufficient for liberation (this, however, is what the Southern school appears to be committed to). With respect to Ramanuja's main works, there is clear textual evidence that he regarded individuals as impotent, apart from God (cf. *Shri Bhashya*, II.i.34. pp.478-9). As noted, on Ramanuja's account, God's role as creator is to grant us the fruits of our desires. Without God actually acting on our behalf to simulate a world in which *it seems as if we are doers*, we would be nothing but isolated persons with many desires, and largely incorrect beliefs, cut off from our peers, with no way to work through our predilections. God's creative role, on this account, serves the purpose of bridging the gap between ourselves and the rest of reality. On this picture of the human condition, it is quite clear that we as individuals are literally helpless, but for the creative dispensation of God.

Another response to Lester's argument is to invoke Ramanuja's own doctrine of co-ordinate predication, while defending the view that Ramanuja in his main works holds that *prapatti* is sufficient for liberation. Ramanuja in the *Vedarthasangraha* writes:

The heart of the whole *shastra* [body of authoritative texts] is this: The individual selves are essentially of the nature of pure knowledge, devoid of restriction and limitation. They get covered up by nescience in the shape of karma. The consequence is that the scope and breadth of their knowledge is curtailed in accordance with their karma. They get embodied in the multifarious varieties of bodies from [the deity] Brahma down to, the lowest species. Their knowledge is limited in accordance with their specific embodiment. They are deluded into identification with their bodies. In accordance with them they become subject to joys and sorrows, which, in essence constitute what is termed "the river of transmigratory existence" [*samsara*]. For these individual selves, so lost in *samsara, there is no way of emancipation, other than surrender* to the supreme Lord [*bhagavatprapattimanthrena*]. For the purpose of inculcating that sole way of emancipation, the first truth to be taught by the *shastra* is that the individual souls are not intrinsically divided into several kinds, like gods, men, etc., and that they are fundamentally alike and are equal in having knowledge as their essential nature. The essential nature of the individual self is such that it is wholly subservient and instrumental to God and therefore God is its inner self. The nature of the supreme Being is unique, on, account of his absolute perfection and absolute antithesis to everything that is evil. God is the ocean of countless, infinitely excellent attributes. The *shastras* further assert that all sentient and non sentient entities are sustained and operated by the supreme Being. Therefore, the Supreme is the ultimate self of all. *They teach meditation along with its accessory conditions as the means for attaining him*. (*Vedarthasangraha* §99, my italics)

It is noteworthy that while Ramanuja avails himself of the notion that surrendering to God *is the only way to emancipation*, he is also clear to emphasise that disciplines such as *"meditation" and accessory conditions* are essential to attaining liberation. One might argue, thus, that Ramanuja did hold that *prapatti* or *sharanagati* are the "only" way to liberation, but this way is not *substantially* distinct from the way of *bhakti* yoga. Rather, *"bhakti"* and *"prapatti"* are distinct qualities that qualify one path. On this interpretation, Ramanuja is assuming that the reader will appreciate the phenomenon of co-ordinate predication, which is the putative semantic phenomenon that Ramanuja appeals to elsewhere to argue that all individuals are *Brahman*, while being essentially distinct modes or attributes of *Brahman*, and not identical to the totality of *Brahman*. In this way, *prapatti* and *bhakti* both denote the same path, but they emphasize different points along the path.

8. CONCLUSION: RAMANUJA'S PLACE IN THE HISTORY OF INDIAN PHILOSOPHY

Ramanuja stands in the Indian philosophical tradition as one of its most important figures. He is the first thinker in this tradition to provide a systematic theistic interpretation of the import of the Vedas. His uncompromising stand on the side of common sense and moral realism stands as a striking contrast to stereotyped accounts of Indian philosophical thought as otherworldly and amoral. And while his significance in the history of Indian philosophy may be under appreciated, his greater influence on the character and form of popular Hinduism may also be under-recognized, despite the fact that he is regarded as a saint in many parts of Southern India. According to Karl Potter, "...Ramanuja's tradition can be said to represent one of the main arteries through which philosophy reached down to the masses, and it may be that Vishishtadvaita is today the most powerful philosophy in India in terms of numbers of adherents, whether they know themselves by that label or not" (Potter p.253). Whether Potter is correct or not, Ramanuja is an Indian philosopher who defended the symbiosis of the spiritual, moral and practically earnest life.

REFERENCES

a. Primary Sources

1.Ramanuja (*acarya*) (11th Century). *Shri Bhashyam* (Critical Edition). Melkote: Academy of Sanskrit Research, 1985.

2.Ramanuja (*acarya*) (11th Century). *Shri Ramanuja Gita Bhashya* (*Bhagavad Gita Bhashya.*) Trans. and Ed. Svami Adidevananda. Madras: Sri Ramakrishna Math, 1991.

3.Ramanuja (*acarya*) (11th Century). *Shrimad Bhagavad Ramanuja Granthamala.* (Complete works.) Ed. Prativadi Bhayankara Annangaracharya. Kancheepuram: available at Granthamala Karyalaya, 1974.

4.Ramanuja (*acarya*) (11th Century). *Vedanta Sutras with the Commentary of Ramanuja* (*Shri Bhashya*). Trans. (English) George Thibaut. Sacred Books of the East. Vol. 48. Delhi: Motilal Banarsidass, 1996.

5.Ramanuja (*acarya*) (11th Century). *Vedarthasamgraha* (*Vedarthasangraha*). Trans. and Ed. S.S. Ragavachar. Mysore: Shri RamaKrishna Ashrama, 1968.

6.Russell, Bertrand (20th Century). "On Denoting." *Mind* 14.56 (1905): 479-93.

7.Shankara (*acarya*) (9th Century). *Bhagavadgita with the Commentary of Shankaracarya (Bhagavad Gita Bhashya)*. Trans. and Ed. Swami Gambhirananda. Calcutta: Advaita Ashrama, 1991.

8.Shankara (*acarya*) (9th Century). *Brahma Sutra Bhashya*. Trans. Swami Gambhirananda. Calcutta: Advaita Ashrama, 1983.

9.Shrinivasadasa (17th Century). *Yatidramatadipika*. Trans. Svami Adidevananda. Madras: Sri Ramakrishna Math, 1978.

10.Yamuna (*acarya*) (11th Century). *Sri Yamunacharya's Siddhi Trayam*. Trans. K. Shrinivasacharya. Ed. R. Ramanujachari: N.p., 1970.

b. Secondary Sources on Ramanuja

1.Buitenen, J. A. B. van. "Introduction." Trans. J. A. B. van Buitenen. *Ramanuja's Vedarthasangraha*. Ed. J. A. B. van Buitenen. 1st , reprint. ed. Pune: Deccan College Postgraduate and Research Institute, 1956. viii, 316.

2.Carman, John B. *The Theology of Ramanuja; an Essay in Interreligious Understanding*. Yale Publications in Religion, 18. New Haven: Yale University Press, 1974.

3.Govindacarya, A. "The Astadasa-Bedas, or the Eighteen Points of Doctrinal Differences Between the Tengalais (Southerners) and the Vadagalais (Northerners) of the Vishishtadvaita Vaishnava School, South India." *Journal of the Royal Asiatic Society of Great Britain and Ireland* (1910): 1103-12.

4.Lester, Robert C. "Ramanuja and Shri Vaishnavism: the Concept of *Prapatti* or *Sharanagati*." *History of Religion* 5.2 (1966): 266-82.

5.Potter, Karl H. *Presuppositions of India's Philosophies*. Prentice-Hall Philosophy Series. Englewood Cliffs, N.J.: Prentice-Hall, 1963.

6.Tapasyananda. *Bhakti Schools of Vedanta*. Madras: Ramakrishna Math, 1990.

15

Dvaita Philosophy

Madhva (1238-1317): The Dvaita or "dualist" school of Hindu Vedanta philosophy originated in 13th-century South India with Sri Madhvacarya (Madhva). Madhva, who considered himself an avatara of the wind-god Vayu, argued that a body of canonical texts called the "Vedanta" or "end of the Veda" taught the fundamental difference between the individual self or *atman* and the ultimate reality, *brahman*. According to Madhva there are two orders of reality: 1. *svatantra,* independent reality, which consists of Brahman alone and 2. *paratantra,* dependent reality, which consists of jivas (souls) and jada (lifeless objects). Although dependent reality would not exist apart from brahman's will, this very dependence creates a fundamental distinction between brahman and all else, implying a dualist view. By interpreting the Vedanta materials (especially the Upanisads, the Bhagavadgita and the Brahmasutras) along these lines, Madhva deliberately challenged the non-dualist reading in which the *atman* was identified with *brahman*. Madhva argued that the scriptures could not teach the identity of all beings because this would contradict ordinary perception, which tells us that we are different both from one another and from God. Madhva and his followers call their system *tattvavada,* "the realist viewpoint".

1. MADHVA AND SANKARA

The main tenet of Madhva's *Dvaita Vedanta* is that the Vedic tradition teaches a fundamental difference between the human soul or *atman* and the ultimate reality, *brahman*. This is markedly different from the earlier *Advaita Vedanta,* which Madhva often vociferously attacked. Sankara's *A-dvaita* or "non-dualist" *Vedanta* (9th century) argued that the atman is completely identical with brahman. According to Sankara, the *atman* experiences a false sense of plurality and individuality when under the influence of the delusive power of *maya.* While *maya* has the ambiguous ontological status of being neither real nor unreal, the only true reality is *brahman.* A soul becomes liberated from the cycle of rebirth (*punar-janma*) by realizing that its very experience of *samsara* is an illusion; its true identity is the singular objectless consciousness that constitutes pure being or *brahman.*

2. MADHVA AND RAMANUJA

While Ramanuja's system of *Visistadvaita Vedanta* or "qualified non-dualism" modifies Sankara's position on the soul's identity with *brahman,* Madhva also rejected it. Ramanuja assumes a plurality of individual souls whose identity remains intact even after liberation but maintains that the souls share the essential nature of *brahma.* The souls are eternal particles issuing from *brahman,* who as their source retains its transcendence. Ramanuja maintains Visnu's distinct difference from the human soul and his supremacy as creator and redeemer. Ramanuja identifies brahman with Visnu, holding that *brahman* is *saguna,* i.e. possesses attributes, in contrast to Sankara's attributeless or *"nirguna" brahman.*

3. DVAITA VEDANTA

Like Ramanuja, Madhva identifies *brahman* with Visnu. However, he argues that any system that allows for any identification of the *atman* with *brahman* undermines Visnu's supremacy, compromises His status, and strips devotional acts of their meaning. Madhva's insistence on the modal distinction between the*atman* and *brahman,* wherein the former is inalterably dependent upon–and therefore, fundamentally different from–the latter, insures Visnu-as-*brahman*'s complete and utter transcendence of the human soul. For Madhva, this view alone makes devotion [bhakti] an essential component of religious belief and practice. Attaining Visnu's grace is the soul's only hope of achieving liberation [moksa] from the cycle of rebirth (*samsara*).

Like Ramanuja, Madhva opposes Sankara's conception of Brahman as *nirguna* or without qualities and as a pure self-consciousness. Madhva views Visnu as preeminent above all other deities on the basis of His unique characteristics. This emphasis on Visnu's particular collocation of attributes that renders Him distinct from all other gods, human souls, and the material world reveals another critical component of Madhva's philosophy which is his acceptance of an ontological plurality as a fundamental facet of being. Indeed, Madhva rejects the notion that *brahman* is the only truly existent entity (tattva) and he maintains that, even though living beings and inert matter are dependent upon *Brahman*, such dependence differentiates them from Him and makes them discrete entities (tattvas). Thus, reality in Madhva's system consists of three basic elements: God, the souls (*jivasi*), and insentient matter (*jada*).

Madhva's pluralistic ontology is founded on his realist epistemology, which in turn affects his Vedic hermeneutics. He argues that God and the human soul are separate because our daily experience of separateness from God and of plurality in general is presented to us as an undeniable fact, fundamental to our knowledge of all things. Madhva's emphasis on the validity of experience as a means of knowledge is intended to refute the nondualist position that the differences we experience in daily life are ultimately a shared illusion with the ambiguous ontological status of being neither real nor unreal. In Madhva's view, Advaita's denial of the innate validity of knowledge acquired through sense perception completely undermines our ability to know anything since we must always question the content of our knowledge. This questioning would encompass our knowledge of the sacred canon, which is accessible to us only through our ability to perceive it and to draw inferences from it. Madhva argues that perception and inference must be innately valid and the reality they present us with must be actually and ultimately real since such a position is the only one that allows us to know the content of the Vedas. The Vedas alone are responsible for teaching us about the nature of the self and *brahman*.

This aspect of Madhva's realist epistemology is important not only because it bolsters Madhva's claim that the *atman* and *brahman* are permanently distinct as revealed to us by experience, but because it means that the sacred texts must be read in consonance with the data we receive from our everyday experience, even though the Vedas present us with knowledge of a supra-sensible realm. Madhva argues that the Vedas cannot teach non-difference between the *atman* and *brahman* or a lack of true plurality since this would directly contradict our experience. In Madhva's view the sacred texts teach *pancabheda,* the five-fold difference between 1. Visnu and jivas 2. Visnu and jada 3. jiva and jada 4. one jiva and another and 5. one form of jada and another.

Madhva's belief in the innate difference of one soul from another led to some interesting doctrines in his system. He believed in a hierarchy of jivas, based upon their innate configurations of virtues (*gunas*) and faults (*dosas*). For example, Visnu is supreme because He possesses all qualities in their most fulfilled and perfect form. Furthermore, because Madhva believed that souls possess innate characteristics and capacities, he also maintained that they were predestined to achieve certain ends. This perspective put Madhva at odds with traditional Hindu views of the *karma* theory wherein differences in social and religious status are explained via past moral or immoral acts. For Madhva, each individual being possesses an innate moral propensity and *karma* is merely the mechanism by which a given soul is propelled towards his or her destiny.

4. CANONICAL SOURCES

Madhva's attempts to locate his controversial views in the canonical Vedanta texts often proved difficult. He is perhaps most famous for his idiosyncratic rendering of the Chandogya Upanisad's statement *tat tvam asi* or "you (the *atman*) are that (*brahman*)." By carrying over the 'a' from the preceding word, Madhva rendered the phrase *atat tvam asi* or "you are not that." Some scholars have speculated on "foreign," particularly Christian, influences on Madhva's thought but current scholarly consensus maintains that political and social changes in Madhva's region prompted a new approach to old religious convictions.

Madhva's Dvaita Vedanta is recognized as one of the three major schools of Vedanta (besides Sankara's Advaita and Ramanuja's Visistadvaita Vedanta). It has been further developed by such major figures as Jayatirtha (1356-1388) and Vyasaraya (1478-1589) and is kept alive by a still flourishing community [Madhva sampradaya] in India with its main center at Udipi (Karnataka).

5. REFERENCES :

1.Sharma, B. N. K. *Philosophy of Sri Madhvacarya.* Rev. ed. Delhi: Motilal Banarsidass, 1986.

2.Sharma, B. N. K. *Madhva's Teachings in His Own Words.* Bombay: Bharatiya Vidya Bhavan, 1961.

3.Siauve, Suzanne. *La Doctrine de Madhva.* Pondicherry: Institut Francais d'Indologie, 1968.

Conclusion

In relation to Western philosophical thought, Indian philosophy offers both surprising points of affinity and illuminating differences. The differences highlight certain fundamentally new questions that the Indian philosophers asked. The similarities reveal that, even when philosophers in India and the West were grappling with the same problems and sometimes even suggesting similar theories, Indian thinkers were advancing novel formulations and argumentations. Problems that the Indian philosophers raised for consideration, but that their Western counterparts never did, include such matters as the origin (*utpatti*) and apprehension (*jnapti*) of truth(*pramanya*). Problems that the Indian philosophers for the most part ignored but that helped shape Western philosophy include the question of whether knowledge arises from experience or from reason and distinctions such as that between analytic and synthetic judgments or between contingent and necessary truths. Indian thought, therefore, provides the historian of Western philosophy with a point of view that may supplement that gained from Western thought. A study of Indian thought, then, reveals certain inadequacies of Western philosophical thought and makes clear that some concepts and distinctions may not be as inevitable as they may otherwise seem. In a similar manner, knowledge of Western thought gained by Indian philosophers has also been advantageous to them.

Vedic hymns, Hindu scriptures dating from the 2nd millennium BCE, are the oldest extant record from India of the process by which the human mind makes its gods and of the deep psychological processes of mythmaking leading to profound cosmological concepts. The Upanishads (speculative philosophical texts) contain one of the first conceptions of a universal, all-pervading, spiritual reality leading to a radical monism (absolute nondualism, or the essential unity of matter and spirit). The Upanishads also contain early speculations by Indian philosophers about nature, life, mind, and the human body, not to speak of ethics and social philosophy. The classical, or orthodox, systems (darshanas) debate, sometimes with penetrating insight and often with a degree of repetition that can become tiresome to some, such matters as the status of the finite individual; the distinction as well as the relation between the body, mind, and the self; the nature of knowledge and the types of valid knowledge; the nature and origin of truth; the types of entities that may be said to exist; the relation of realism to idealism; the problem of whether universals or relations are basic; and the very important problem of moksha, or liberation (literally "release")—its nature and the paths leading up to it.

The various Indian philosophies contain such a diversity of views, theories, and systems that it is almost impossible to single out characteristics that are common to all of them. Acceptance of the authority of the Vedas characterizes all the orthodox (astika) systems—but not the unorthodox (*nastika*) systems, such as Charvaka (radical materialism), Buddhism, and Jainism. Moreover, even when philosophers professed allegiance to the Vedas, their allegiance did little to fetter the freedom of their speculative ventures. On the contrary, the acceptance of the authority of the Vedas was a convenient way for a philosopher's views to become acceptable to the orthodox, even if a thinker introduced a wholly new idea. Thus, the Vedas could be cited to corroborate a wide diversity of views; they were used by the Vaisheshika thinkers (i.e., those who believe in ultimate particulars, both individual souls and atoms) as much as by the Advaita (monist) Vedanta philosophers.

In most Indian philosophical systems, the acceptance of the ideal of moksha, like allegiance to the authority of the scriptures, was only remotely connected with the systematic doctrines that were being propounded. Many epistemological, logical, and even metaphysical doctrines were debated and decided on purely rational grounds that did not directly bear upon the ideal of *moksha*. Only the Vedanta ("end of the Vedas") philosophy and the Samkhya (a system that accepts a real matter and a plurality of the individual souls) philosophy may be said to have a close relationship to the ideal of *moksha*. The logical systems—Nyaya, Vaisheshika, and Purva-Mimamsa—are only very remotely related. Also, both the philosophies and other scientific treatises, including even the *Kama-sutra* ("Aphorisms on Love") and the *Artha-shastra* ("The Science of Material Gain"), recognized the same ideal and professed their efficacy for achieving it.

When Indian philosophers speak of intuitive knowledge, they are concerned with making room for it and demonstrating its possibility, with the help of logic—and there, as far as they are concerned, the task of philosophy ends. Indian philosophers do not seek to justify religious faith; philosophic wisdom itself is accorded the dignity of religious truth. Theory is not subordinated to practice, but theory itself, as theory, is regarded as being supremely worthy and efficacious.

Three basic concepts form the cornerstone of Indian philosophical thought: the self or soul (atman), works (karma), and liberation (moksha). Leaving the Charvakas aside, all Indian philosophies concern themselves with these three concepts and their interrelations, though this is not to say that they accept the objective validity of these concepts in precisely the same manner. Of these, the concept of karma, signifying moral efficacy of human actions, seems to be the most typically Indian. The concept of atman, not altogether absent in Western thought, corresponds in a certain sense to the Western concept of a transcendental or absolute spirit self—important differences notwithstanding. The concept of moksha as the concept of the highest ideal has likewise been one of the concerns of Western thought, especially during the Christian era, though it probably has never been as important as for the Hindu mind. Most Indian philosophies assume that *moksha* is possible, and the "impossibility of *moksha*" (*anirmoksha*) is regarded as a material fallacy likely to vitiate a philosophical theory.

In addition to karma, the lack of two other concerns further differentiates Indian philosophical thought from Western thought in general. Since the time of the Greeks, Western thought has been concerned with mathematics and, in the Christian era, with history. Neither mathematics nor history has ever raised philosophical problems for the Indian. In the lists of pramanas, or ways of knowing accepted by the different schools, there is none that includes mathematical knowledge or historical knowledge. Possibly connected with their indifference toward mathematics is the significant fact that Indian philosophers have not developed formal logic. The theory of the syllogism (a valid deductive argument having two premises and a conclusion) is, however, developed, and much sophistication has been achieved in logical theory. Indian logic offers an instructive example of a logic of cognitions (*jnanani*) rather than of abstract propositions—a logic not sundered and kept isolated from psychology and epistemology, because it is meant to be the logic of actual human striving to know what is true of the world.

Bibliography

Primary Sources

1.*Âcâramga Sûtra*. Trans. Harmann Georg Jacobi. Jaina Sûtras. Ed. Harmann Georg Jacobi. Vol. 1. 2 vols. Delhi: AVF Books, 1987.

2.*Aiterya Brâhmana. Aiterya Brâhmana of the Zg Veda*. Trans. Martin Haug. Sacred Books of the Hindus. Ed. B.D. Basu. Allahabad: Sudhindra Nath Vasu, 1922.

3.*Bhâgavata Purâna. Srîmad Bhâgavatam*. Trans. Tapasyânanda. Madras: Sri Ramakrishna Math, 1981.

4.Chandrakânta. *Vaisesika Sûtra (Gloss)*. Trans. Nandal Sinha. Allahabad: Sudhindra Nath Basu, 1923.

5.*Dhammapada. A Source Book in Indian Philosophy*. Eds. S. Radhakrishnan and Charles Alexander Moore. Princeton, N.J.: Princeton University Press, 1967. 292-325.

6.Gautama. *Nyâya Sûtra*. Trans. Satisa Chandra Viyabhusana. Sacred Books of the Hindus. Ed. Nandalal Sinha. 2nd rev. and enl. ed. Vol. 8. Allahabad: Panini Office, 1930.

7.Gautama, Vâtsyâyana, and *Uddyotakara. The Nyâya-Sûtras of Gautama: with the Bhâsya of Vâtsyâyana and the Vârtika of Uddyotakara*. Trans. Ganganatha Jha. Delhi: Motilal Banarsidass, 1984.

8.*Gîtâ. Srîmad Bhagavad Gîtâ; the Scripture of Mankind*. Trans. and Ed. Swâmi Tapasyânanda. Madras: Srî Ramakrishna Math, 1986.

9.GuGaratna. *Tarkarahasyadîpika*. Cârvâka/Lokâyata: an Anthology of Source Materials and Some Recent Studies. Ed. Debiprasad Chattopadhyaya. New Delhi: Indian Council of Philosophical Research in association with Rddhi-India Calcutta, 1990.

10.Îsvarakr&sna. *Sânkhya Kârikâ*. Trans. S.S. Suryanârâyana-Sastri. Madras University Philosophical Series. no. 3. Ed. S.S. Suryanârâyana-Sastri. 2nd rev. ed. Madras: University of Madras, 1948.

11.Jaimini. *Mîmâmsâ Sûtra*. Trans. and Ed. Mohan Lal Sandal. Sacred Books of the Hindus. Vol. 27. Allahabad: Sudhindre Nath Basu, 1923.

12.Khana. *Vaisesika Sûtra*. Trans. and Ed. Nandalal Sinha. Sacred Books of the Hindus. Ed. Nandal Sinha. 2nd rev. and enl. ed. Vol. 6. Allahabad: Sudhindra Nath Basu, Panini Office, 1923.

13.*Katha Upanisad*. Trans. and Ed. Swami Gambirananda. *Eight Upanisads, With the Commentary of Sankarâcârya*. Ed. Swami Gambirananda. Vol. 2: Advaita Ashrama, 1977. 91-220.

14.Kumârila. *Slokavârtika*. 1909 Bibliotheca Indica. Calcutta: Asiatic Society. Trans. Ganganatha Jha. Srî Garib Das Oriental Series. Vol. 8. Delhi: Srî Satguru, 1983.

15.Madhva. *Mahâbhâratâtparyanirnayah*. Trans. and Ed. K.T. Pandurang. Vol. 1. Chirtanur: Sriman Madhva Siddhantonnanhini Sabha, 1993. Madhva. *Vedânta Sûtras with the commentary of Srî Madhwacharya (Madva Brahma Sûtra Bhâsya)*. Trans. S. Subba Rau. Madras: Thompson and Co., 1904.

16.*Majjhima Nikâya. The Collection of the Middle Length Sayings*. Trans. I. B. Horner. Pali Text Society Translation Series. Vol. 29–31. 3 vols. London: Published for the Pali Text Society by Luzac, 1957.

17.Manu. *The Laws of Manu (ManavaDharmasâstra)*. Trans. G.Buhler. Sacred Books of the East. Ed. Max Müller. Vol. xxv. Oxford: Oxford University Press, 1886.

18.*Mundaka Upanisad*. Trans. and Ed. Swami Gambirananda. *Eight Upanisads, With the Commentary of Sankarâcârya*. Vol. 2: Advaita Ashrama, 1977. 77-172.

19.Patañjali. *Yoga Sûtra*. Trans. and Ed. Swâmi Prabhavananda. Madras: Ramakrishna Math., 1953.

20.Plato. *Phaedo*. Trans. Hugh Tredennick. The Collected Dialogues of Plato, Including the Letters. Bollingen Series 71. Eds. Edith Hamilton and Huntington Cairns. New York: Pantheon Books, 1966. 40-99.

21.Plato. *Phaedrus*. Trans. R. Hackforth. The Collected Dialogues of Plato, Including the Letters. Bollingen Series 71. Eds. Edith Hamilton and Huntington Cairns. New York: Pantheon Books, 1966. 475-525.

22.Plato. *Republic*. Trans. Paul Shorey. The Collected Dialogues of Plato, Including the Letters. Bollingen Series 71. Eds. Edith Hamilton and Huntington Cairns. New York: Pantheon Books, 1966. 575-844.

23.*Purusa Sûkta. Srî Rudram and Purusasûktam.* Trans. and Ed. Swami Amritananda. Ed. Swami Amritananda. Chennai: Sri Ramakrishna Math, 1997.

24.Radhakrishnan, S. *The Hindu View of Life.* Books that matter. London: G. Allen & Unwin, 1961.

25.Radhakrishnan, S., and Charles Alexander Moore, eds. *A Source Book in Indian Philosophy.* Princeton, N.J.: Princeton University Press, 1967.

26.Râmânuja. Srî Râmânuja *Gîtâ Bhâsya.* Trans. and Ed. Swâmi Âdidevânada. Madras: Sri Ramakrishna Math, 1991.

27.Râmânuja. *Vedânta Sûtras with the commentary of Râmânuja (Râmânuja Brahma Sûtra Bhâsya; Srî Bhâsya).* Trans. George Thibaut. Sacred Books of the East. Vol. 48. Delhi: Motilal Banarsidass, 1996.

28.Râmânuja. *Vedârthasangraha.* Trans. and Ed. S.S. Ragavachar. Mysore: Sri Ramakrishna Ashrama, 1968.

29.*Zg Veda. Vedic hymns.* Trans. Hermann Oldenberg. Sacred books of the East. Ed. F. Max Müller. Vol. 32, 46. 2 vols. Oxford: The Clarendon Press, 1891.

30. Sabara. *Sabara Bhâsya.* Trans. Ganganatha Jha. Gaekwad's Oriental Series. Vol. 66, 70, 73. Baroda: Oriental Institute, 1933.

31.*Samyutta Nikâya. The Connected Discourses of the Buddha : a New Translation of the Samyutta Nikâya; translated from the Pâli.* Trans. Bhikkhu Bodhi. 2 vols. Somerville, MA: Wisdom Publications, 2000.

32.Sankara (*âcârya*). *Bhagavad Gîtâ with the commentary of Sankarâcârya.* Trans. Swâmi Gambhirânanda. Calcutta: Advaita Ashrama, 1991.

33.Sankara (*âcârya*). "Taittitrîya *Upanisad* Bhâsya." Trans. Swami Gambirananda. *Eight Upanisads, With the Commentary of Sankarâcârya.* Vol. 1: Advaita Ashrama, 1977. 3-29.

34.Sankara (*âcârya*). *The Vedânta Sûtras (Brahma Sûtra Bhâsya).* Sacred books of the East, vol.38. Delhi: Motilal Banarsidass, 1994.

35.Sankara-Misra. *Vaiúecika Sûtra Bhâsya.* Trans. Nandalal Sinha. Sacred Books of the Hindus. Ed. Nandal Sinha. 2nd rev. and enl. ed. Vol. 6. Allahabad: Sudhindra Nath Basu, Panini Office, 1923.

36.*Sûtrakrtânga* . Trans. Harmann Georg Jacobi. Jaina Sûtras. Ed. Harmann Georg Jacobi. Vol. 2. Delhi: AVF Books, 1987. 235–436.

37.Tapasyânanda, Swâmi. *Bhakti Schools of Vedânta*. Madras: Ramakrishna Math, 1990.

38.Udayanâcârya and Haridâsa Nyâyâlamkâra. *The Kusumâñjali: or, Hindu Proof of the Existence of a Supreme Being (10th Century)*. (Udayanâcârya's *Nyâyausumâñjali* with Haridâsa's Nyâyâlamkâra's Vyâkhyâ). Trans. and Ed. E.B. Cowell. Varanasi: Bharat-Bharati, 1980.

39.Vivekânanda. *The Complete Works of Swami Vivekânanda*. Mayavati memorial ed. Calcutta: Advaita Ashrama, 1964.

Secondary Sources

1.Bharadwaja, V.K. "A Non-Ethical Concept of Ahimsâ." *Indian Philosophical Quarterly*. xi.2 (1984): 171-77.

2.Chaterjee, Satischandra, and Dhirendramohan Data. *An Introduction to Indian Philosophy*. Calcutta: University of Calcutta, 1960.

3.Dasgupta, Surendranath. *A History of Indian Philosophy*. 5 vols. Delhi: Motilal Banarsidas, 1975.

4.Deutsch, Eliot. *Advaita Vedânta: a Philosophical Reconstruction*. 1st ed. Honolulu: East-West Center Press, 1969.

5.Dundas, Paul. *The Jains*. New York: Routledge, 1992.

6.Flintoff, Everard. "Pyrrho and India." *Phronesis* 25 (1980): 88-106.

7.Fox, Michael W. *Bringing Life to Ethics: Global Bioethics for a Humane Society*. Albany: State University of New York Press, 2001.

8.Hacker, Paul. *Philology and Confrontation*. Ed. Wilhelm Halbfass. Albany: State Universisty of New York, 1995.

9.Halbfass, Wilhelm. *India and Europe: an Essay in Understanding*. *Indien und Europa: Perspektiven ihrer geistigen Begegnung*. Basel; Stuttgart: Schwabe, 1981. Albany, N.Y.: State University of New York Press, 1988.

10.Halbfass, Wilhelm. *Tradition and Reflection: Explorations in Indian Thought*. Albany, N.Y.: State University of New York Press, 1991.

11.Jha, Ganganatha. *Purva Mîmâmsâ in its Sources*. Trans. Jha, Ganganatha. Library of Indian Philosophy and Religion. Benares: Benares Hindu University, 1942.

12.Kane, Pandurang Vaman. *History of Dharmasâstra: Ancient and Medi¿val Religious and Civil Law in India*. Government Oriental Series. Class B. no. 6. 2nd rev. and enl. ed. 5 vols. Poona: Bhandarkar Oriental Research Institute, 1990.

13.Klostermaier, Klaus. "*Dharmamegha samâdhi*: Comments on *Yoga Sûtra* IV.29." *Philosophy East and West* 36.3 (1986:): 253-62.

14.Larson, Gerald James, and Ram Shankar Bhattacharya. *Samkhya: a Dualist Tradition in Indian Philosophy*. Encyclopedia of Indian Philosophies. Ed. Karl H. Potter. Vol. 4. Princeton, N.J.: Princeton University Press, 1987.

15.Monier-Williams, Monier. *A Sanskrit-English Dictionary: Etymologically and Philologically Arranged, with Special Reference to Cognate Indo-European Languages*. Oxford University Press 1872, enlarged 1899. "greatly enlarged and improved" ed. Delhi: Motilal Banarsidass Publishers, 1995.

16.Potter, Karl H., ed. *Encyclopedia of Indian Philosophies*. 5 vols. Princeton NJ; Delhi: Princeton University Press; Motilal Banarsidass, 1970–1995.

17.Potter, Karl H., ed. *Presuppositions of India's Philosophies*. Prentice-Hall Philosophy Series. Englewood Cliffs, N.J.: Prentice-Hall, 1963.

18.Potter, Karl H., and Sibajiban Bhattacharya. *Indian Metaphysics and Epistemology: The Tradition of Nyâya–Vaisesika up to Gangesa*. The Encyclopedia of Indian Philosophies. Ed. Karl H. Potter. Vol. 2. Princeton NJ: Princeton University, 1977.

19.Sharma, B. N. Krsnamurti. *The Brahma Sûtras and their Principal Commentaries; a Critical Exposition*. 2nd ed. New Delhi: Munshiram Manoharlal, 1986.

20.Thapar, Romila. *A History of India*. Vol. 1. London: Penguin Books, 1990.

21.Whicher, Ian. *The Integrity of the Yoga Darsana*. Albany: State University of New York, 1998.

Index